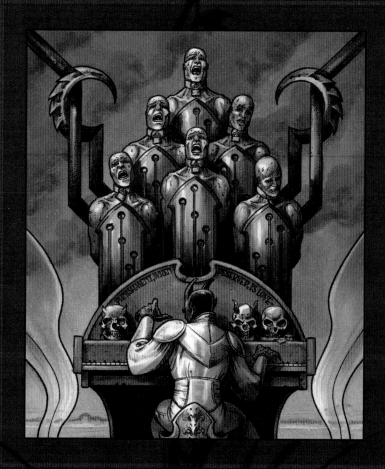

PUNISHMENT, WHEN DESERVED, IS LOVE.

"Punishment,
when deserved,
is love."

-Saint
Thomas
Aquinas

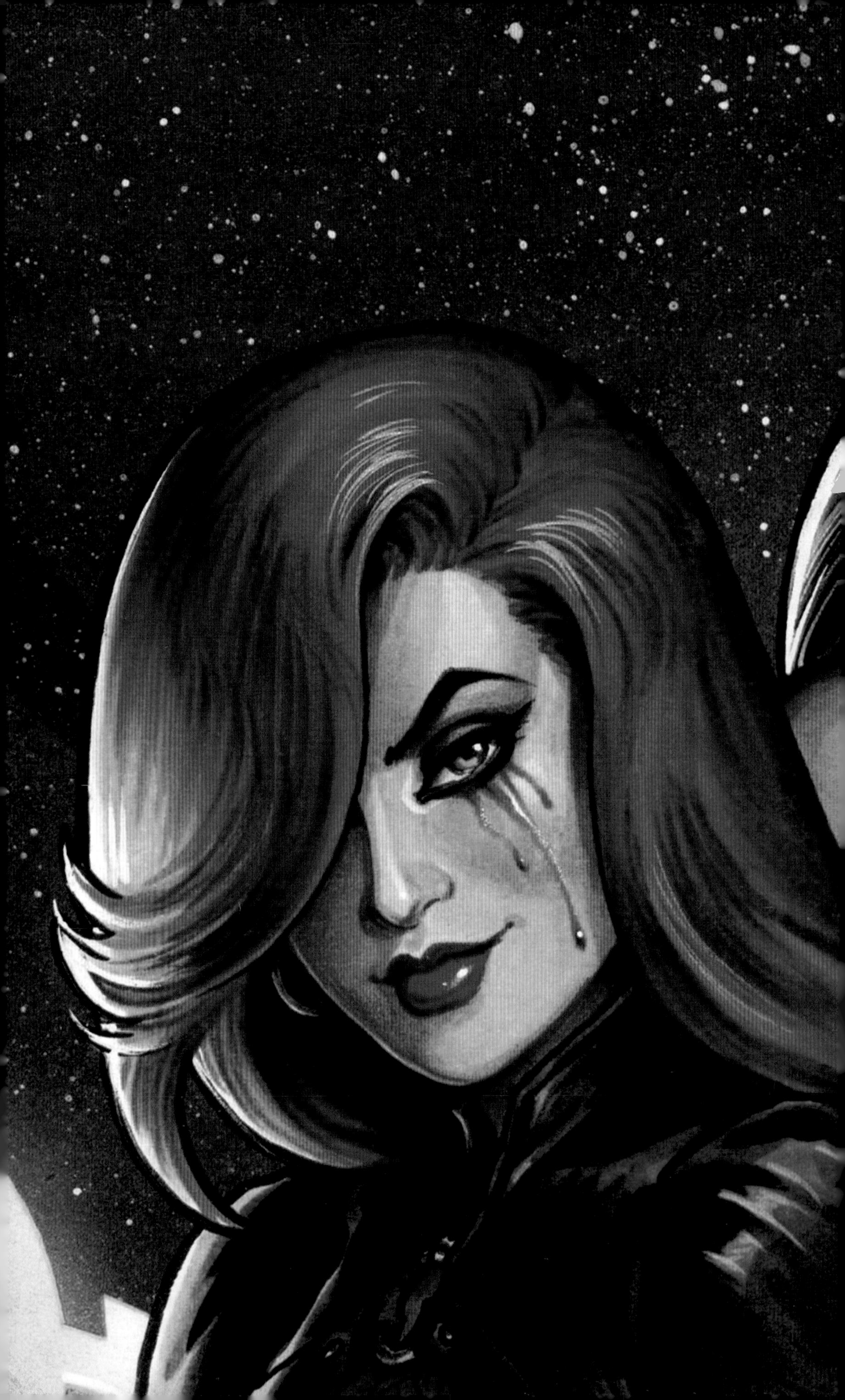

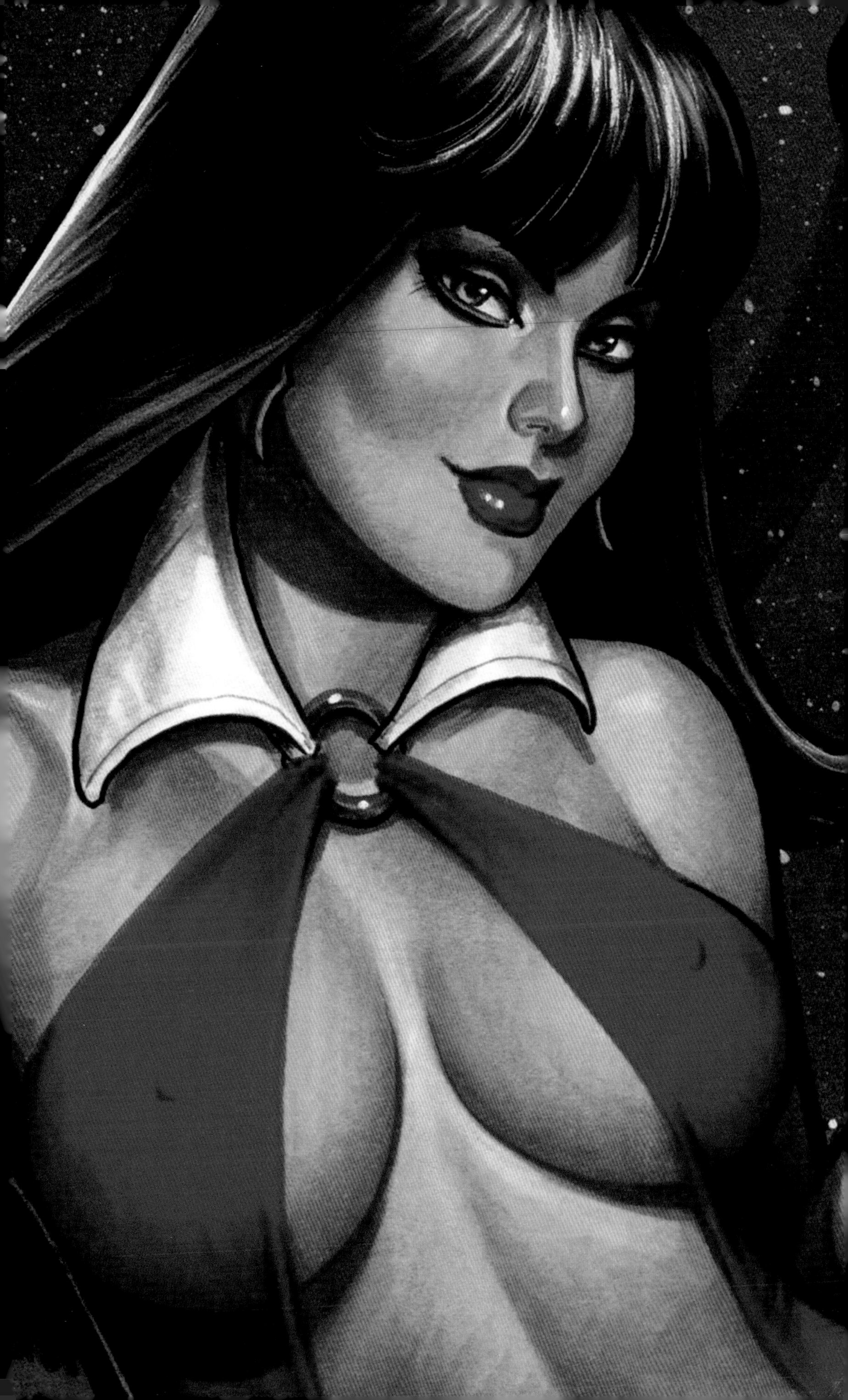

DAWN·VA

WRITTEN & ILLUSTRATED BY

Issues 1, 2, 3 colored by VALENTINA PINTO
from guides by JML

Issues 3, 4, 5 colored by
JOSEPH MICHAEL LINSNER

VAMPIRELLA

JOSEPH MICHAEL LINSNER

letters by
JEFF ECKLEBERRY

creative editor
KRISTINA DEAK-LINSNER

NICK BARRUCCI
CEO / Publisher

JUAN COLLADO
President / COO

JOE RYBANDT
Senior Editor

RACHEL PINNELAS
Associate Editor

KEVIN KETNER
Editorial Assistant

JASON ULLMEYER
Art Director

GEOFF HARKINS
Graphic Designer

ALEXIS PERSSON
Production Artist

CHRIS CANIANO
Digital Associate

RACHEL KILBURY
Digital Assistant

BRANDON DANTE PRIMAVERA
Director of IT/Operations

RICH YOUNG
Director of Business Development

KEITH DAVIDSEN
Marketing Manager

PAT O'CONNELL
Sales Manager

Online at www.DYNAMITE.com
On Facebook /Dynamitecomics
On Instagram /Dynamitecomics
On Tumblr dynamitecomics.tumblr.com
On Twitter @Dynamitecomics
On YouTube /Dynamitecomics

Standard Edition: ISBN-10: 1-60690-889-8   ISBN-13: 978-1-60690-889-1
Signed Edition: ISBN-10: 1-52410-107-9   ISBN-13: 978-1-52410-107-7

First Printing   10 9 8 7 6 5 4 3 2 1   Printed in China

INTRODUCTION

I've been admiring the beauty of Vampirella since before I could read.

I remember first seeing her ads in an issue of Warren's Famous Monsters that my aunt had gotten me (I grew up loving Frankenstein and all things that go bump in the night). That was probably 1974 when I was 5 years old.

Everything she projected in the classic Jose Gonzalez door poster just knocked my socks off. She was a grand and powerful figure, classy and yet sexy as all hell. What a body, what legs. And regal -- one look at her and you knew instantly that she was a queen. Her stance, her manner, the sly look in her eye all commanded respect. Her slight smile was the key for me. It seemed to say that this was all a game to her. She would let her little bat do her bidding for her, and only get involved if she needed to -- or wanted to.

I am sure my young brain didn't pull all of that out of my first view of the Jose Gonzalez painting, but it did make a very strong emotional impact on me. What she projected stuck with me, and helped me form my tastes. I believe that a woman can be strong, smart and sexy without sacrificing anything. Those are the women I find attractive and the ones I try to portray in my stories.

That flowed out of me when I created Dawn in the late 80's.

I wasn't trying to imitate or pay homage to Vampirella when I put out a comic called **Cry For Dawn** in 1989. But it was a horror anthology where Dawn served as hostess and introduced the stories...just like Vampirella did in her Warren days. With Dawn's creation I was taking my influences and mixing them all together. My love of Vargas girls, classic glamour queens like Marilyn Monroe, Sophia Loren and Ann Margret, comic art maestros like Frank Frazetta, Barry Smith, Richard Corben, Moebius, P. Craig Russell all came together and filtered out through my brain in the form of Dawn.

Frazetta was already firmly embedded in my psyche as my favorite artist when I learned that he designed Vampirella. Trina Robbins came up with a great basic costume concept, and Frazetta breathed life into it. Jose Gonzalez took her a step further, gave her the grace and dignity of a queen. I knew I had to tap into that when drawing Dawn and that's consistently been a high-water mark that I've aimed for over these past 25 years. In many ways, Dawn meeting and sharing a stage with Vampirella is bringing things full circle.

Dawn means the world to me, and I swore that I would never do a crossover with her. It seemed like a cheap marketing ploy. Those things are almost never any good -- why waste my time? Dawn had made a cameo in the 100th issue of Witchblade, but that was just a lark done mostly for the absurd fun of it. But a few years ago, Nick Barrucci of Dynamite Entertainment approached me with the idea of a Dawn & Vampirella crossover. At first I was hesitant, but the more I thought about it, the seed of a story took root and started to grow. And now 2 years later, here's the first issue. Thanks Nick for making this happen. I'm glad that Dawn's first crossover is a royal one -- nothing else would do.

It's the perfect way to celebrate 25 years of Dawn.

To Hell and back -- where else does one take a goddess or a vampire queen on a rendezvous?

Working on this series has been a childhood dream come true. As a life long reader of comic books, it doesn't get any cooler than having the character you created go on an adventure with an iconic heroine that you grew up loving. What a thrill it's been seeing **Dawn** rub elbows with **Vampirella**. I love my girl, but Vampi is the one who started it all.

I'd like to thank **Nick Barrucci** and the folks at **Dynamite** for their support and input. **Jeff Eckleberry**, as always, you've done another fine job. And a big thank you to **Kristina Deak** for shining a light on the feminine mystery and helping me understand girls a little bit better. From occasionally posing as a cover model to pointing out whenever the dialogue went off character -- '*girls don't talk like that to each another*' -- this series would be much weaker without your valuable contributions and guidance.

And thanks to you for reading.

Joe Linsner,
January, 2016

'Like' my official Linsner page on FACEBOOK
https://www.facebook.com/josephmichaellinsner

& Follow me on TWITTER
@JosephLinsner - Twitter

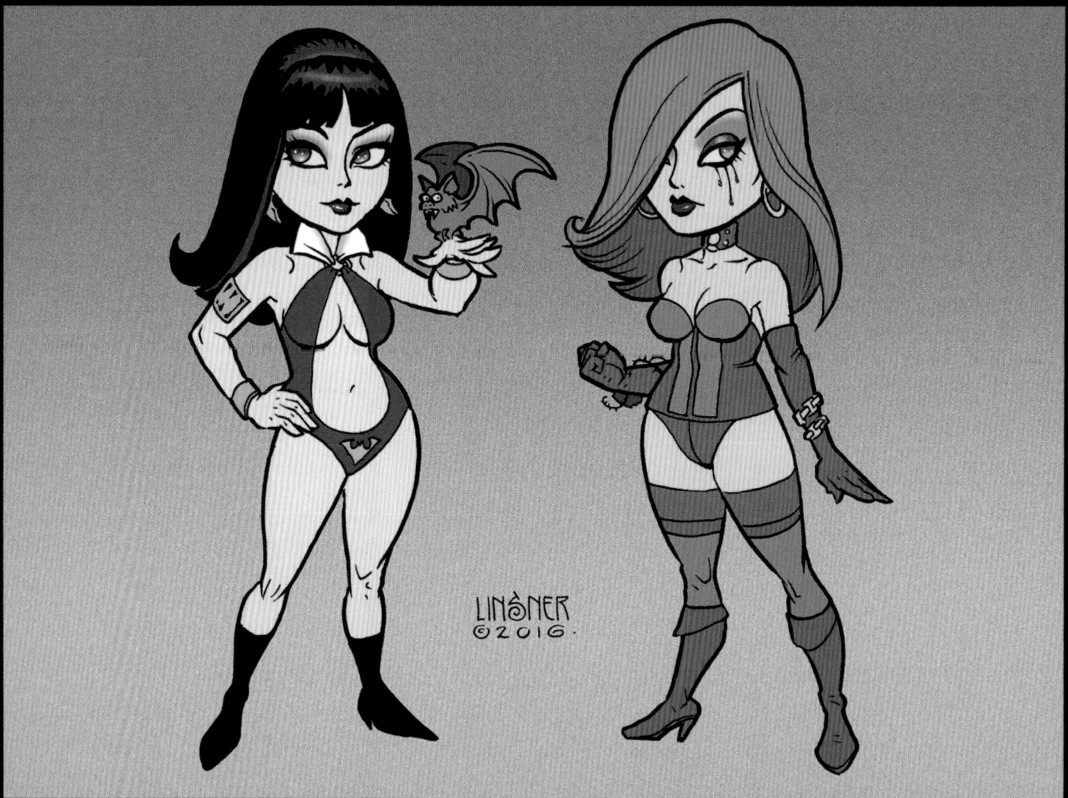
LINSNER
©2016.

CHAPTER • ONE

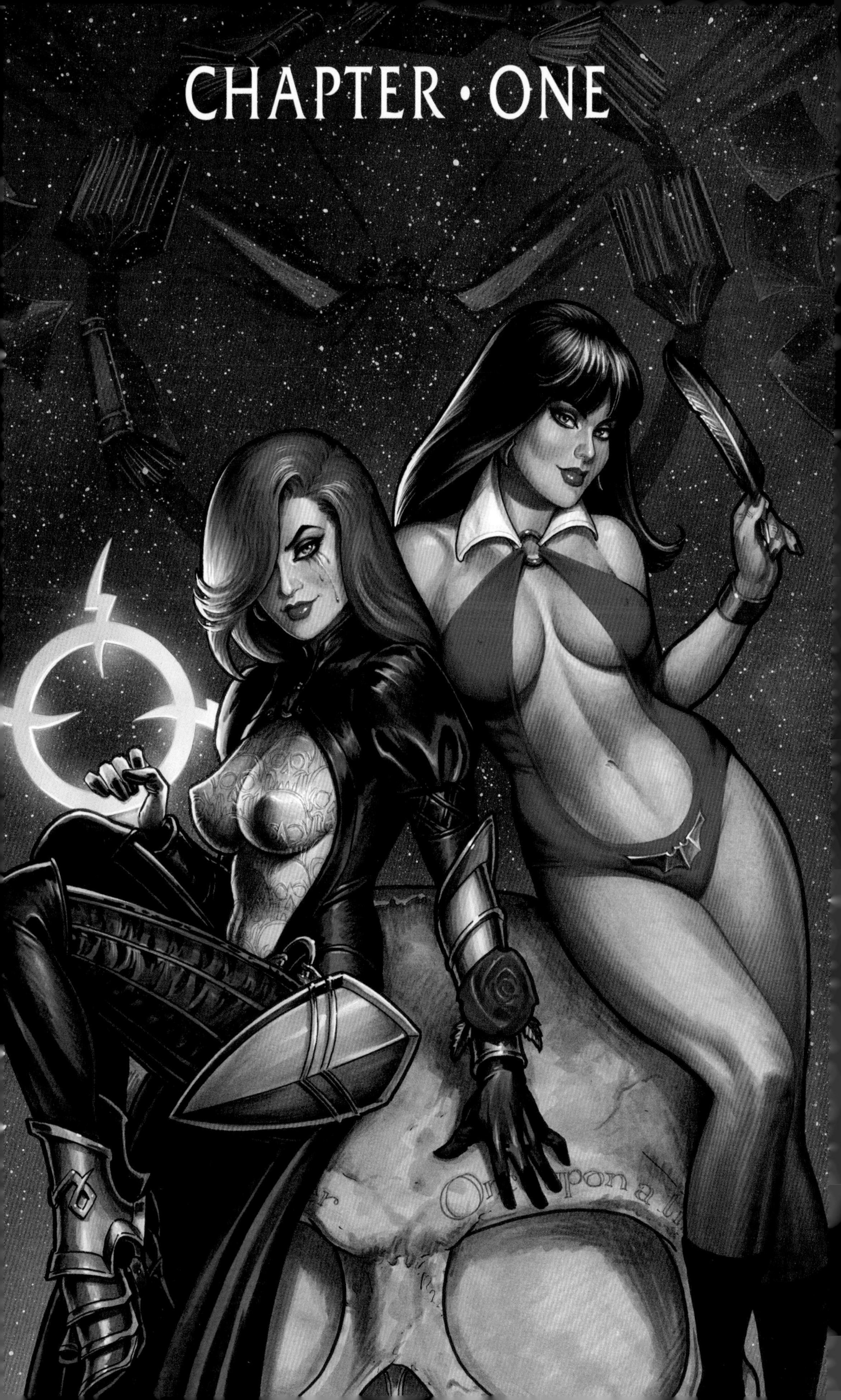

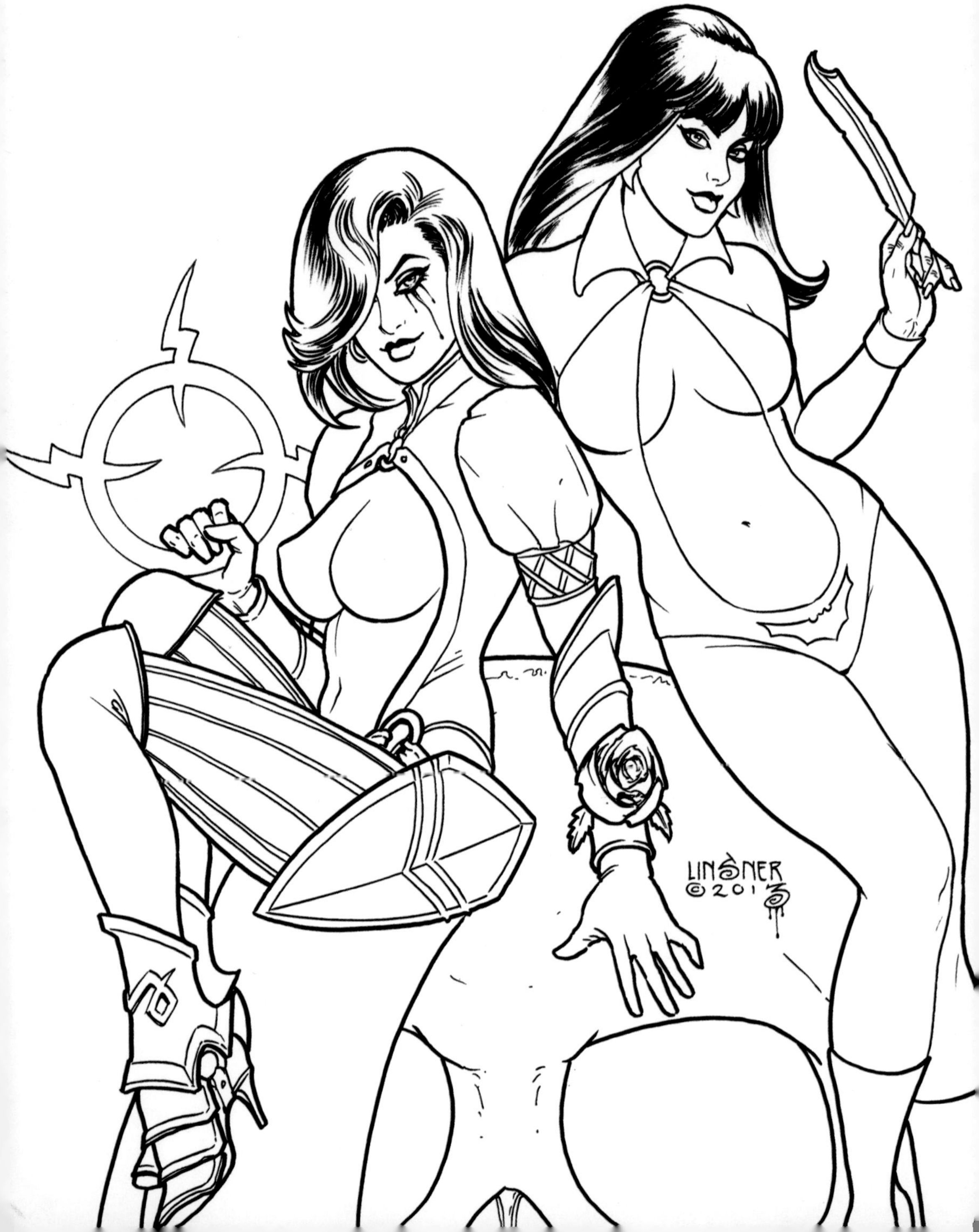
LINSNER
©2013

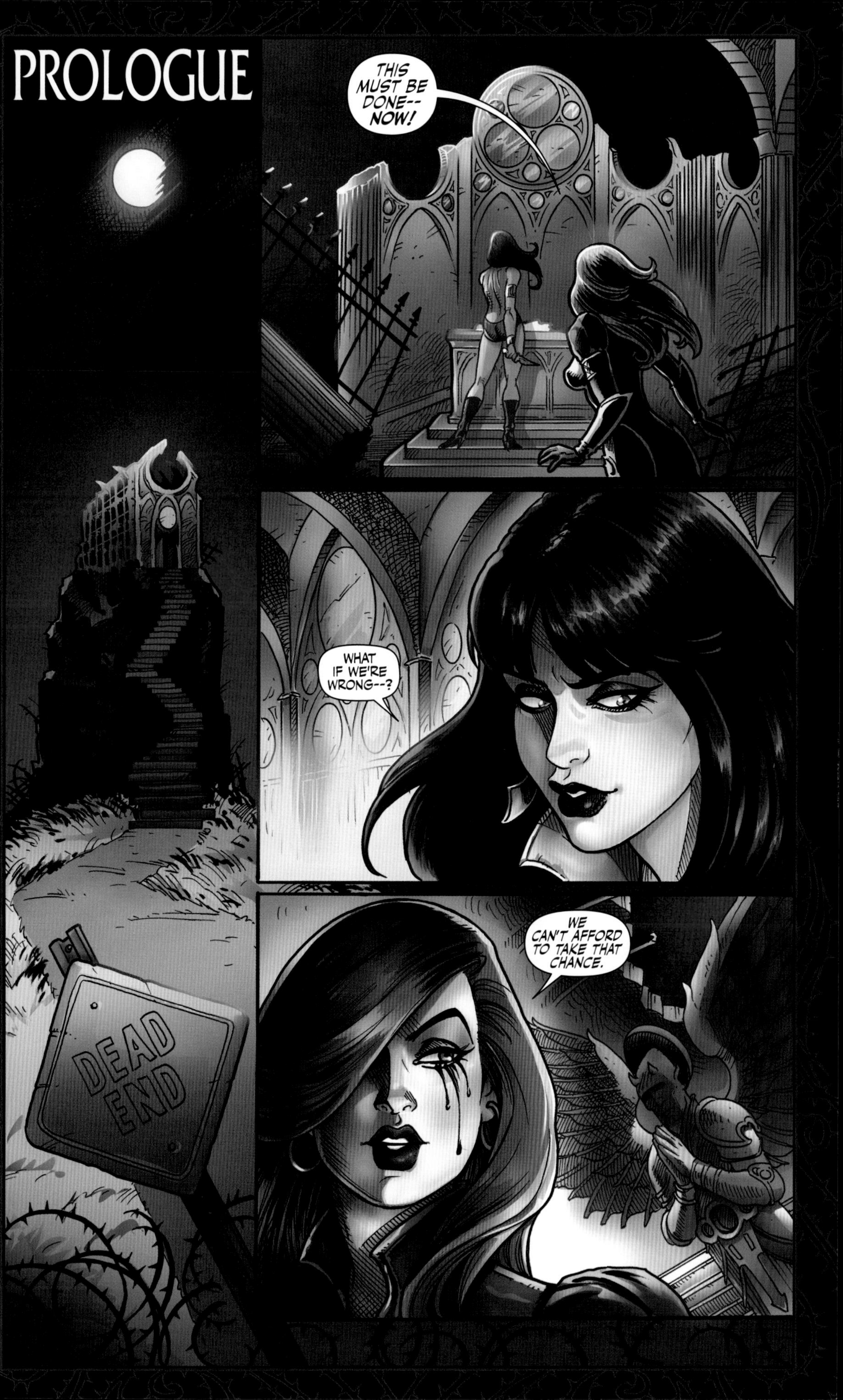
PROLOGUE
THIS MUST BE DONE--NOW!
WHAT IF WE'RE WRONG--?
WE CAN'T AFFORD TO TAKE THAT CHANCE.
DEAD END

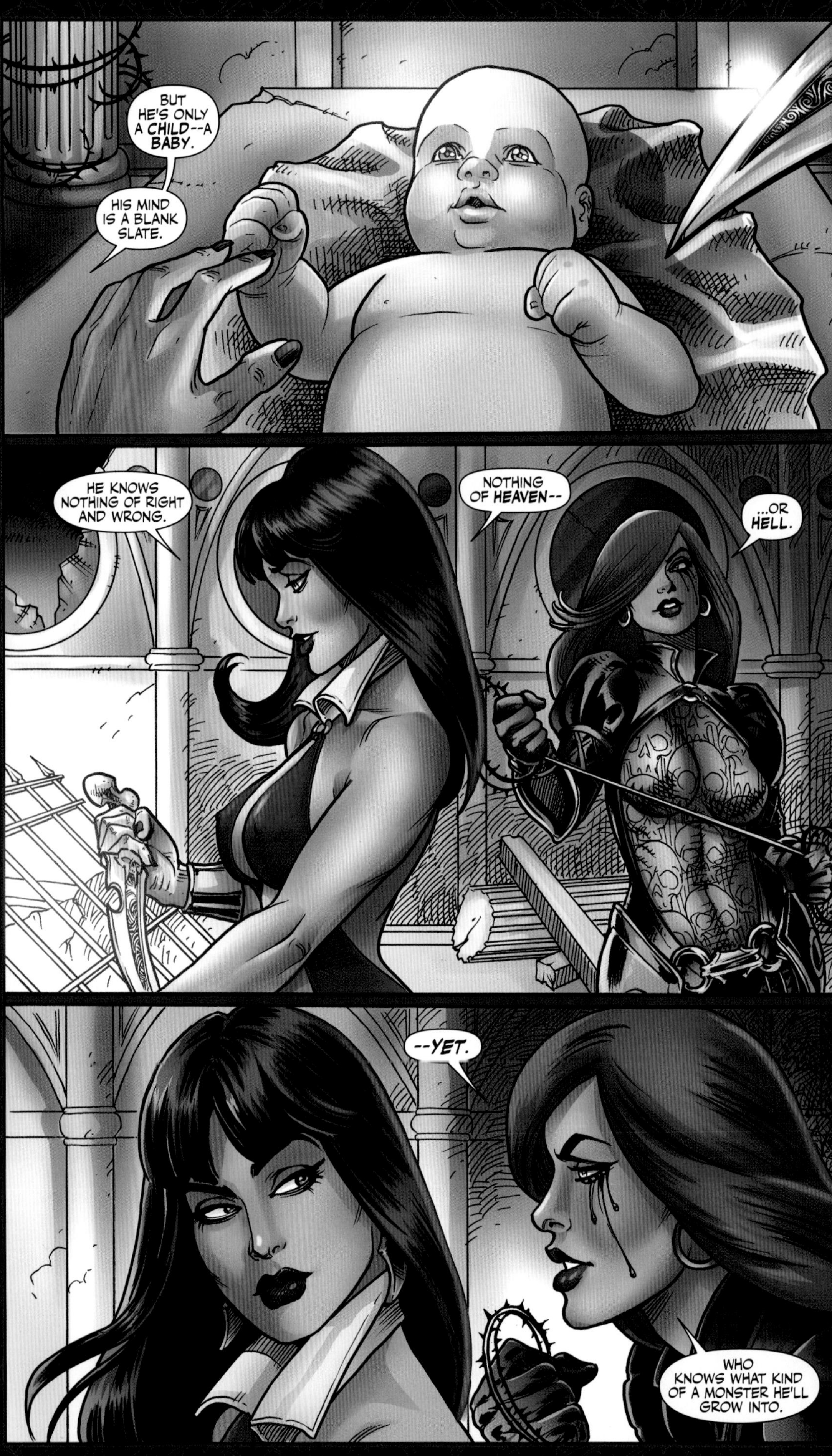
BUT HE'S ONLY A CHILD--A BABY.
HIS MIND IS A BLANK SLATE.
HE KNOWS NOTHING OF RIGHT AND WRONG.
NOTHING OF HEAVEN--
...OR HELL.
--YET.
WHO KNOWS WHAT KIND OF A MONSTER HE'LL GROW INTO.

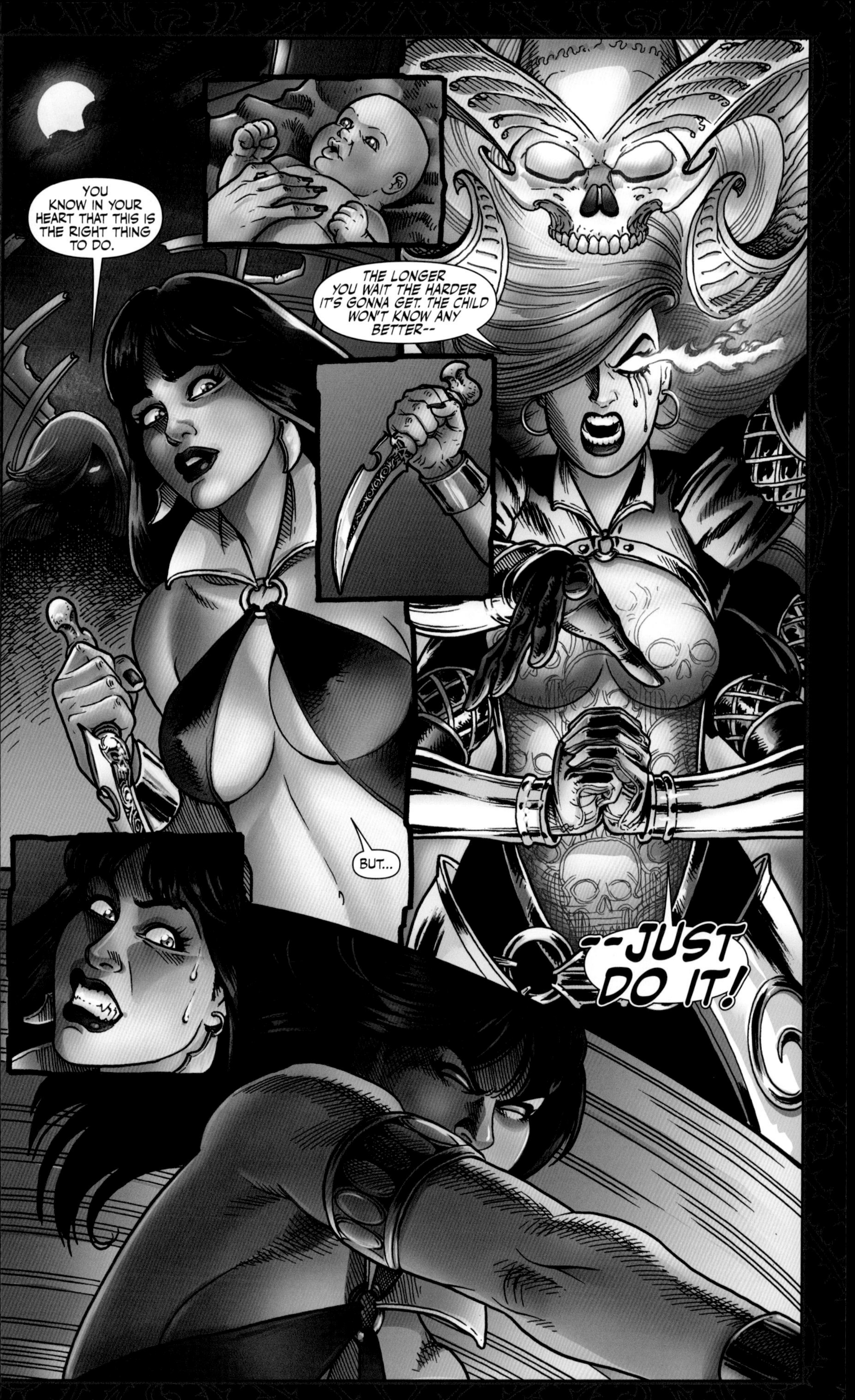
YOU KNOW IN YOUR HEART THAT THIS IS THE RIGHT THING TO DO.
THE LONGER YOU WAIT THE HARDER IT'S GONNA GET. THE CHILD WON'T KNOW ANY BETTER--
BUT...
--JUST DO IT!

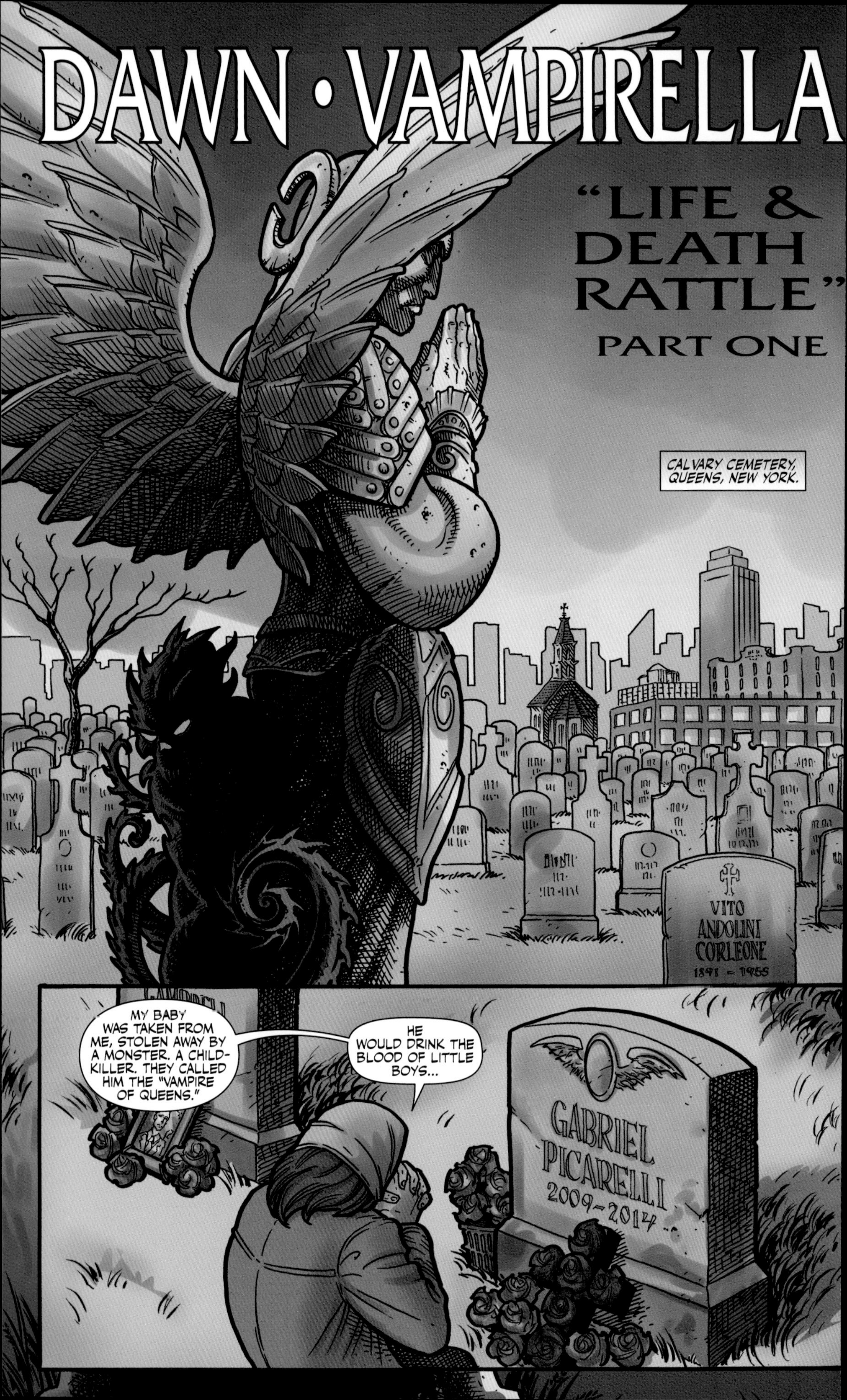
DAWN • VAMPIRELLA
"LIFE & DEATH RATTLE"
PART ONE
CALVARY CEMETERY, QUEENS, NEW YORK.
VITO ANDOLINI CORLEONE
MY BABY WAS TAKEN FROM ME, STOLEN AWAY BY A MONSTER. A CHILD-KILLER. THEY CALLED HIM THE "VAMPIRE OF QUEENS."
HE WOULD DRINK THE BLOOD OF LITTLE BOYS...
GABRIEL PICARELLI 2009-2014

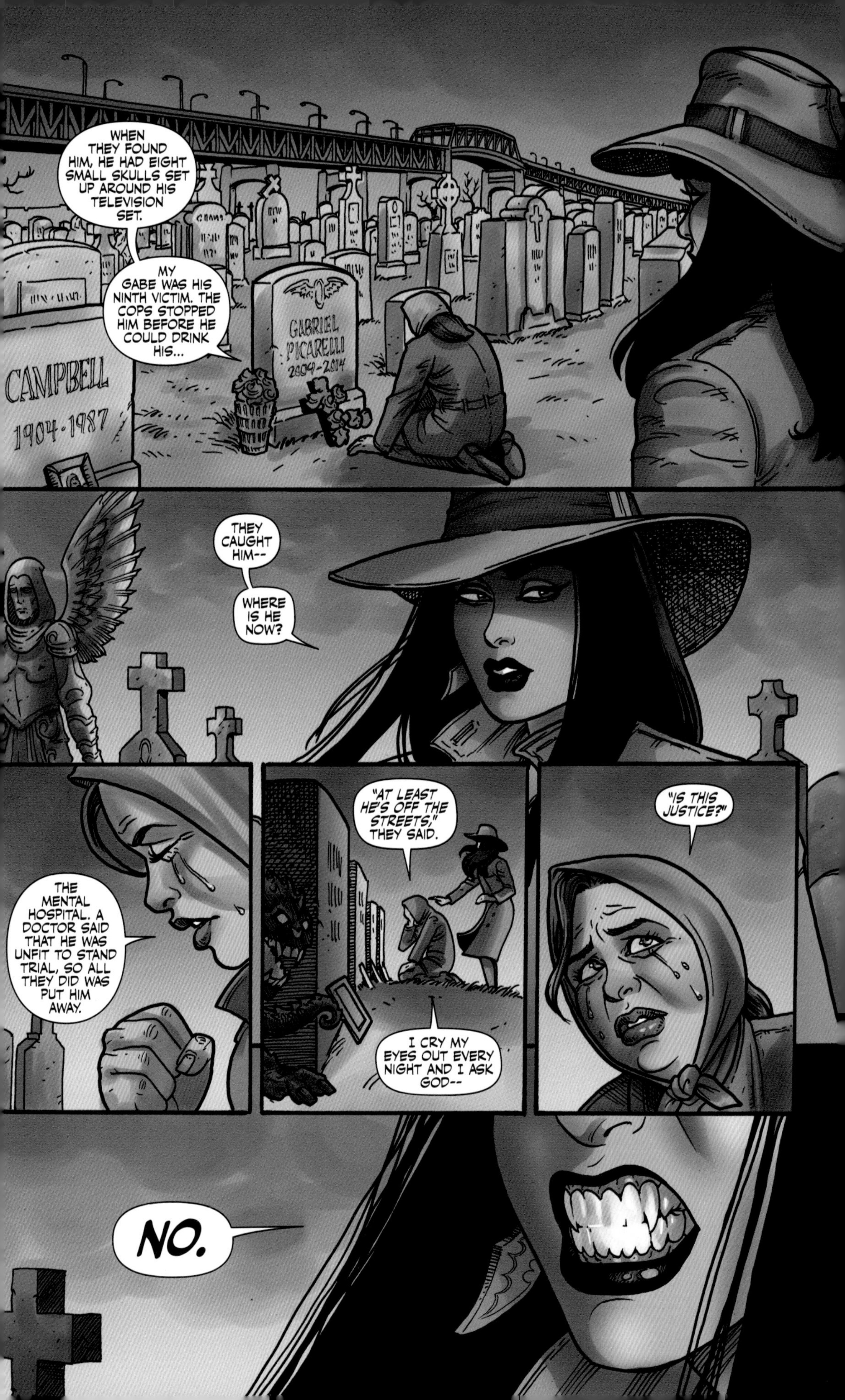
WHEN THEY FOUND HIM, HE HAD EIGHT SMALL SKULLS SET UP AROUND HIS TELEVISION SET.
MY GABE WAS HIS NINTH VICTIM. THE COPS STOPPED HIM BEFORE HE COULD DRINK HIS...
GABRIEL PICARELLI 2009-2014
CAMPBELL 1904-1987
THEY CAUGHT HIM--
WHERE IS HE NOW?
THE MENTAL HOSPITAL. A DOCTOR SAID THAT HE WAS UNFIT TO STAND TRIAL, SO ALL THEY DID WAS PUT HIM AWAY.
"AT LEAST HE'S OFF THE STREETS," THEY SAID.
I CRY MY EYES OUT EVERY NIGHT AND I ASK GOD--
"IS THIS JUSTICE?"
NO.

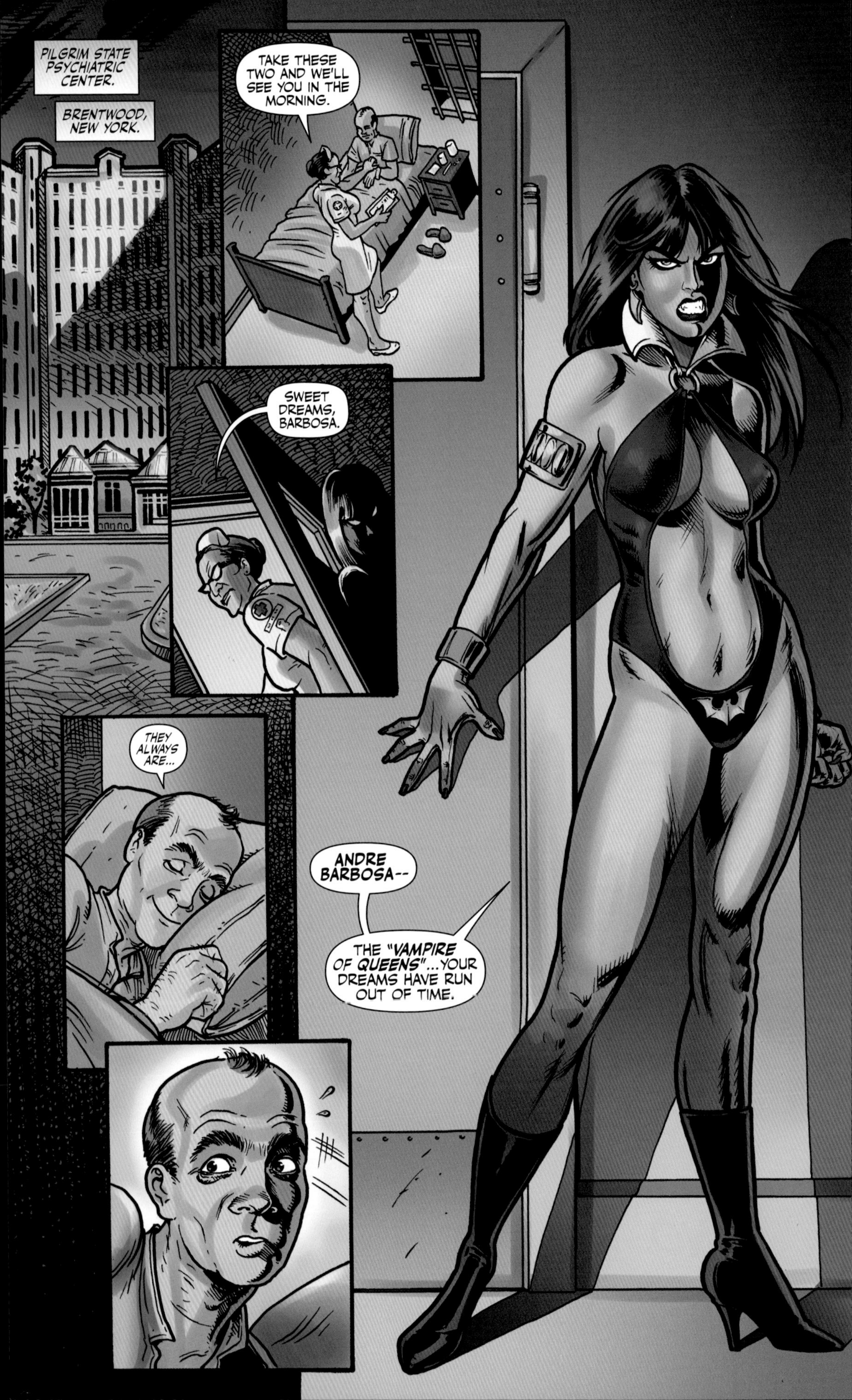
PILGRIM STATE PSYCHIATRIC CENTER.
BRENTWOOD, NEW YORK.
TAKE THESE TWO AND WE'LL SEE YOU IN THE MORNING.
SWEET DREAMS, BARBOSA.
THEY ALWAYS ARE...
ANDRE BARBOSA--
THE "VAMPIRE OF QUEENS"...YOUR DREAMS HAVE RUN OUT OF TIME.

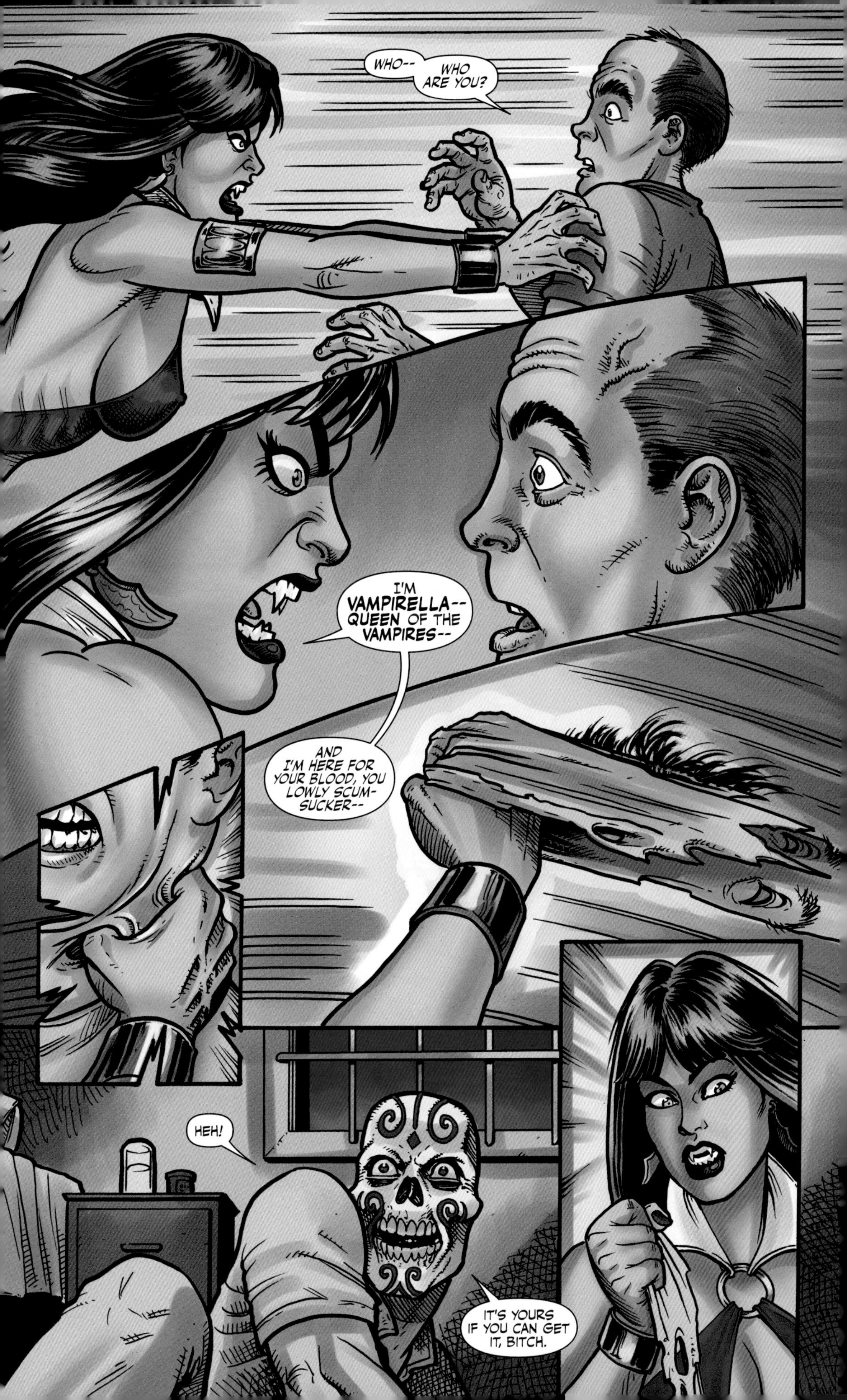
WHO--
WHO ARE YOU?
I'M VAMPIRELLA-- QUEEN OF THE VAMPIRES--
AND I'M HERE FOR YOUR BLOOD, YOU LOWLY SCUM-SUCKER--
HEH!
IT'S YOURS IF YOU CAN GET IT, BITCH.

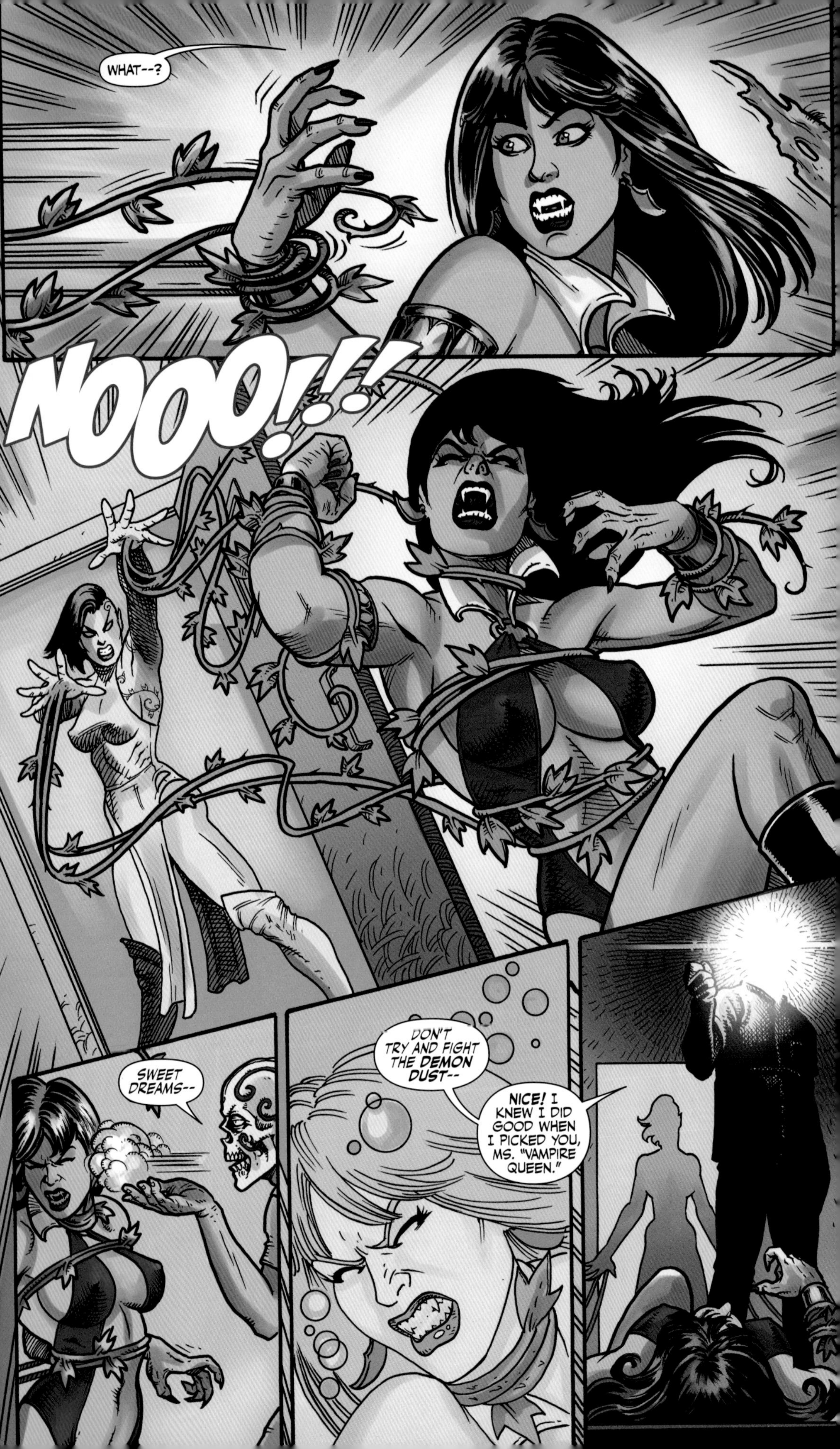
WHAT--?
NOOO!!!
SWEET DREAMS--
DON'T TRY AND FIGHT THE DEMON DUST--
NICE! I KNEW I DID GOOD WHEN I PICKED YOU, MS. "VAMPIRE QUEEN."

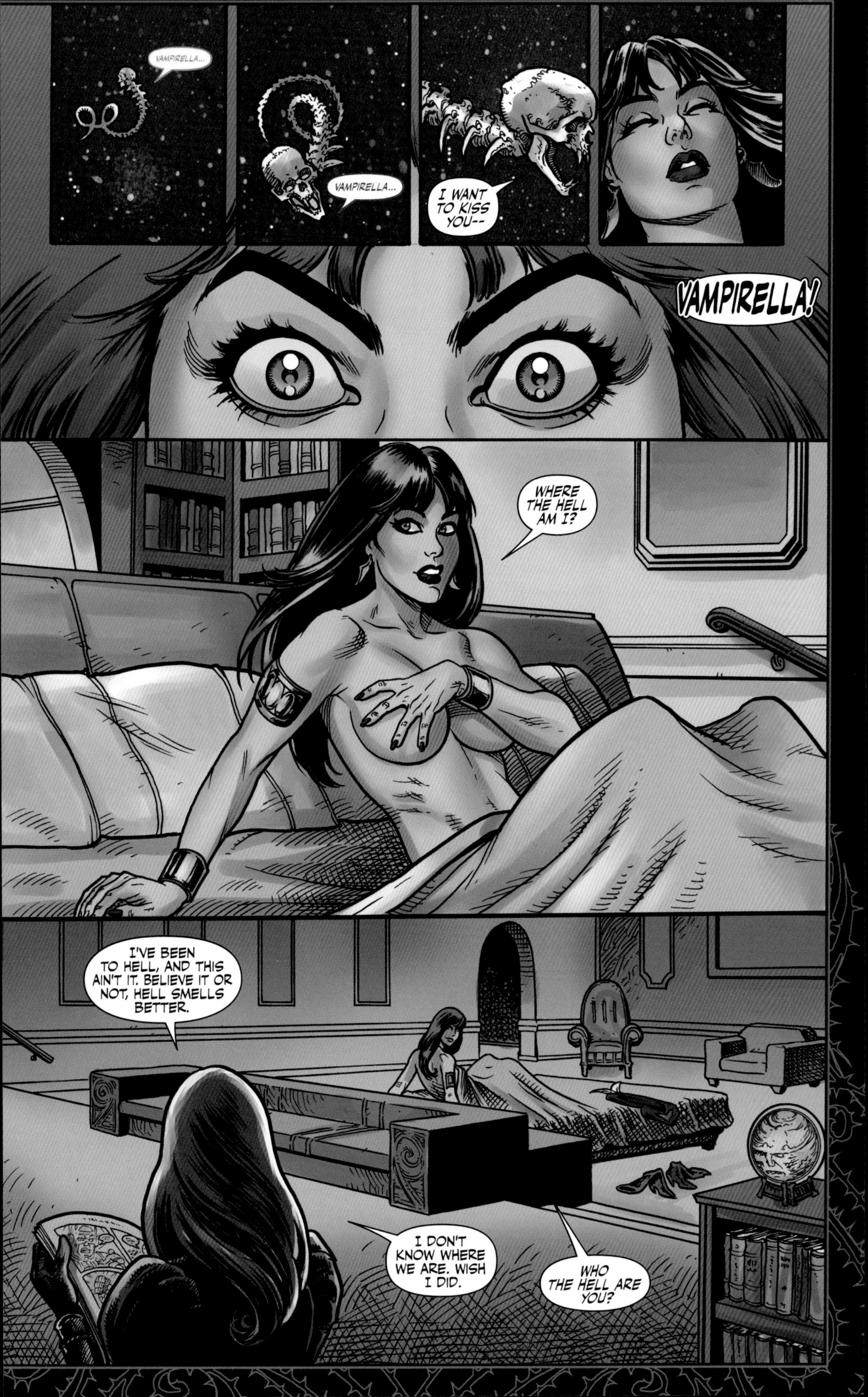
VAMPIRELLA...
VAMPIRELLA...
I WANT TO KISS YOU--
VAMPIRELLA!
WHERE THE HELL AM I?
I'VE BEEN TO HELL, AND THIS AIN'T IT. BELIEVE IT OR NOT, HELL SMELLS BETTER.
I DON'T KNOW WHERE WE ARE. WISH I DID.
WHO THE HELL ARE YOU?

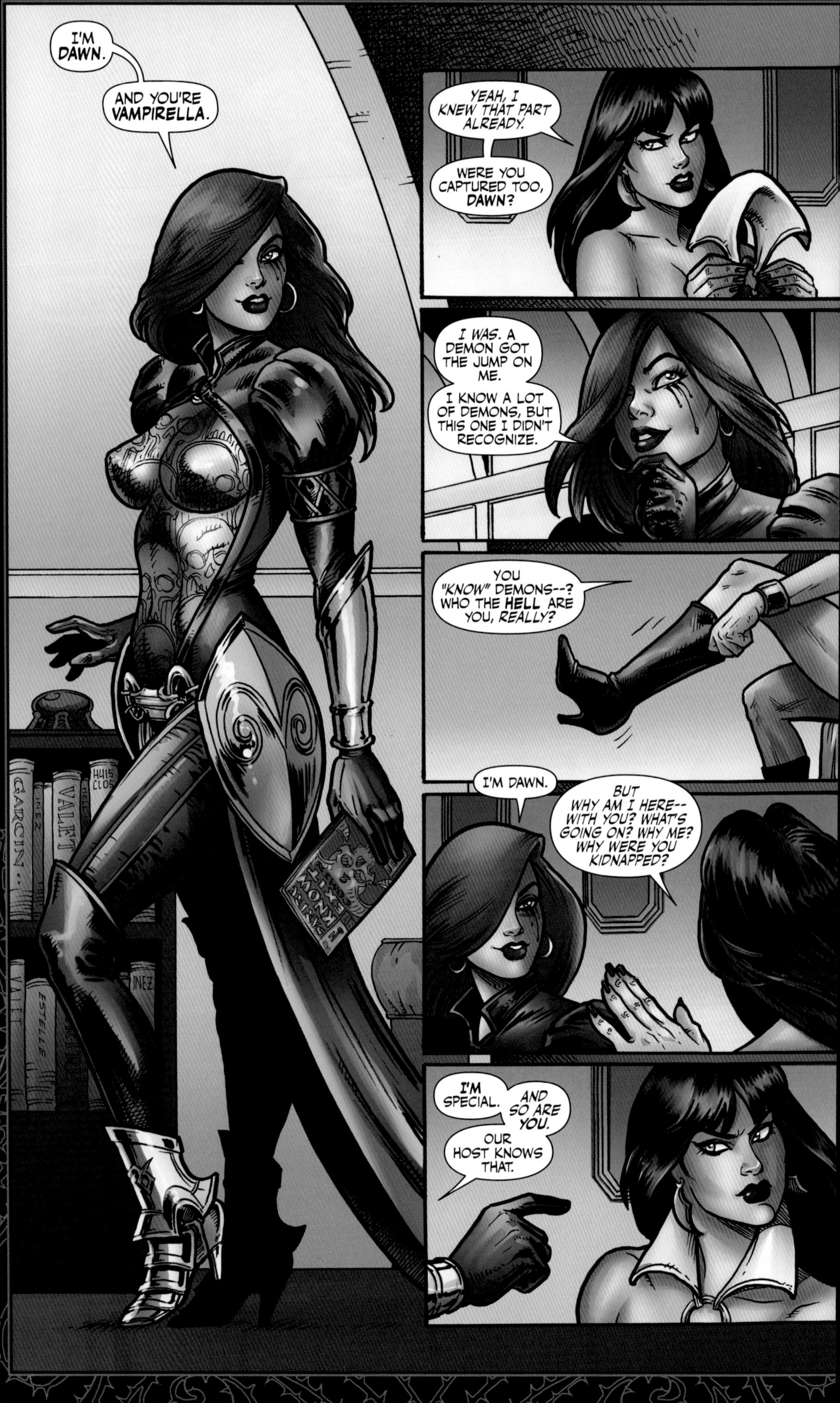
I'M DAWN.
AND YOU'RE VAMPIRELLA.
YEAH, I KNEW THAT PART ALREADY.
WERE YOU CAPTURED TOO, DAWN?
I WAS. A DEMON GOT THE JUMP ON ME.
I KNOW A LOT OF DEMONS, BUT THIS ONE I DIDN'T RECOGNIZE.
YOU "KNOW" DEMONS--? WHO THE HELL ARE YOU, REALLY?
I'M DAWN.
BUT WHY AM I HERE-- WITH YOU? WHAT'S GOING ON? WHY ME? WHY WERE YOU KIDNAPPED?
I'M SPECIAL.
AND SO ARE YOU.
OUR HOST KNOWS THAT.

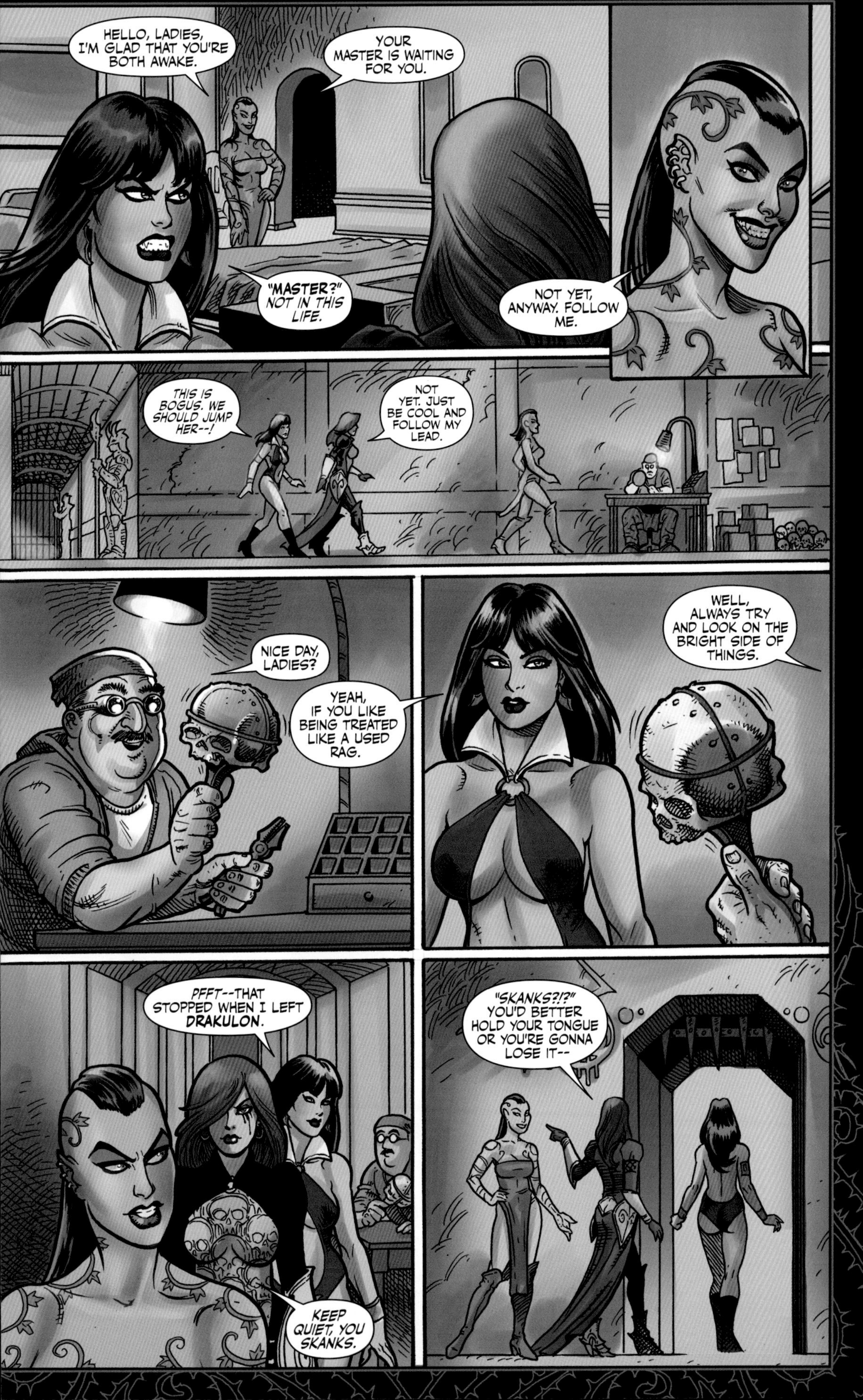
HELLO, LADIES, I'M GLAD THAT YOU'RE BOTH AWAKE.
YOUR MASTER IS WAITING FOR YOU.
"MASTER?" NOT IN THIS LIFE.
NOT YET, ANYWAY. FOLLOW ME.
THIS IS BOGUS. WE SHOULD JUMP HER--!
NOT YET. JUST BE COOL AND FOLLOW MY LEAD.
NICE DAY, LADIES?
YEAH, IF YOU LIKE BEING TREATED LIKE A USED RAG.
WELL, ALWAYS TRY AND LOOK ON THE BRIGHT SIDE OF THINGS.
PFFT--THAT STOPPED WHEN I LEFT DRAKULON.
KEEP QUIET, YOU SKANKS.
"SKANKS?!?" YOU'D BETTER HOLD YOUR TONGUE OR YOU'RE GONNA LOSE IT--

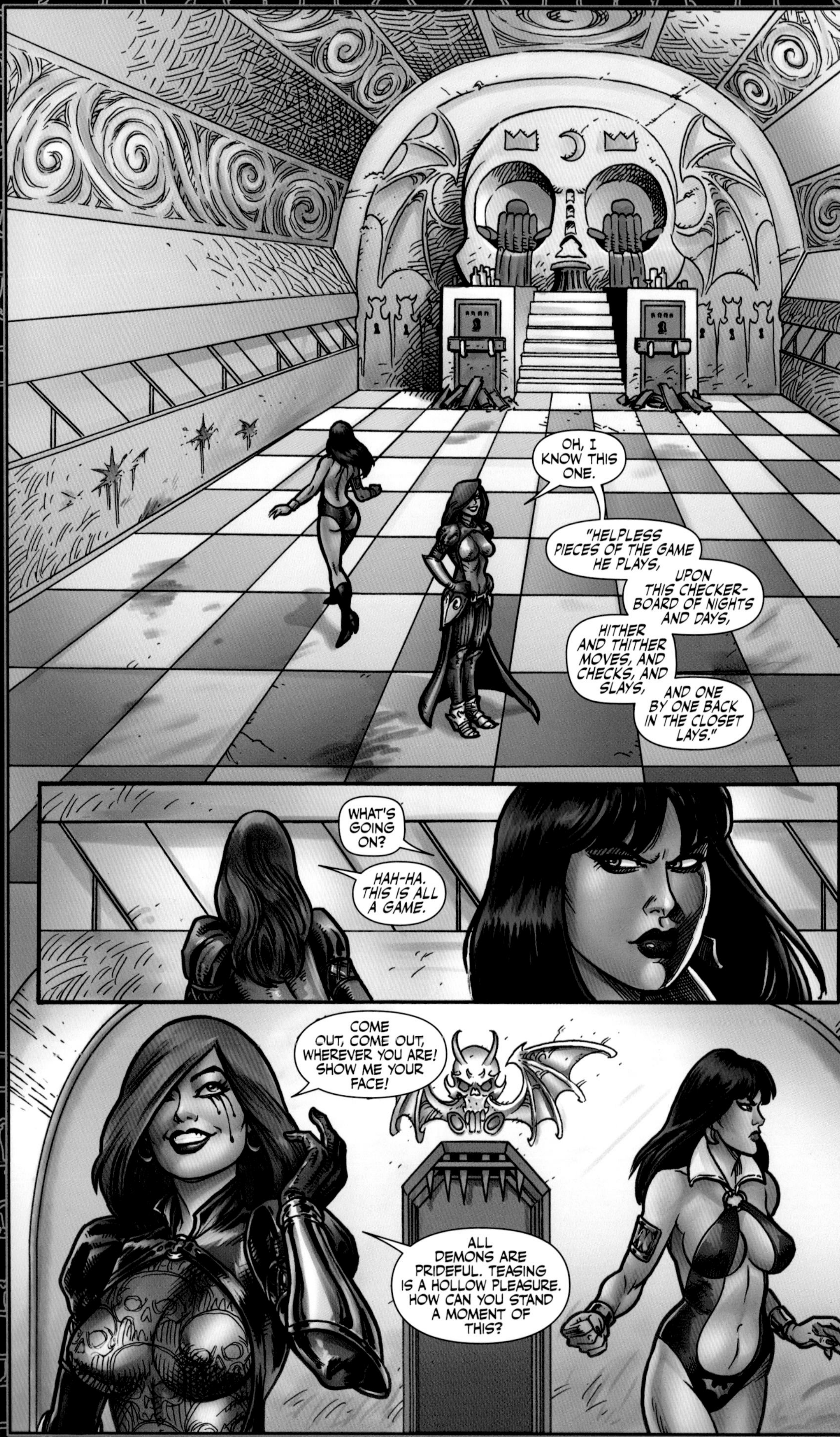
OH, I KNOW THIS ONE.
"HELPLESS PIECES OF THE GAME HE PLAYS,
UPON THIS CHECKER-BOARD OF NIGHTS AND DAYS,
HITHER AND THITHER MOVES, AND CHECKS, AND SLAYS,
AND ONE BY ONE BACK IN THE CLOSET LAYS."
WHAT'S GOING ON?
HAH-HA. THIS IS ALL A GAME.
COME OUT, COME OUT, WHEREVER YOU ARE! SHOW ME YOUR FACE!
ALL DEMONS ARE PRIDEFUL. TEASING IS A HOLLOW PLEASURE. HOW CAN YOU STAND A MOMENT OF THIS?

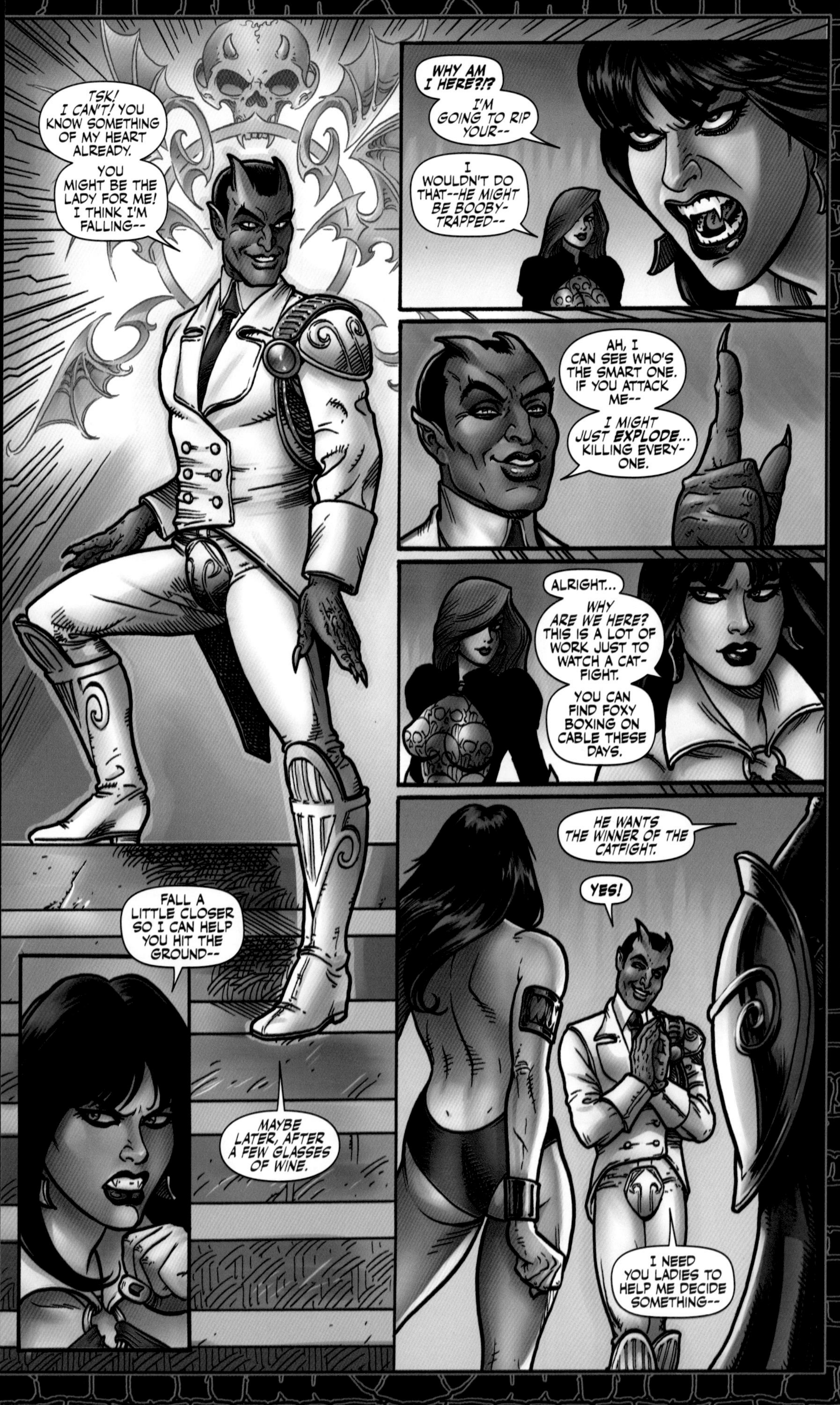
TSK! I CAN'T! YOU KNOW SOMETHING OF MY HEART ALREADY.
YOU MIGHT BE THE LADY FOR ME! I THINK I'M FALLING--
FALL A LITTLE CLOSER SO I CAN HELP YOU HIT THE GROUND--
MAYBE LATER, AFTER A FEW GLASSES OF WINE.
WHY AM I HERE?!?
I'M GOING TO RIP YOUR--
I WOULDN'T DO THAT--HE MIGHT BE BOOBY-TRAPPED--
AH, I CAN SEE WHO'S THE SMART ONE. IF YOU ATTACK ME--
I MIGHT JUST EXPLODE... KILLING EVERY-ONE.
ALRIGHT...
WHY ARE WE HERE? THIS IS A LOT OF WORK JUST TO WATCH A CAT-FIGHT.
YOU CAN FIND FOXY BOXING ON CABLE THESE DAYS.
HE WANTS THE WINNER OF THE CATFIGHT.
YES!
I NEED YOU LADIES TO HELP ME DECIDE SOMETHING--

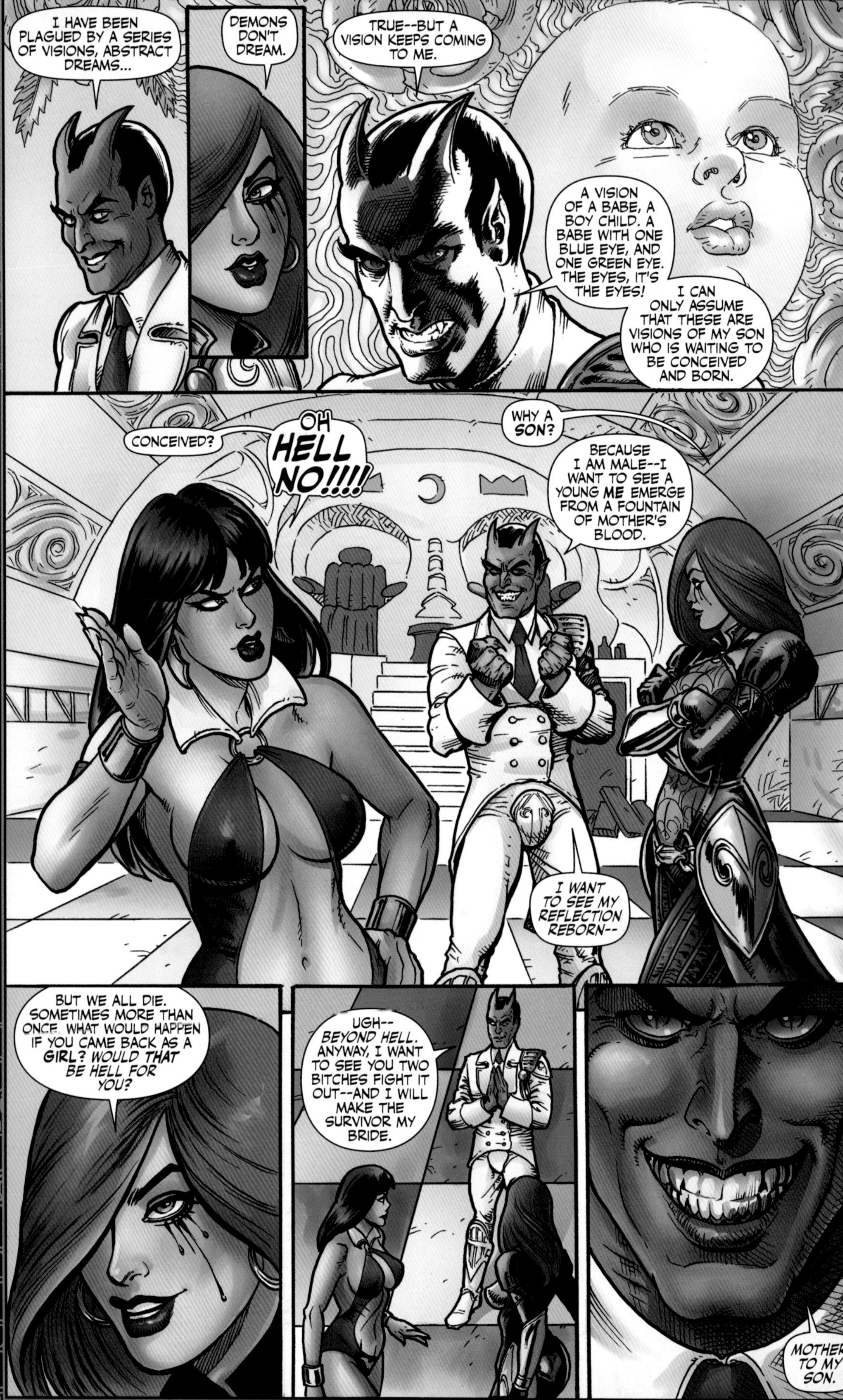
I HAVE BEEN PLAGUED BY A SERIES OF VISIONS, ABSTRACT DREAMS...
DEMONS DON'T DREAM.
TRUE--BUT A VISION KEEPS COMING TO ME.
A VISION OF A BABE, A BOY CHILD. A BABE WITH ONE BLUE EYE, AND ONE GREEN EYE. THE EYES, IT'S THE EYES!
I CAN ONLY ASSUME THAT THESE ARE VISIONS OF MY SON WHO IS WAITING TO BE CONCEIVED AND BORN.
CONCEIVED?
OH HELL NO!!!!
WHY A SON?
BECAUSE I AM MALE--I WANT TO SEE A YOUNG ME EMERGE FROM A FOUNTAIN OF MOTHER'S BLOOD.
I WANT TO SEE MY REFLECTION REBORN--
BUT WE ALL DIE. SOMETIMES MORE THAN ONCE. WHAT WOULD HAPPEN IF YOU CAME BACK AS A GIRL? WOULD THAT BE HELL FOR YOU?
UGH-- BEYOND HELL. ANYWAY, I WANT TO SEE YOU TWO BITCHES FIGHT IT OUT--AND I WILL MAKE THE SURVIVOR MY BRIDE.
MOTHER TO MY SON.

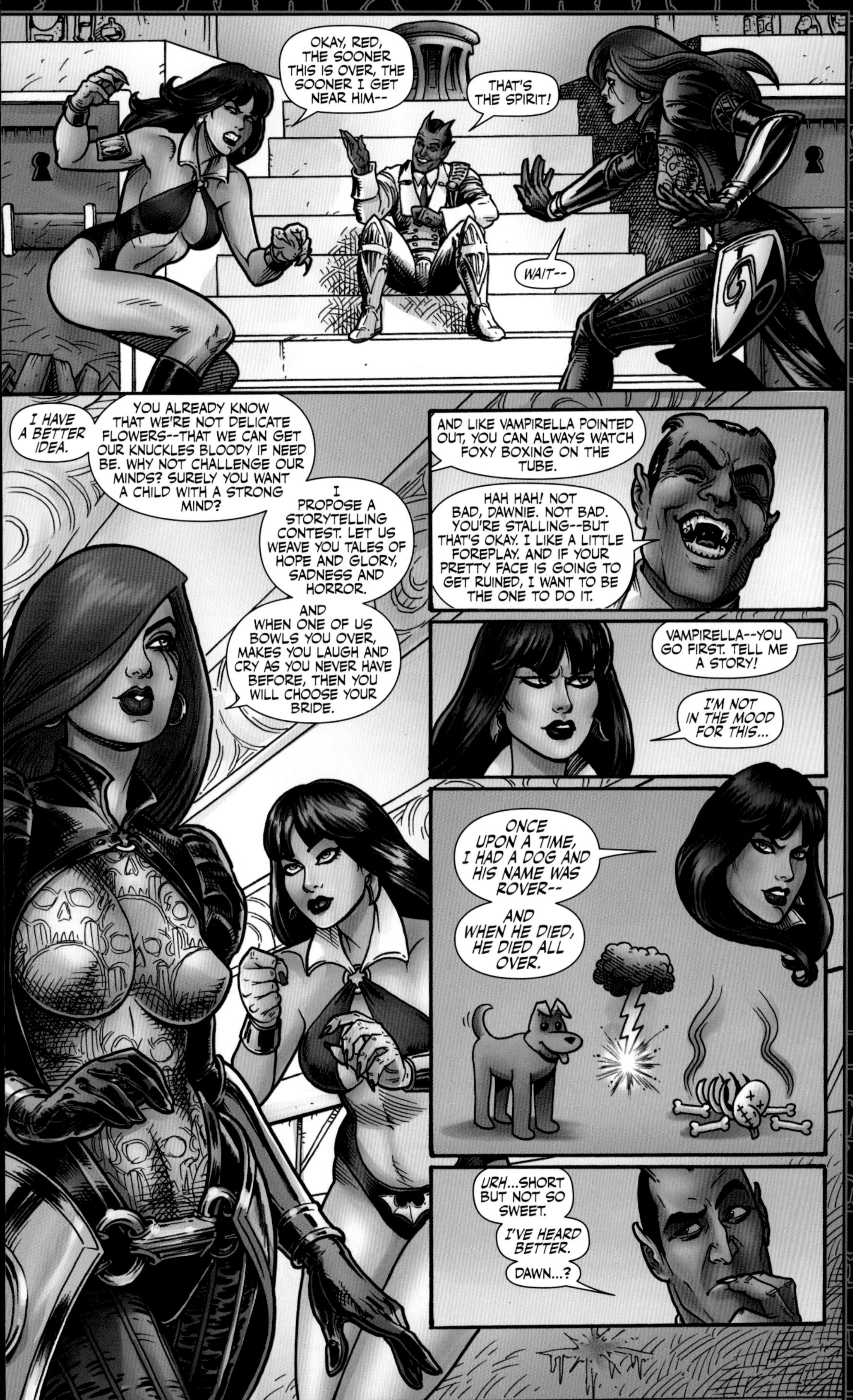

OKAY, RED, THE SOONER THIS IS OVER, THE SOONER I GET NEAR HIM--
THAT'S THE SPIRIT!
WAIT--
I HAVE A BETTER IDEA.
YOU ALREADY KNOW THAT WE'RE NOT DELICATE FLOWERS--THAT WE CAN GET OUR KNUCKLES BLOODY IF NEED BE. WHY NOT CHALLENGE OUR MINDS? SURELY YOU WANT A CHILD WITH A STRONG MIND?
I PROPOSE A STORYTELLING CONTEST. LET US WEAVE YOU TALES OF HOPE AND GLORY, SADNESS AND HORROR.
AND WHEN ONE OF US BOWLS YOU OVER, MAKES YOU LAUGH AND CRY AS YOU NEVER HAVE BEFORE, THEN YOU WILL CHOOSE YOUR BRIDE.
AND LIKE VAMPIRELLA POINTED OUT, YOU CAN ALWAYS WATCH FOXY BOXING ON THE TUBE.
HAH HAH! NOT BAD, DAWNIE. NOT BAD. YOU'RE STALLING--BUT THAT'S OKAY. I LIKE A LITTLE FOREPLAY. AND IF YOUR PRETTY FACE IS GOING TO GET RUINED, I WANT TO BE THE ONE TO DO IT.
VAMPIRELLA--YOU GO FIRST. TELL ME A STORY!
I'M NOT IN THE MOOD FOR THIS...
ONCE UPON A TIME, I HAD A DOG AND HIS NAME WAS ROVER--
AND WHEN HE DIED, HE DIED ALL OVER.
URH...SHORT BUT NOT SO SWEET.
I'VE HEARD BETTER.
DAWN...?

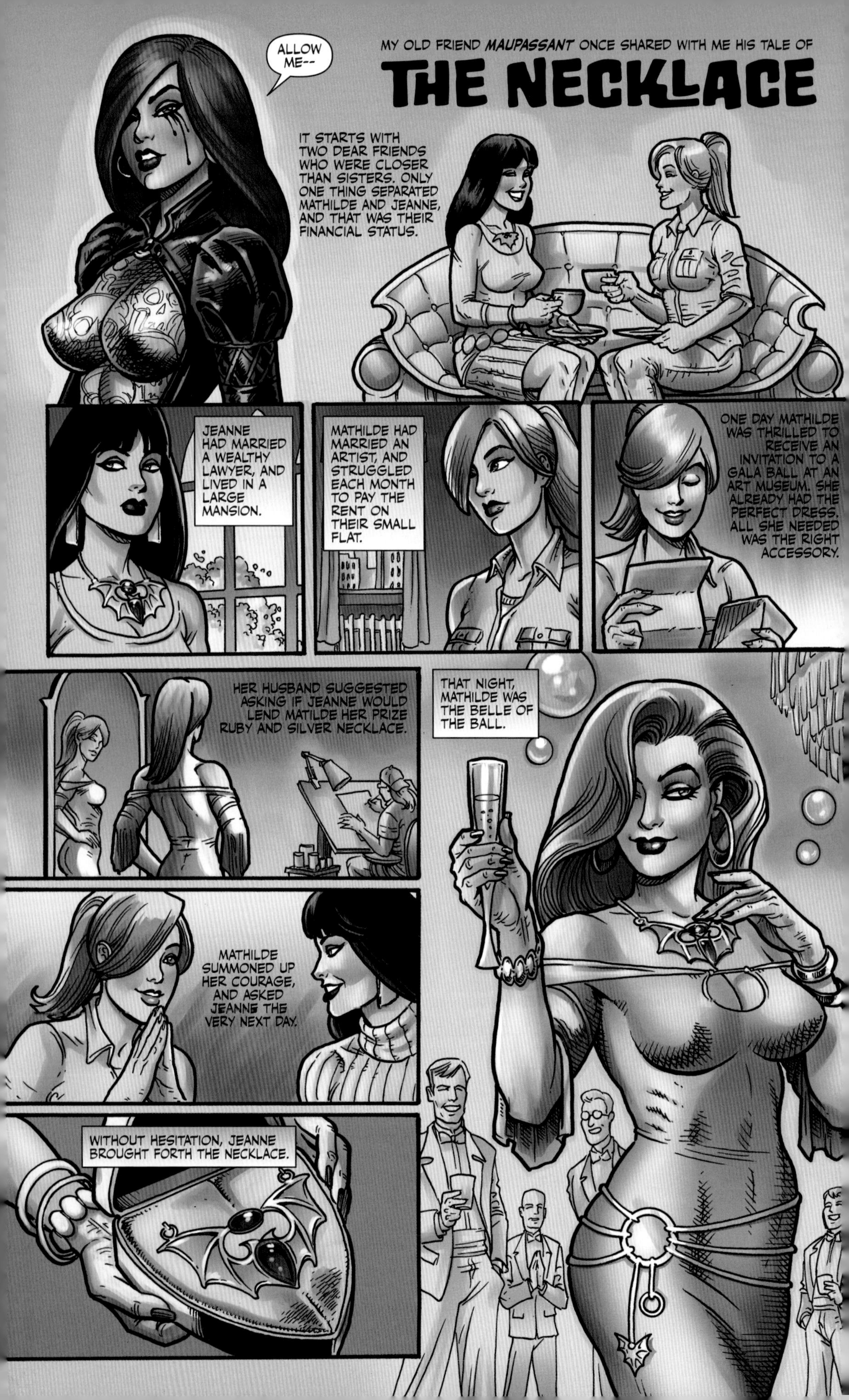
ALLOW ME--
MY OLD FRIEND MAUPASSANT ONCE SHARED WITH ME HIS TALE OF
THE NECKLACE
IT STARTS WITH TWO DEAR FRIENDS WHO WERE CLOSER THAN SISTERS. ONLY ONE THING SEPARATED MATHILDE AND JEANNE, AND THAT WAS THEIR FINANCIAL STATUS.
JEANNE HAD MARRIED A WEALTHY LAWYER, AND LIVED IN A LARGE MANSION.
MATHILDE HAD MARRIED AN ARTIST, AND STRUGGLED EACH MONTH TO PAY THE RENT ON THEIR SMALL FLAT.
ONE DAY MATHILDE WAS THRILLED TO RECEIVE AN INVITATION TO A GALA BALL AT AN ART MUSEUM. SHE ALREADY HAD THE PERFECT DRESS. ALL SHE NEEDED WAS THE RIGHT ACCESSORY.
HER HUSBAND SUGGESTED ASKING IF JEANNE WOULD LEND MATILDE HER PRIZE RUBY AND SILVER NECKLACE.
MATHILDE SUMMONED UP HER COURAGE, AND ASKED JEANNE THE VERY NEXT DAY.
WITHOUT HESITATION, JEANNE BROUGHT FORTH THE NECKLACE.
THAT NIGHT, MATHILDE WAS THE BELLE OF THE BALL.

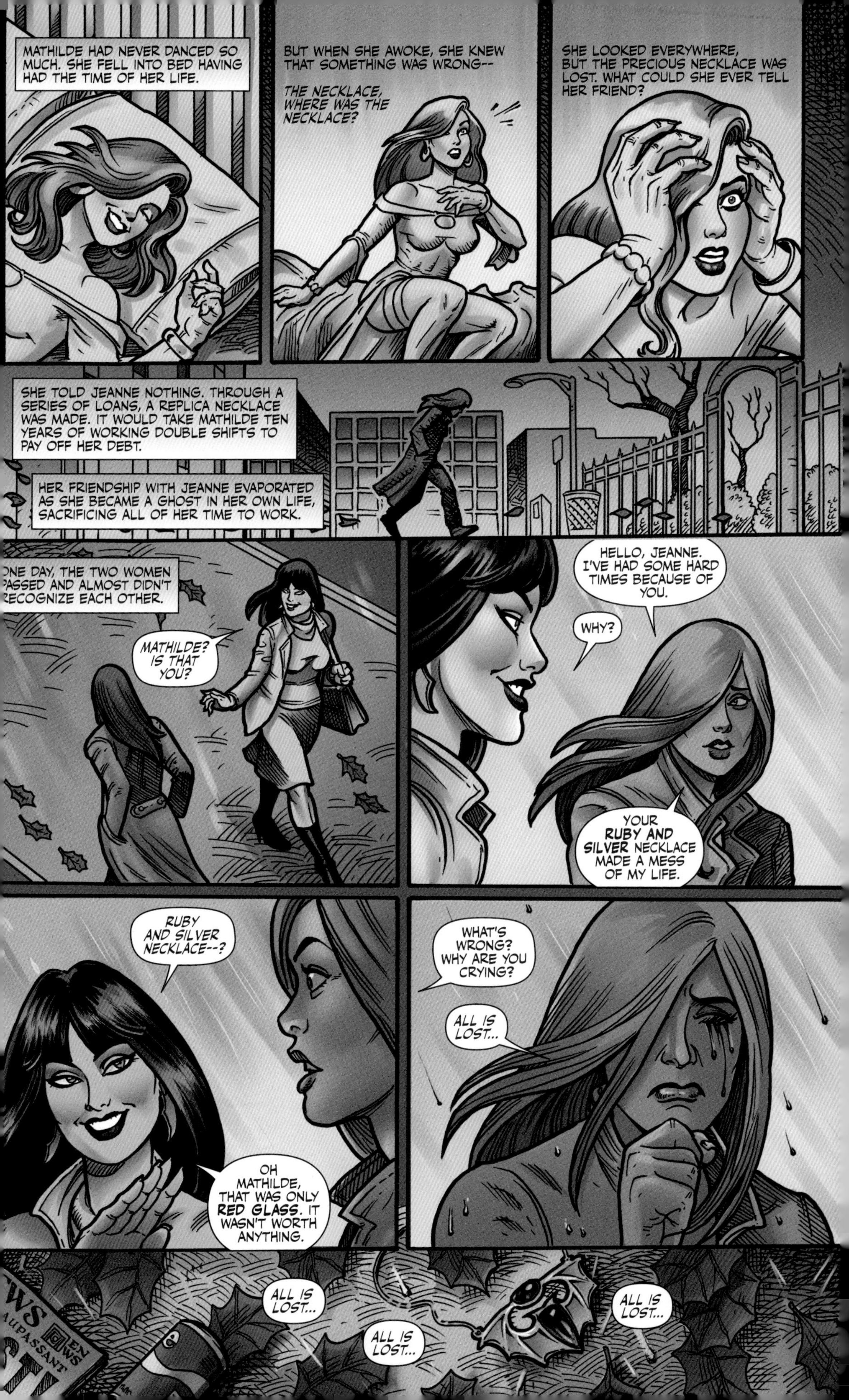
MATHILDE HAD NEVER DANCED SO MUCH. SHE FELL INTO BED HAVING HAD THE TIME OF HER LIFE.
BUT WHEN SHE AWOKE, SHE KNEW THAT SOMETHING WAS WRONG--
THE NECKLACE, WHERE WAS THE NECKLACE?
SHE LOOKED EVERYWHERE, BUT THE PRECIOUS NECKLACE WAS LOST. WHAT COULD SHE EVER TELL HER FRIEND?
SHE TOLD JEANNE NOTHING. THROUGH A SERIES OF LOANS, A REPLICA NECKLACE WAS MADE. IT WOULD TAKE MATHILDE TEN YEARS OF WORKING DOUBLE SHIFTS TO PAY OFF HER DEBT.
HER FRIENDSHIP WITH JEANNE EVAPORATED AS SHE BECAME A GHOST IN HER OWN LIFE, SACRIFICING ALL OF HER TIME TO WORK.
ONE DAY, THE TWO WOMEN PASSED AND ALMOST DIDN'T RECOGNIZE EACH OTHER.
MATHILDE? IS THAT YOU?
HELLO, JEANNE. I'VE HAD SOME HARD TIMES BECAUSE OF YOU.
WHY?
YOUR **RUBY AND SILVER** NECKLACE MADE A MESS OF MY LIFE.
RUBY AND SILVER NECKLACE--?
OH MATHILDE, THAT WAS ONLY **RED GLASS**. IT WASN'T WORTH ANYTHING.
WHAT'S WRONG? WHY ARE YOU CRYING?
ALL IS LOST...
ALL IS LOST...
ALL IS LOST...
ALL IS LOST...

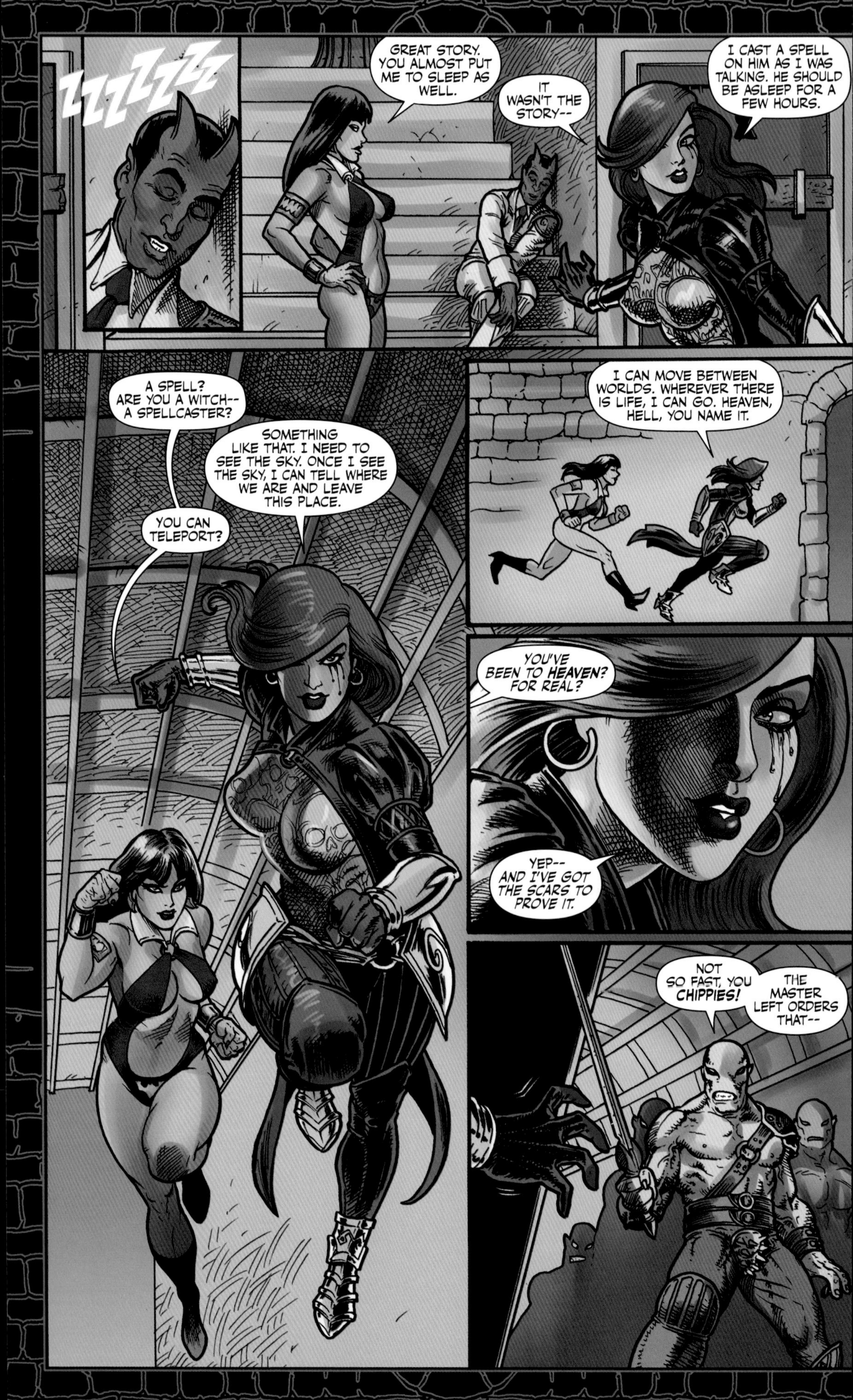
ZZZZZZZZ
GREAT STORY. YOU ALMOST PUT ME TO SLEEP AS WELL.
IT WASN'T THE STORY--
I CAST A SPELL ON HIM AS I WAS TALKING. HE SHOULD BE ASLEEP FOR A FEW HOURS.
A SPELL? ARE YOU A WITCH-- A SPELLCASTER?
SOMETHING LIKE THAT. I NEED TO SEE THE SKY. ONCE I SEE THE SKY, I CAN TELL WHERE WE ARE AND LEAVE THIS PLACE.
YOU CAN TELEPORT?
I CAN MOVE BETWEEN WORLDS. WHEREVER THERE IS LIFE, I CAN GO. HEAVEN, HELL, YOU NAME IT.
YOU'VE BEEN TO HEAVEN? FOR REAL?
YEP-- AND I'VE GOT THE SCARS TO PROVE IT.
NOT SO FAST, YOU CHIPPIES!
THE MASTER LEFT ORDERS THAT--

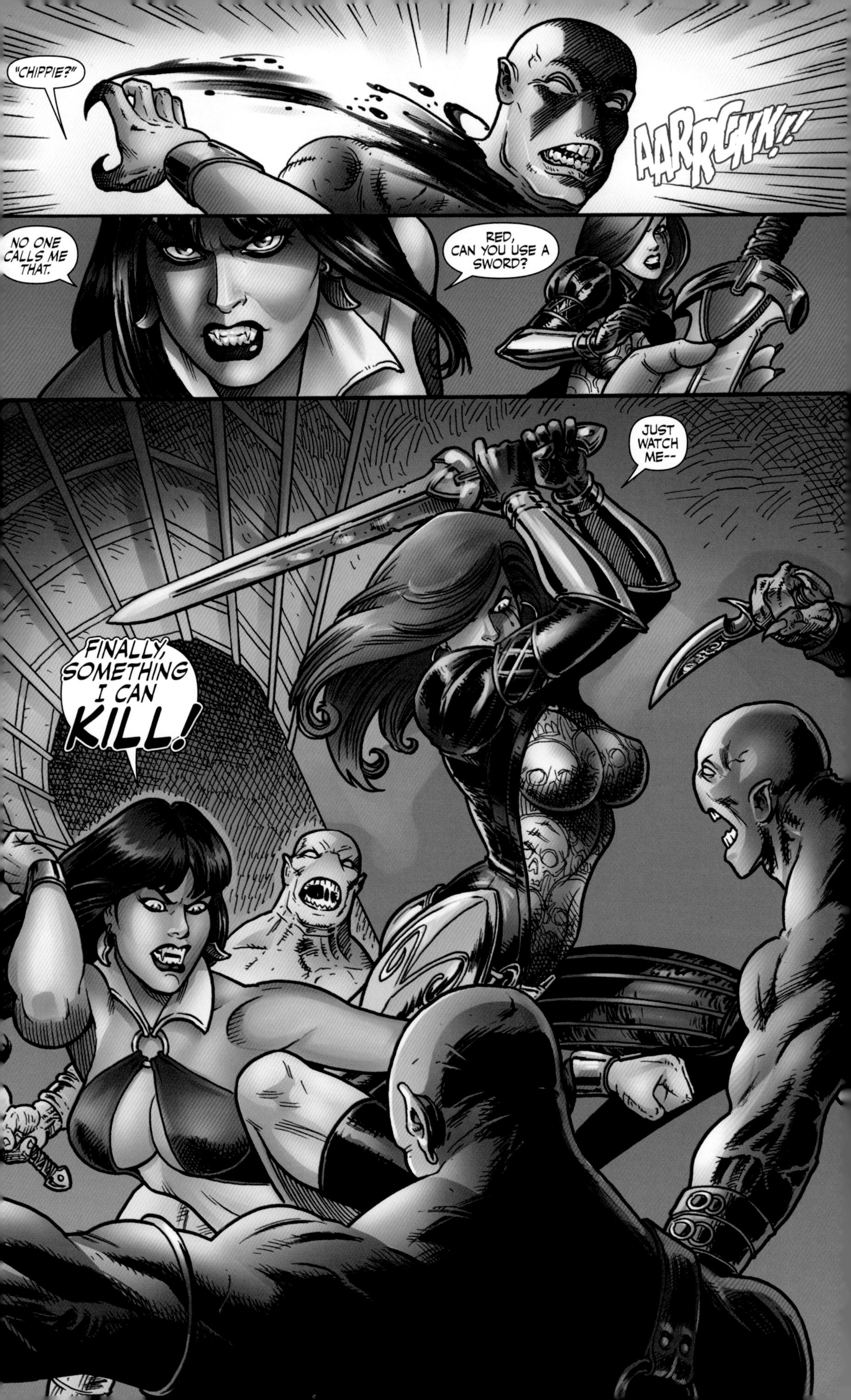
"CHIPPIE?"
AARRGHK!!
NO ONE CALLS ME THAT.
RED, CAN YOU USE A SWORD?
JUST WATCH ME--
FINALLY, SOMETHING I CAN KILL!

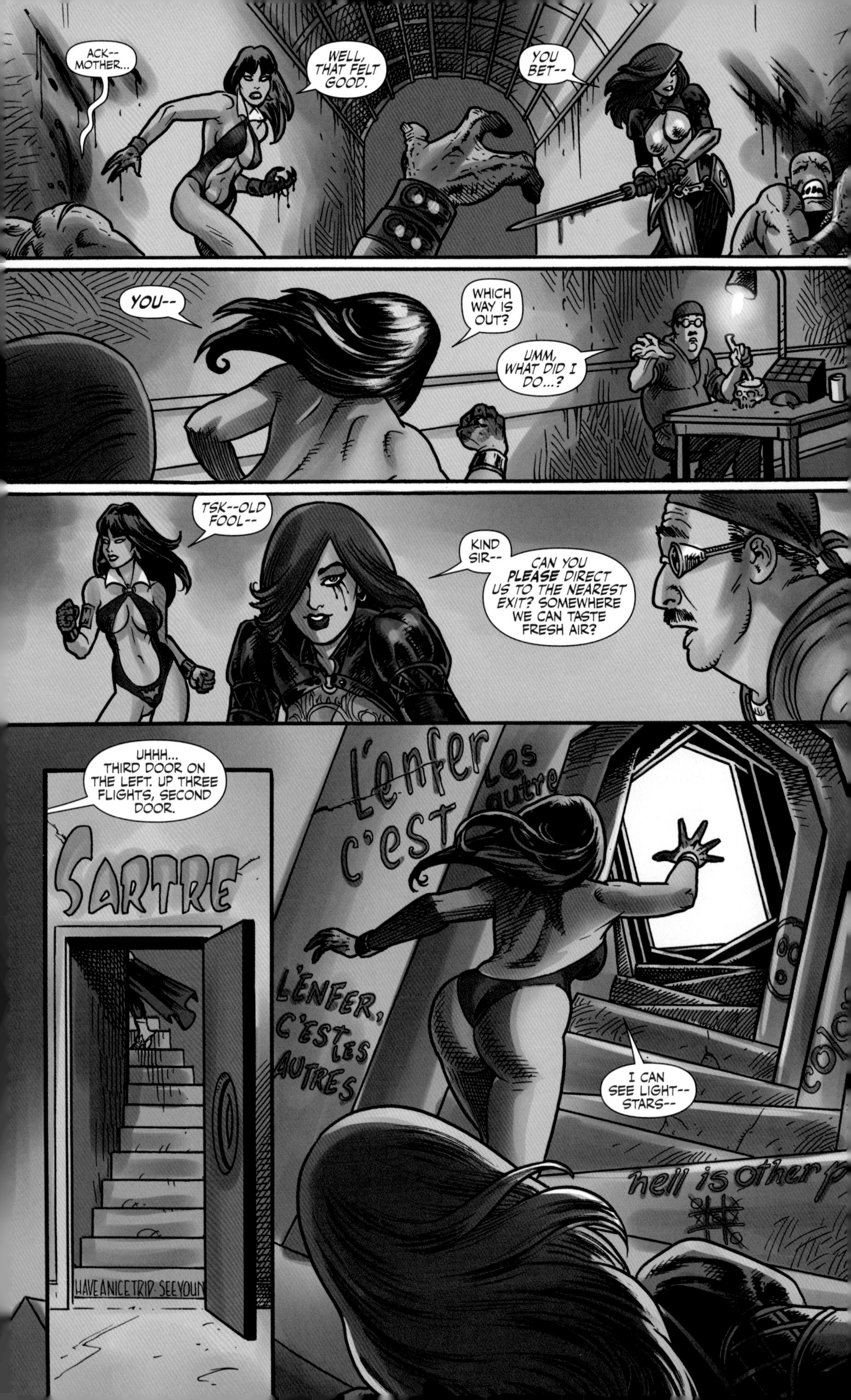
ACK-- MOTHER...
WELL, THAT FELT GOOD.
YOU BET--
YOU--
WHICH WAY IS OUT?
UMM, WHAT DID I DO...?
TSK--OLD FOOL--
KIND SIR--
CAN YOU PLEASE DIRECT US TO THE NEAREST EXIT? SOMEWHERE WE CAN TASTE FRESH AIR?
UHHH... THIRD DOOR ON THE LEFT. UP THREE FLIGHTS, SECOND DOOR.
L'enfer c'est
Les autre
SARTRE
L'ENFER, C'EST LES AUTRES
I CAN SEE LIGHT-- STARS--
hell is other p
HAVE A NICE TRIP. SEE YOU

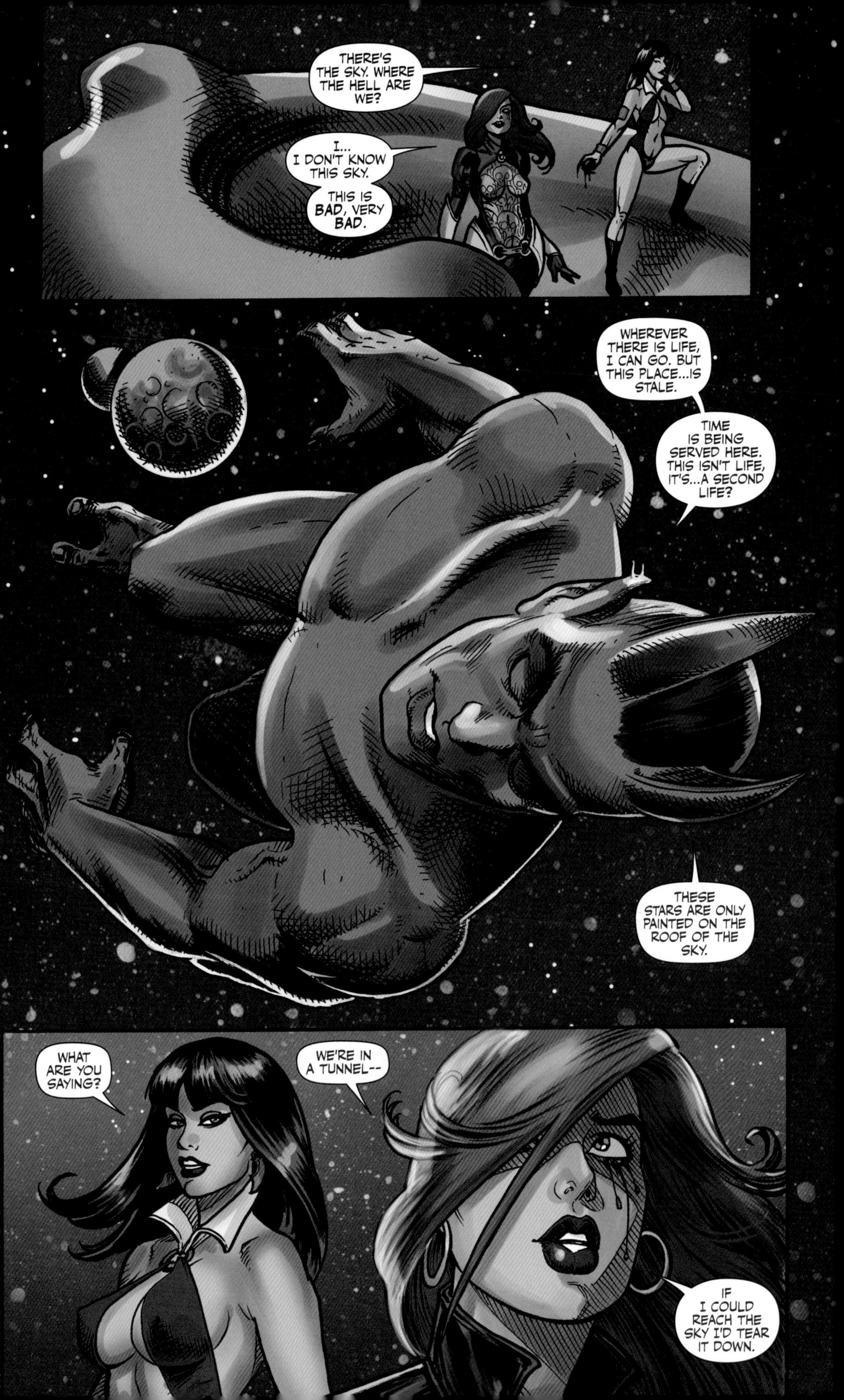
THERE'S THE SKY. WHERE THE HELL ARE WE?
I... I DON'T KNOW THIS SKY.
THIS IS BAD, VERY BAD.
WHEREVER THERE IS LIFE, I CAN GO. BUT THIS PLACE...IS STALE.
TIME IS BEING SERVED HERE. THIS ISN'T LIFE, IT'S...A SECOND LIFE?
THESE STARS ARE ONLY PAINTED ON THE ROOF OF THE SKY.
WHAT ARE YOU SAYING?
WE'RE IN A TUNNEL--
IF I COULD REACH THE SKY I'D TEAR IT DOWN.

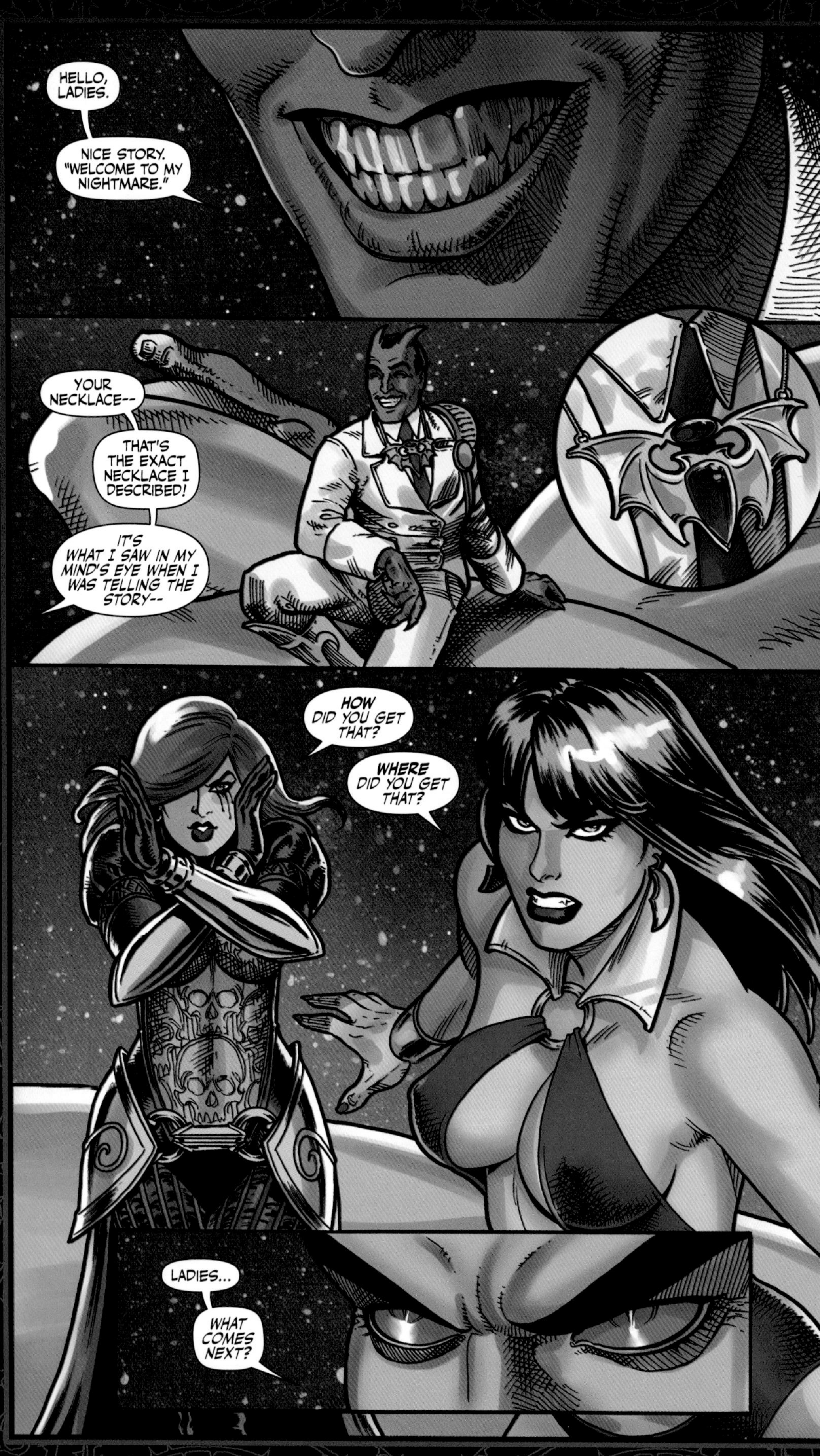
HELLO, LADIES.
NICE STORY. "WELCOME TO MY NIGHTMARE."
YOUR NECKLACE--
THAT'S THE EXACT NECKLACE I DESCRIBED!
IT'S WHAT I SAW IN MY MIND'S EYE WHEN I WAS TELLING THE STORY--
HOW DID YOU GET THAT?
WHERE DID YOU GET THAT?
LADIES...
WHAT COMES NEXT?

CHAPTER · TWO

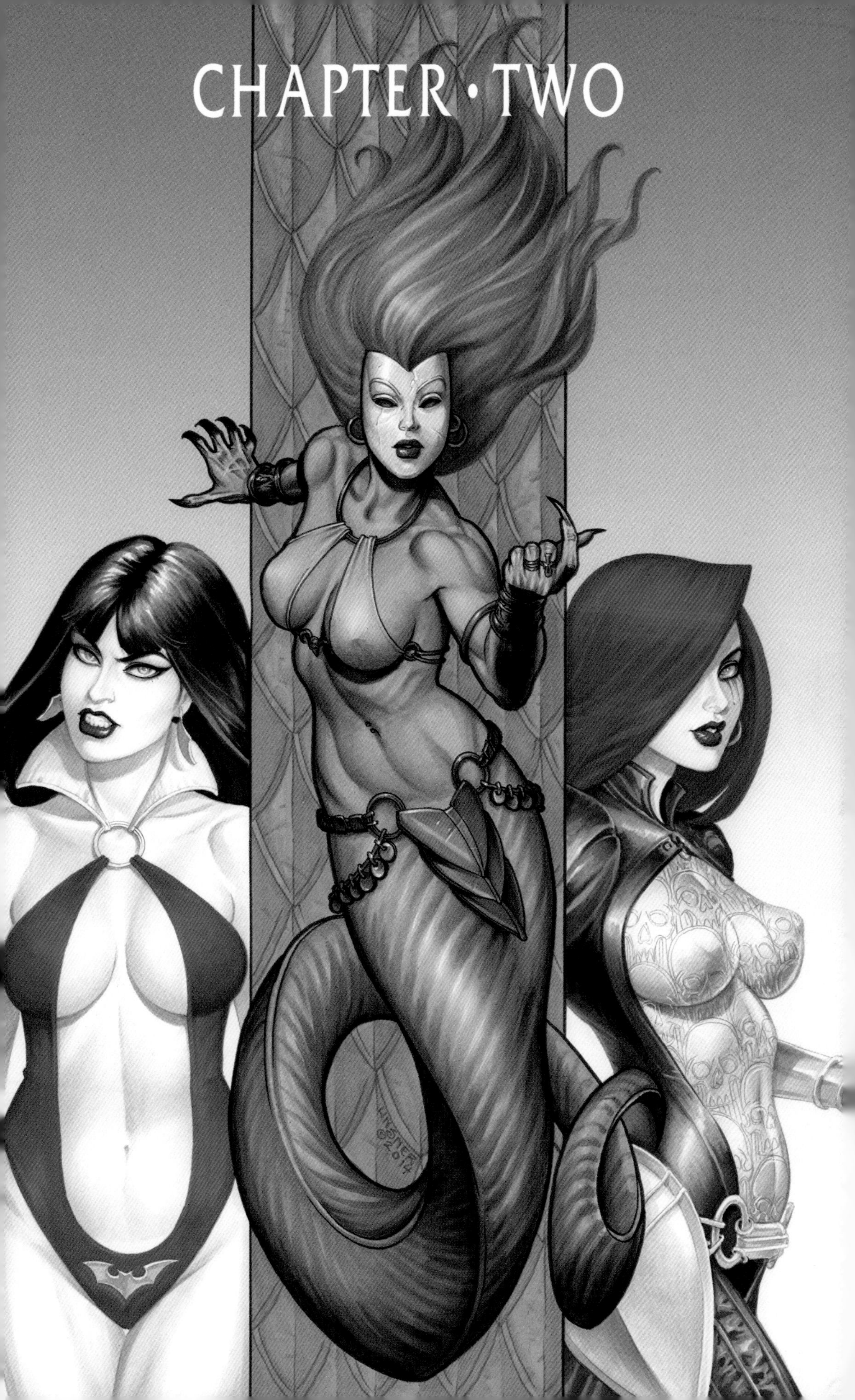

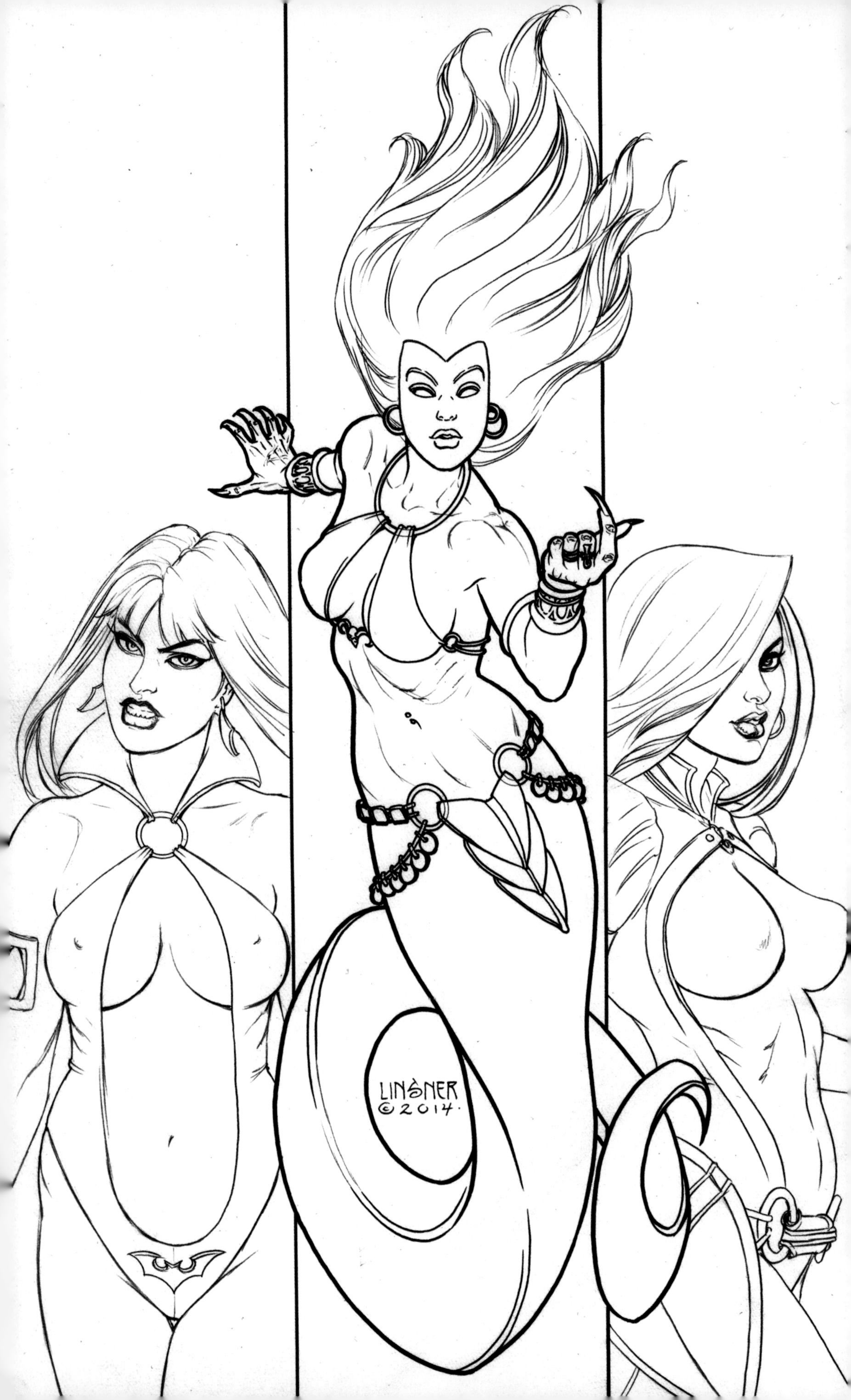
LINSNER
© 2014.

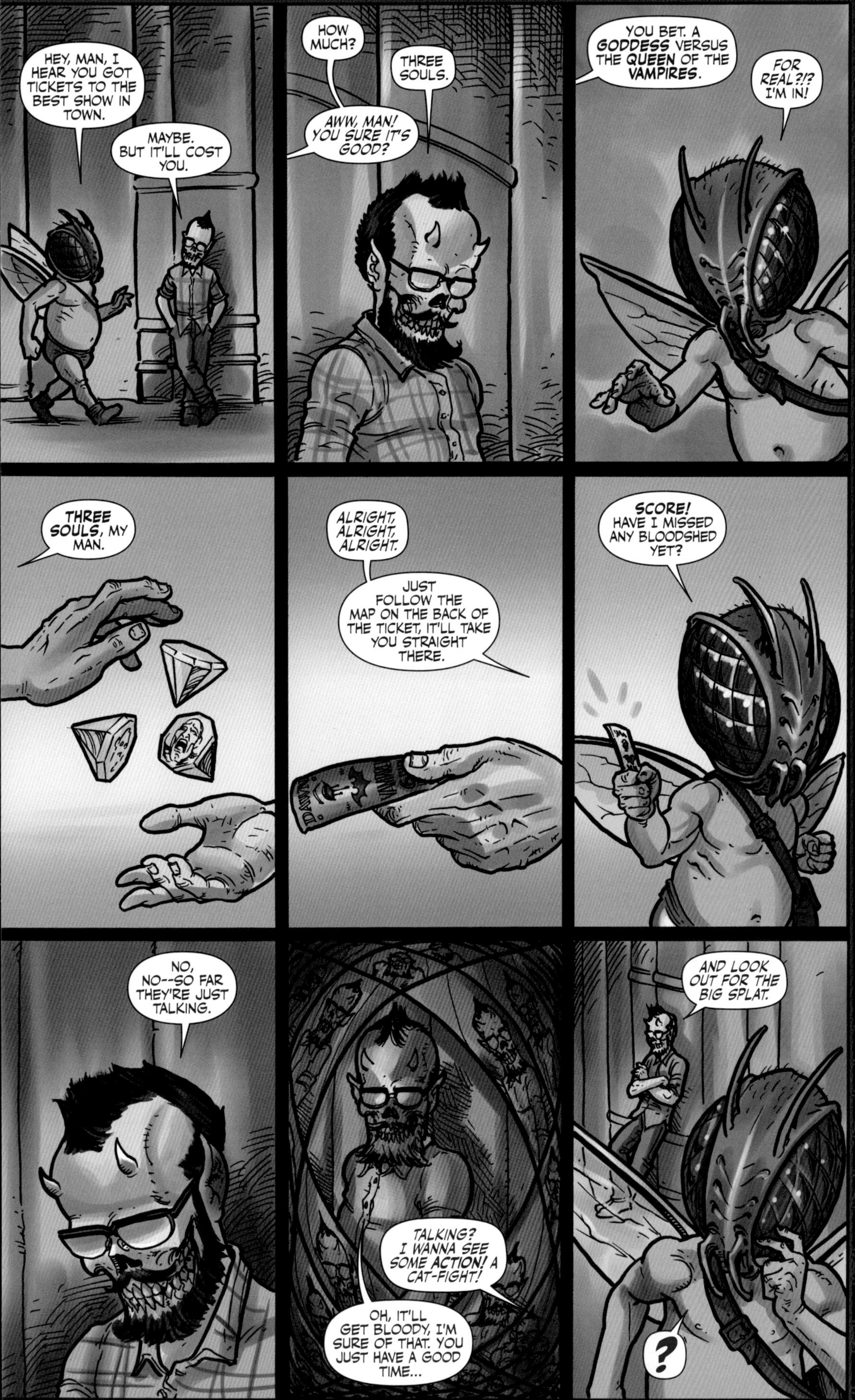
HEY, MAN, I HEAR YOU GOT TICKETS TO THE BEST SHOW IN TOWN.
MAYBE. BUT IT'LL COST YOU.
HOW MUCH?
THREE SOULS.
AWW, MAN! YOU SURE IT'S GOOD?
YOU BET. A GODDESS VERSUS THE QUEEN OF THE VAMPIRES.
FOR REAL?!? I'M IN!
THREE SOULS, MY MAN.
ALRIGHT, ALRIGHT, ALRIGHT.
JUST FOLLOW THE MAP ON THE BACK OF THE TICKET, IT'LL TAKE YOU STRAIGHT THERE.
SCORE! HAVE I MISSED ANY BLOODSHED YET?
NO, NO--SO FAR THEY'RE JUST TALKING.
TALKING? I WANNA SEE SOME ACTION! A CAT-FIGHT!
OH, IT'LL GET BLOODY, I'M SURE OF THAT. YOU JUST HAVE A GOOD TIME...
AND LOOK OUT FOR THE BIG SPLAT.
?

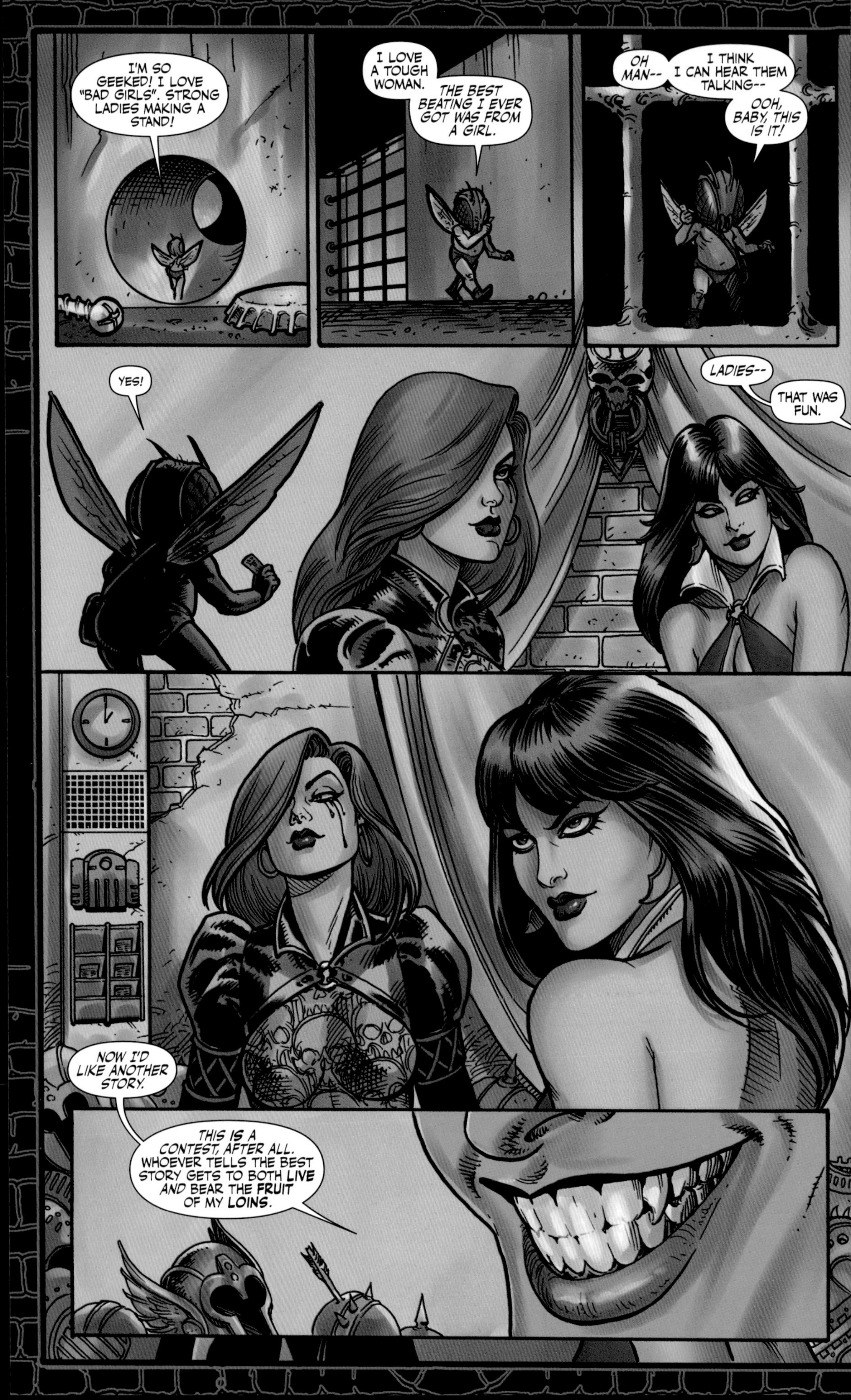
I'M SO GEEKED! I LOVE "BAD GIRLS". STRONG LADIES MAKING A STAND!
I LOVE A TOUGH WOMAN.
THE BEST BEATING I EVER GOT WAS FROM A GIRL.
OH MAN--
I THINK I CAN HEAR THEM TALKING--
OOH, BABY, THIS IS IT!
YES!
LADIES--
THAT WAS FUN.
NOW I'D LIKE ANOTHER STORY.
THIS IS A CONTEST, AFTER ALL. WHOEVER TELLS THE BEST STORY GETS TO BOTH LIVE AND BEAR THE FRUIT OF MY LOINS.

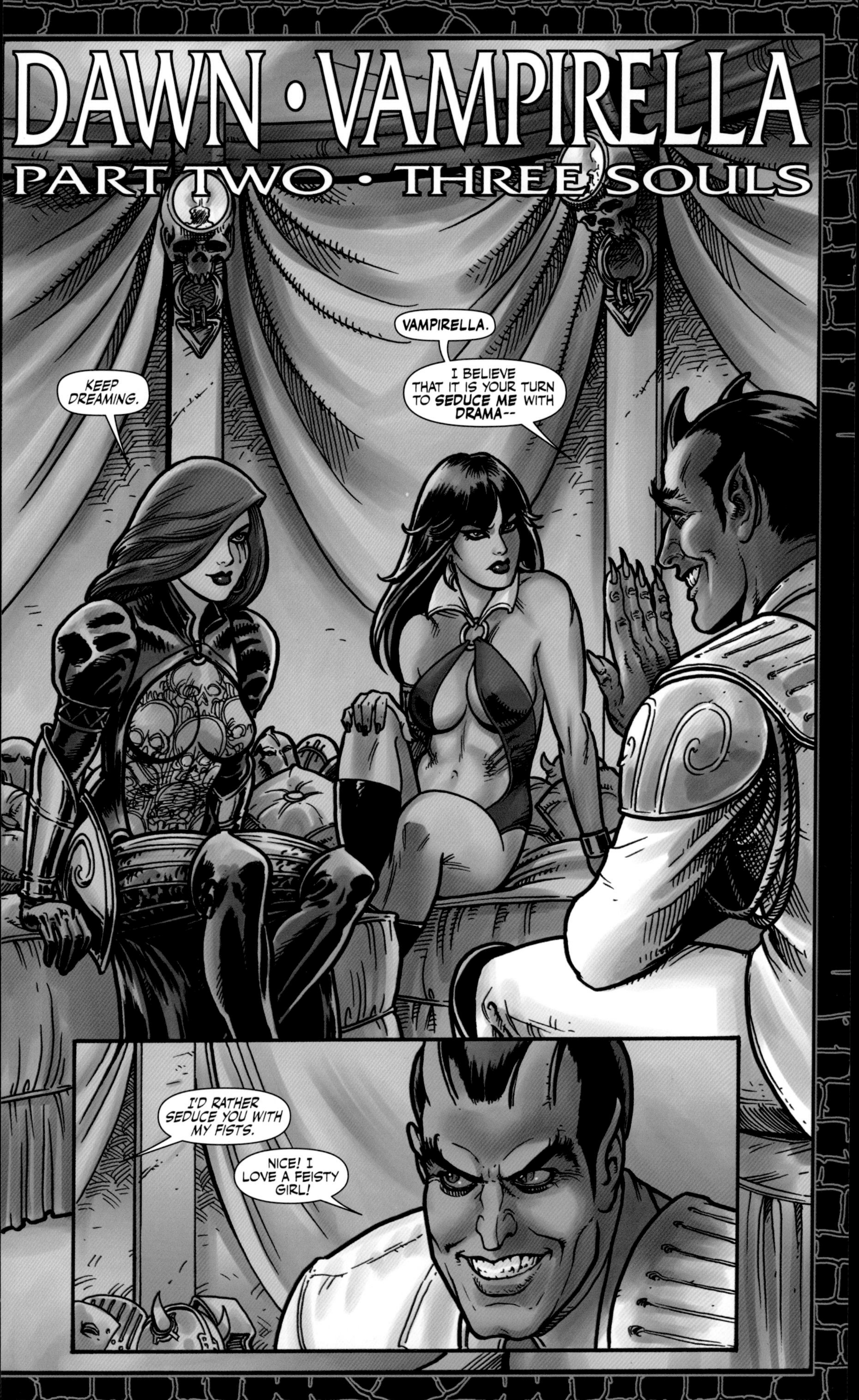
DAWN • VAMPIRELLA
PART TWO • THREE SOULS
KEEP DREAMING.
VAMPIRELLA.
I BELIEVE THAT IT IS YOUR TURN TO SEDUCE ME WITH DRAMA--
I'D RATHER SEDUCE YOU WITH MY FISTS.
NICE! I LOVE A FEISTY GIRL!

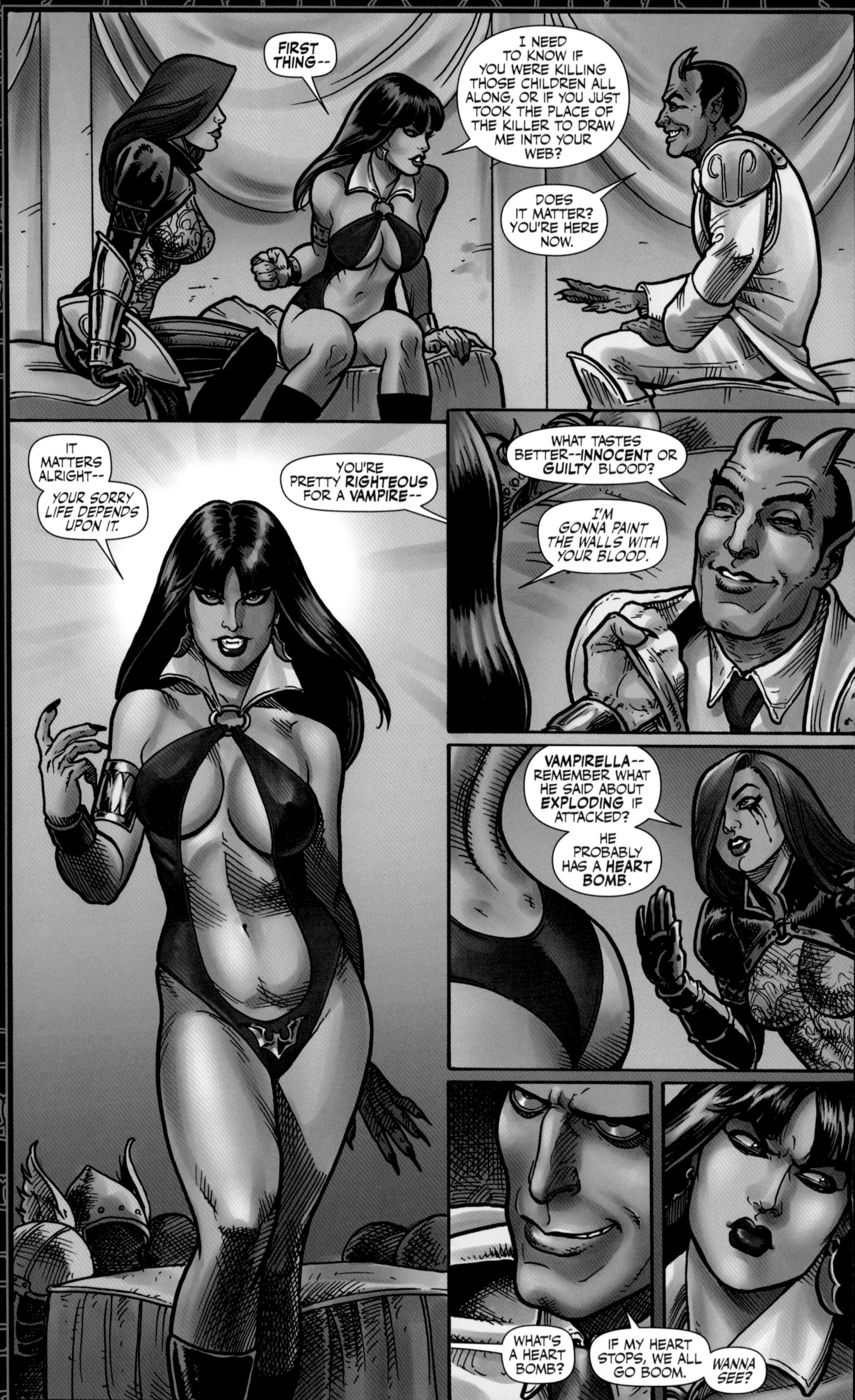
FIRST THING--
I NEED TO KNOW IF YOU WERE KILLING THOSE CHILDREN ALL ALONG, OR IF YOU JUST TOOK THE PLACE OF THE KILLER TO DRAW ME INTO YOUR WEB?
DOES IT MATTER? YOU'RE HERE NOW.
IT MATTERS ALRIGHT--
YOUR SORRY LIFE DEPENDS UPON IT.
YOU'RE PRETTY RIGHTEOUS FOR A VAMPIRE--
WHAT TASTES BETTER--INNOCENT OR GUILTY BLOOD?
I'M GONNA PAINT THE WALLS WITH YOUR BLOOD.
VAMPIRELLA--REMEMBER WHAT HE SAID ABOUT EXPLODING IF ATTACKED?
HE PROBABLY HAS A HEART BOMB.
WHAT'S A HEART BOMB?
IF MY HEART STOPS, WE ALL GO BOOM.
WANNA SEE?

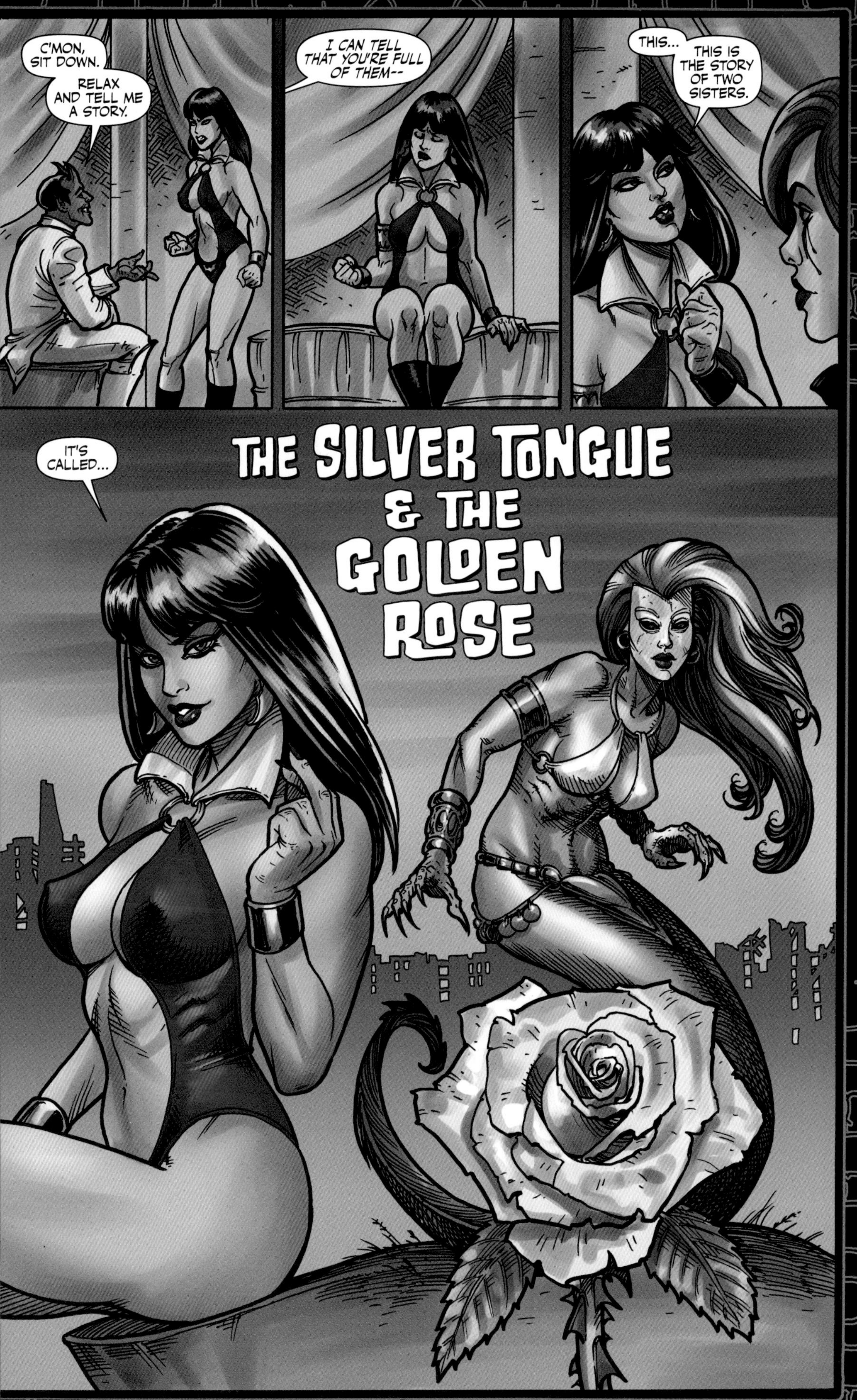
C'MON, SIT DOWN.
RELAX AND TELL ME A STORY.
I CAN TELL THAT YOU'RE FULL OF THEM--
THIS...
THIS IS THE STORY OF TWO SISTERS.
IT'S CALLED...
THE SILVER TONGUE & THE GOLDEN ROSE

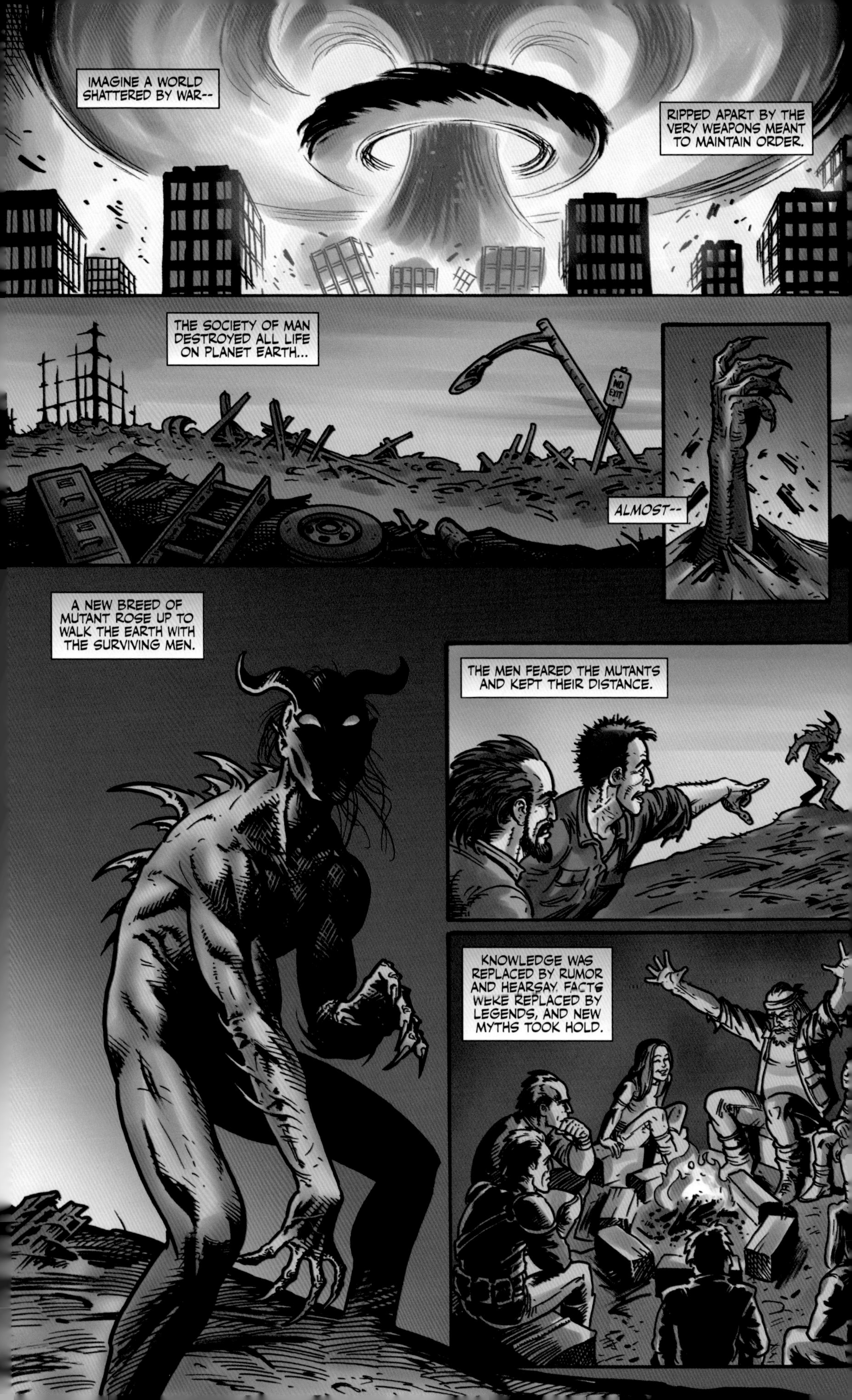

IMAGINE A WORLD SHATTERED BY WAR--
RIPPED APART BY THE VERY WEAPONS MEANT TO MAINTAIN ORDER.
THE SOCIETY OF MAN DESTROYED ALL LIFE ON PLANET EARTH...
NO EXIT
ALMOST--
A NEW BREED OF MUTANT ROSE UP TO WALK THE EARTH WITH THE SURVIVING MEN.
THE MEN FEARED THE MUTANTS AND KEPT THEIR DISTANCE.
KNOWLEDGE WAS REPLACED BY RUMOR AND HEARSAY. FACTS WERE REPLACED BY LEGENDS, AND NEW MYTHS TOOK HOLD.

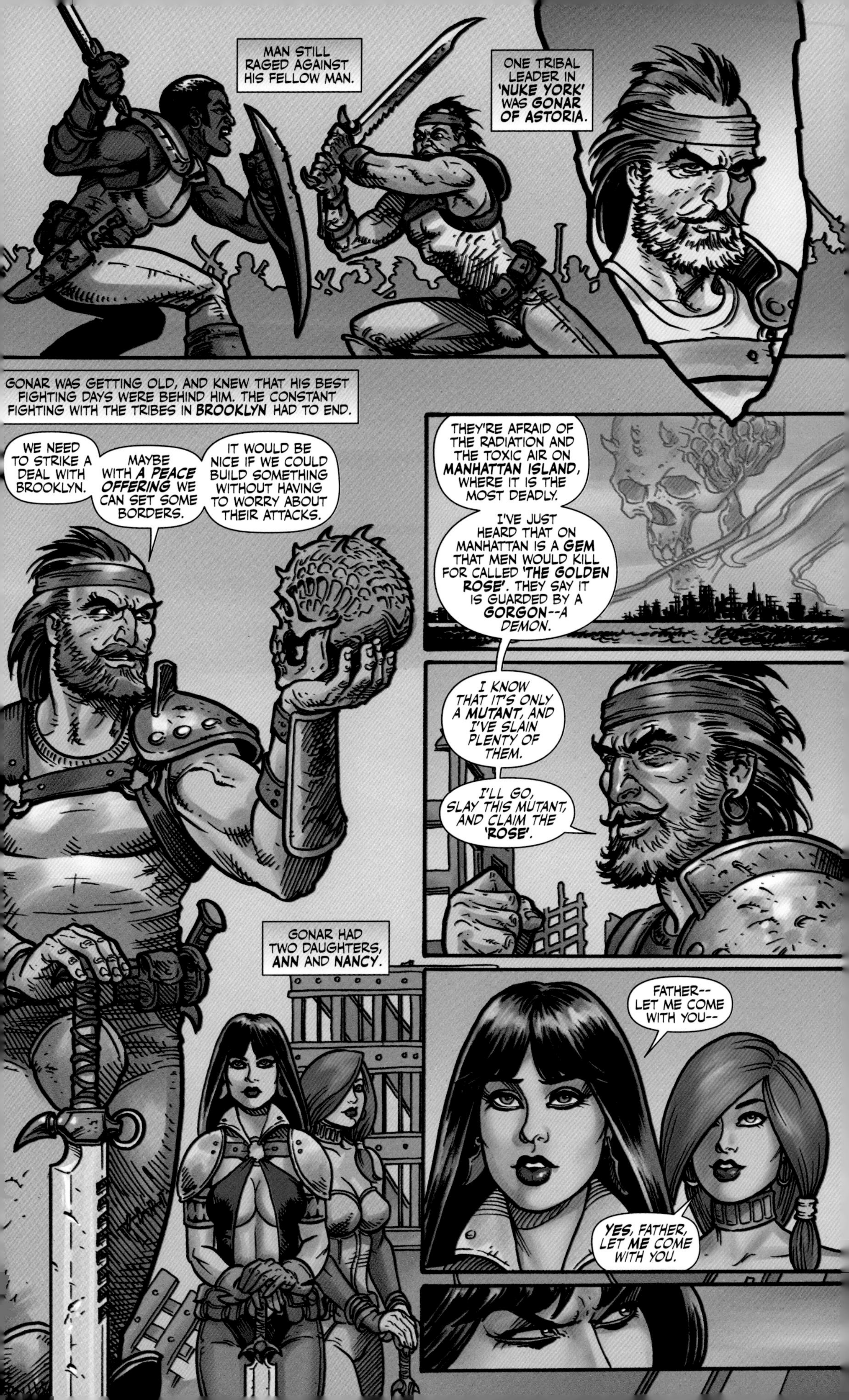
MAN STILL RAGED AGAINST HIS FELLOW MAN.
ONE TRIBAL LEADER IN 'NUKE YORK' WAS GONAR OF ASTORIA.
GONAR WAS GETTING OLD, AND KNEW THAT HIS BEST FIGHTING DAYS WERE BEHIND HIM. THE CONSTANT FIGHTING WITH THE TRIBES IN BROOKLYN HAD TO END.
WE NEED TO STRIKE A DEAL WITH BROOKLYN.
MAYBE WITH A PEACE OFFERING WE CAN SET SOME BORDERS.
IT WOULD BE NICE IF WE COULD BUILD SOMETHING WITHOUT HAVING TO WORRY ABOUT THEIR ATTACKS.
THEY'RE AFRAID OF THE RADIATION AND THE TOXIC AIR ON MANHATTAN ISLAND, WHERE IT IS THE MOST DEADLY.
I'VE JUST HEARD THAT ON MANHATTAN IS A GEM THAT MEN WOULD KILL FOR CALLED 'THE GOLDEN ROSE'. THEY SAY IT IS GUARDED BY A GORGON--A DEMON.
I KNOW THAT IT'S ONLY A MUTANT, AND I'VE SLAIN PLENTY OF THEM.
I'LL GO, SLAY THIS MUTANT, AND CLAIM THE 'ROSE'.
GONAR HAD TWO DAUGHTERS, ANN AND NANCY.
FATHER-- LET ME COME WITH YOU--
YES, FATHER, LET ME COME WITH YOU.

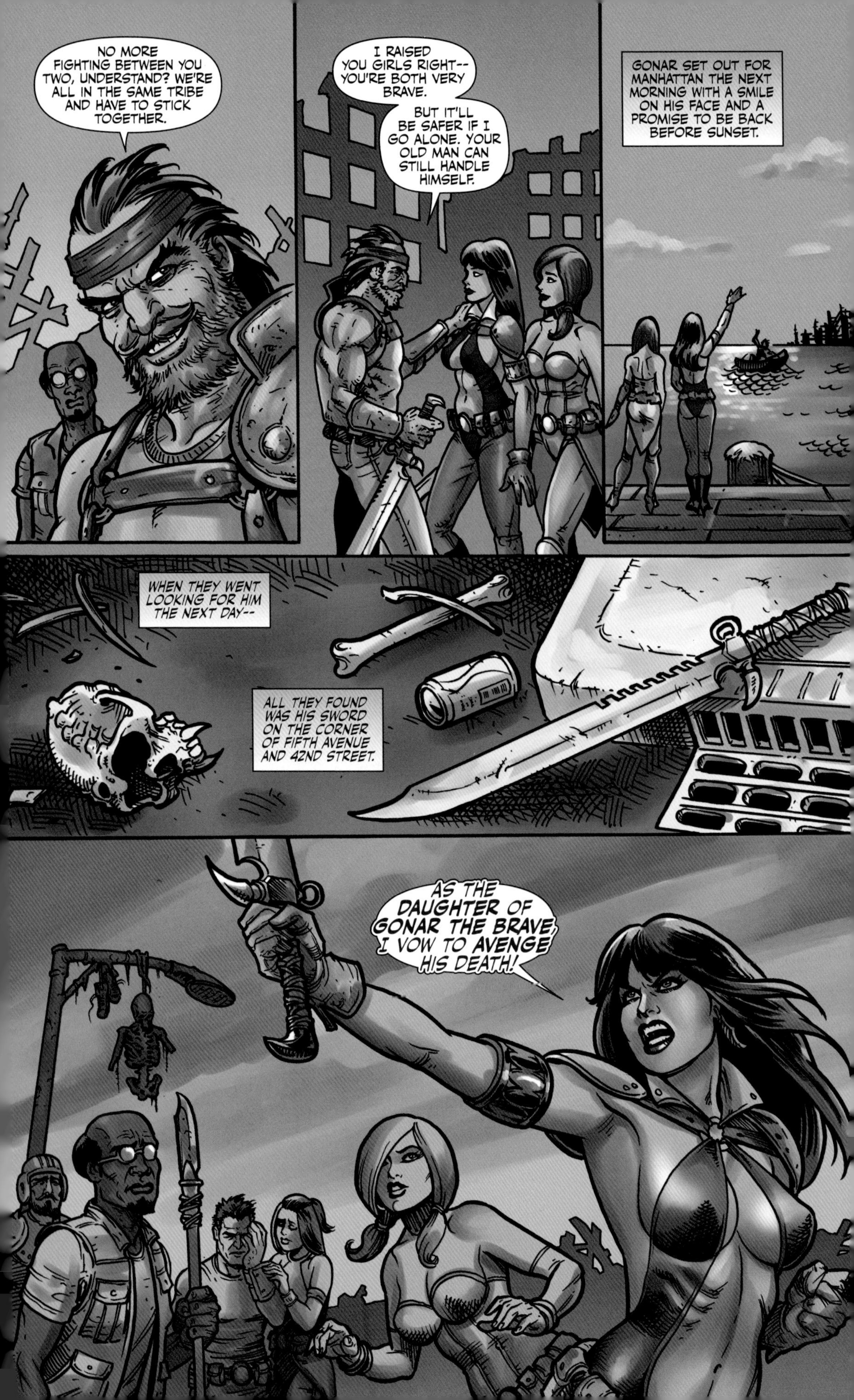

NO MORE FIGHTING BETWEEN YOU TWO, UNDERSTAND? WE'RE ALL IN THE SAME TRIBE AND HAVE TO STICK TOGETHER.
I RAISED YOU GIRLS RIGHT--YOU'RE BOTH VERY BRAVE.
BUT IT'LL BE SAFER IF I GO ALONE. YOUR OLD MAN CAN STILL HANDLE HIMSELF.
GONAR SET OUT FOR MANHATTAN THE NEXT MORNING WITH A SMILE ON HIS FACE AND A PROMISE TO BE BACK BEFORE SUNSET.
WHEN THEY WENT LOOKING FOR HIM THE NEXT DAY--
ALL THEY FOUND WAS HIS SWORD ON THE CORNER OF FIFTH AVENUE AND 42ND STREET.
AS THE DAUGHTER OF GONAR THE BRAVE, I VOW TO AVENGE HIS DEATH!

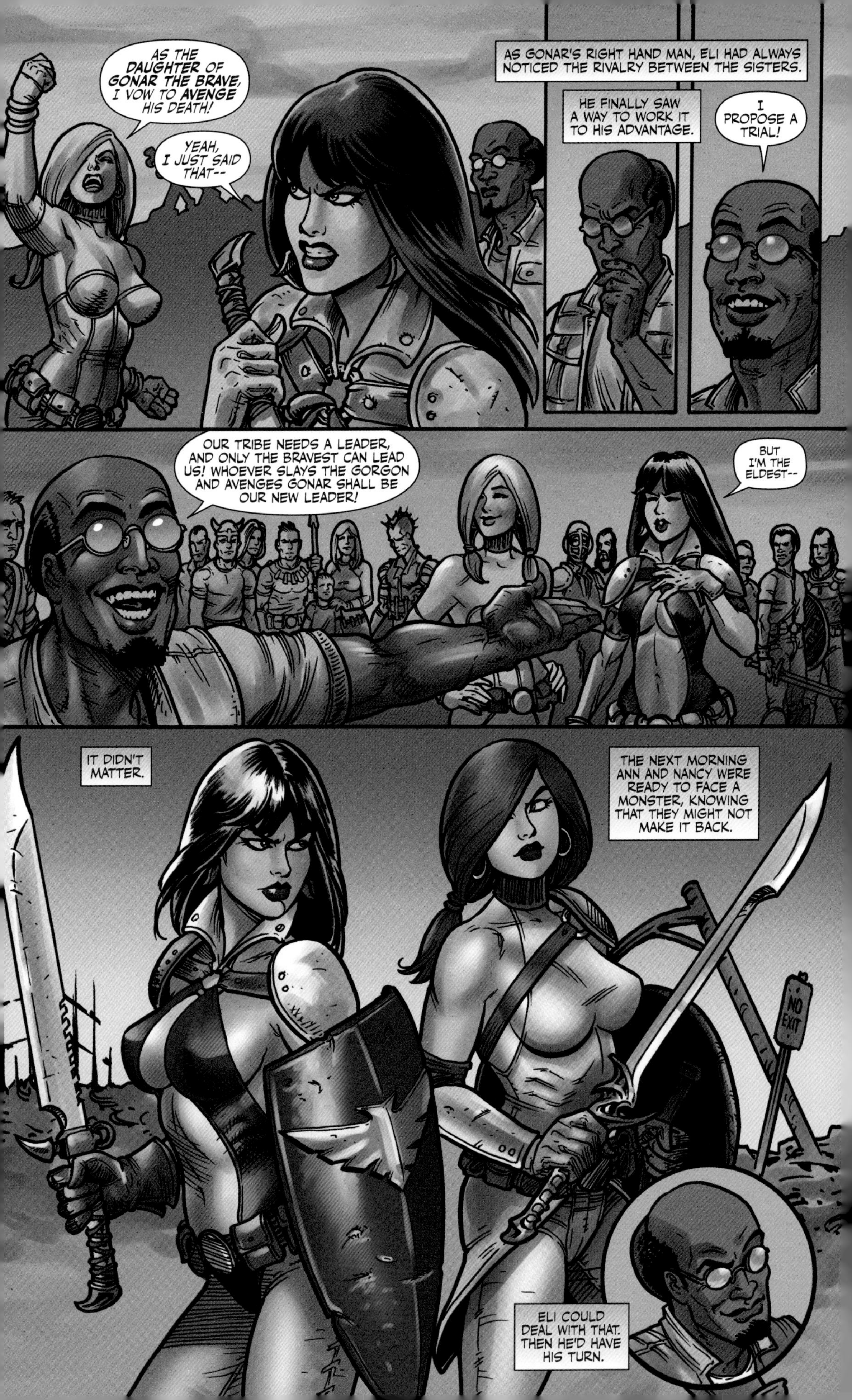
AS THE DAUGHTER OF GONAR THE BRAVE, I VOW TO AVENGE HIS DEATH!
YEAH, I JUST SAID THAT--
AS GONAR'S RIGHT HAND MAN, ELI HAD ALWAYS NOTICED THE RIVALRY BETWEEN THE SISTERS.
HE FINALLY SAW A WAY TO WORK IT TO HIS ADVANTAGE.
I PROPOSE A TRIAL!
OUR TRIBE NEEDS A LEADER, AND ONLY THE BRAVEST CAN LEAD US! WHOEVER SLAYS THE GORGON AND AVENGES GONAR SHALL BE OUR NEW LEADER!
BUT I'M THE ELDEST--
IT DIDN'T MATTER.
THE NEXT MORNING ANN AND NANCY WERE READY TO FACE A MONSTER, KNOWING THAT THEY MIGHT NOT MAKE IT BACK.
NO EXIT
ELI COULD DEAL WITH THAT. THEN HE'D HAVE HIS TURN.

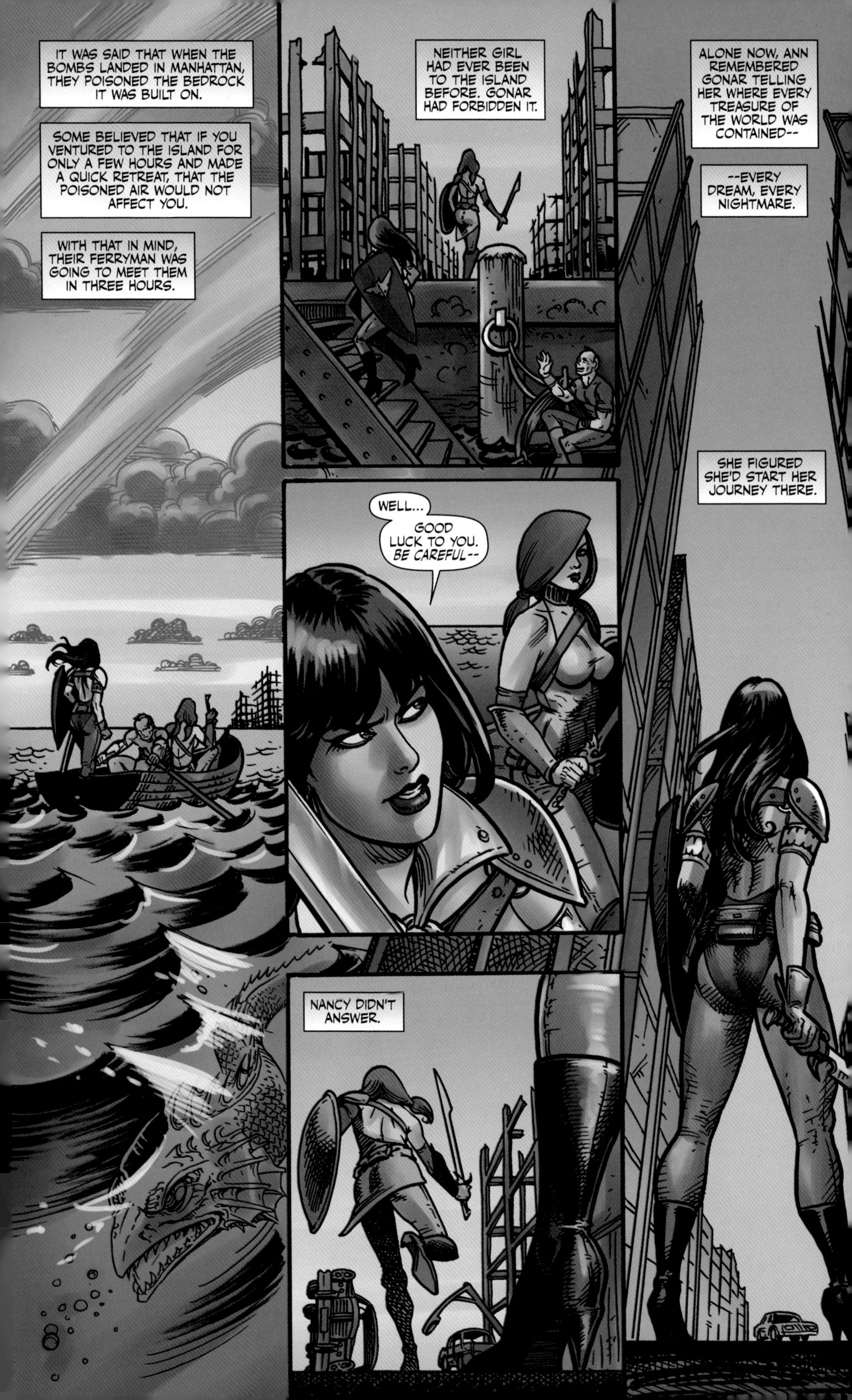
IT WAS SAID THAT WHEN THE BOMBS LANDED IN MANHATTAN, THEY POISONED THE BEDROCK IT WAS BUILT ON.
SOME BELIEVED THAT IF YOU VENTURED TO THE ISLAND FOR ONLY A FEW HOURS AND MADE A QUICK RETREAT, THAT THE POISONED AIR WOULD NOT AFFECT YOU.
WITH THAT IN MIND, THEIR FERRYMAN WAS GOING TO MEET THEM IN THREE HOURS.
NEITHER GIRL HAD EVER BEEN TO THE ISLAND BEFORE. GONAR HAD FORBIDDEN IT.
WELL... GOOD LUCK TO YOU. *BE CAREFUL*--
NANCY DIDN'T ANSWER.
ALONE NOW, ANN REMEMBERED GONAR TELLING HER WHERE EVERY TREASURE OF THE WORLD WAS CONTAINED--
--EVERY DREAM, EVERY NIGHTMARE.
SHE FIGURED SHE'D START HER JOURNEY THERE.

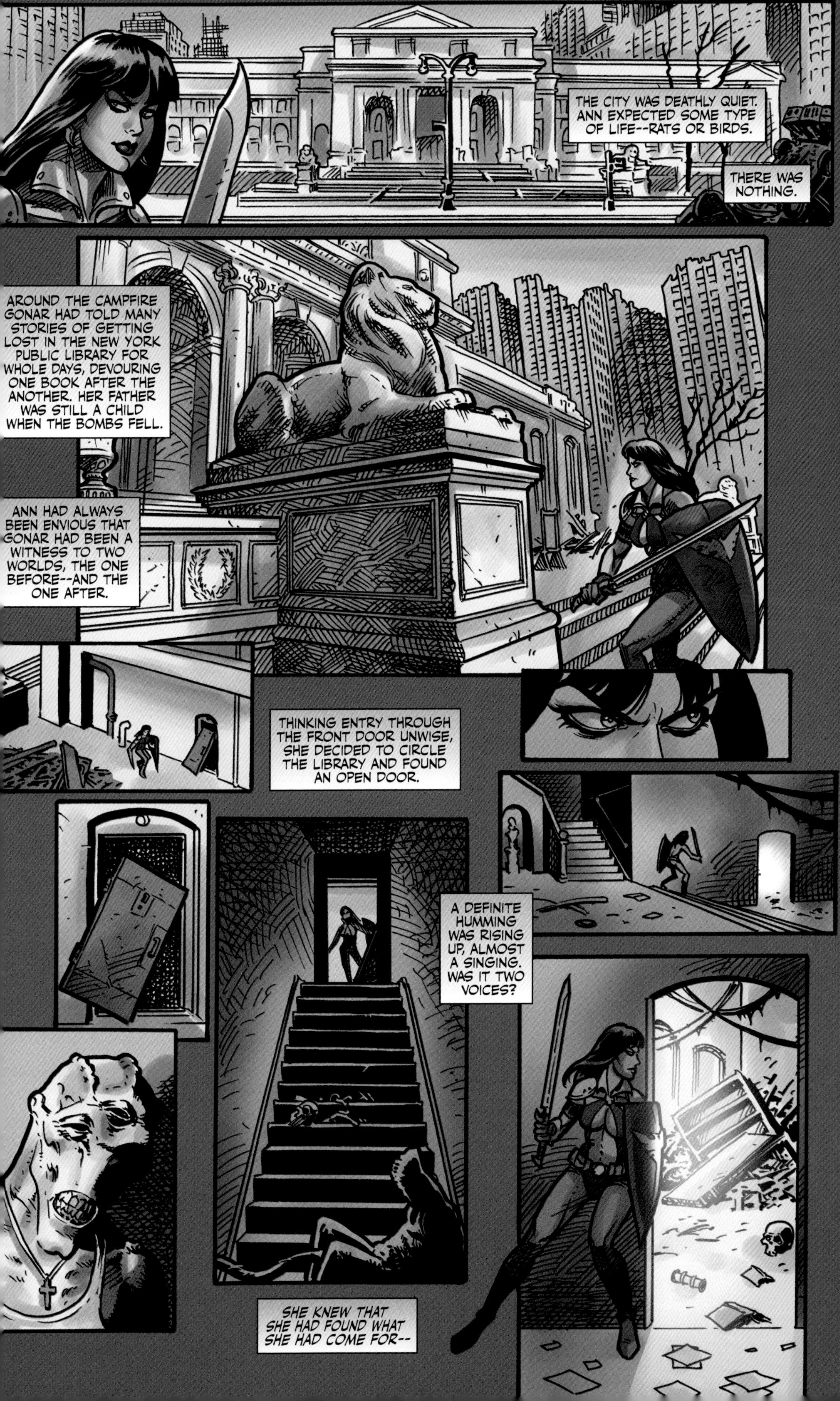
THE CITY WAS DEATHLY QUIET. ANN EXPECTED SOME TYPE OF LIFE--RATS OR BIRDS.
THERE WAS NOTHING.
AROUND THE CAMPFIRE GONAR HAD TOLD MANY STORIES OF GETTING LOST IN THE NEW YORK PUBLIC LIBRARY FOR WHOLE DAYS, DEVOURING ONE BOOK AFTER THE ANOTHER. HER FATHER WAS STILL A CHILD WHEN THE BOMBS FELL.
ANN HAD ALWAYS BEEN ENVIOUS THAT GONAR HAD BEEN A WITNESS TO TWO WORLDS, THE ONE BEFORE--AND THE ONE AFTER.
THINKING ENTRY THROUGH THE FRONT DOOR UNWISE, SHE DECIDED TO CIRCLE THE LIBRARY AND FOUND AN OPEN DOOR.
A DEFINITE HUMMING WAS RISING UP, ALMOST A SINGING. WAS IT TWO VOICES?
SHE KNEW THAT SHE HAD FOUND WHAT SHE HAD COME FOR--

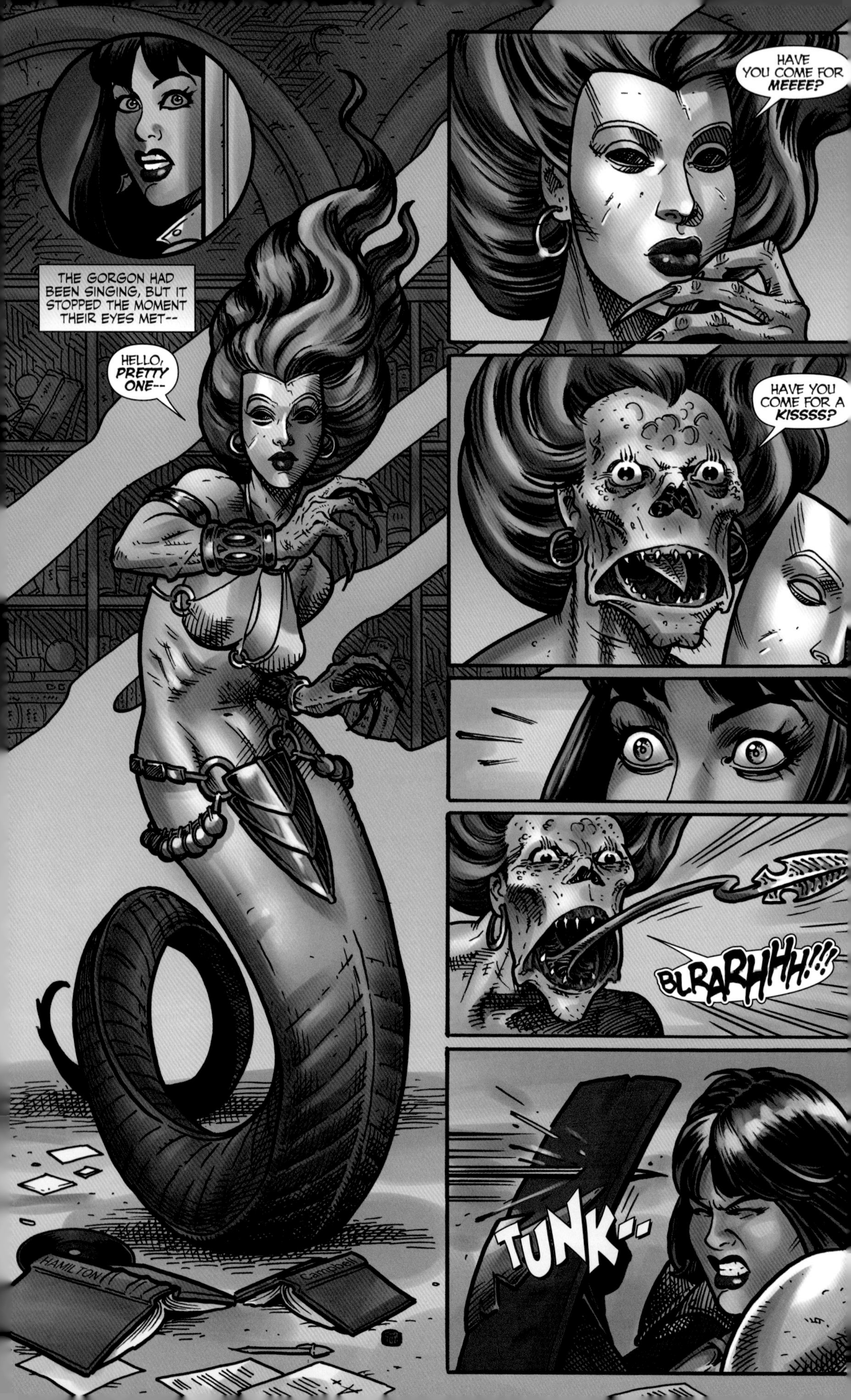
THE GORGON HAD BEEN SINGING, BUT IT STOPPED THE MOMENT THEIR EYES MET--
HELLO, PRETTY ONE--
HAVE YOU COME FOR MEEEE?
HAVE YOU COME FOR A KISSSS?
BLRARHHH!!!
TUNK--
HAMILTON
Campbell

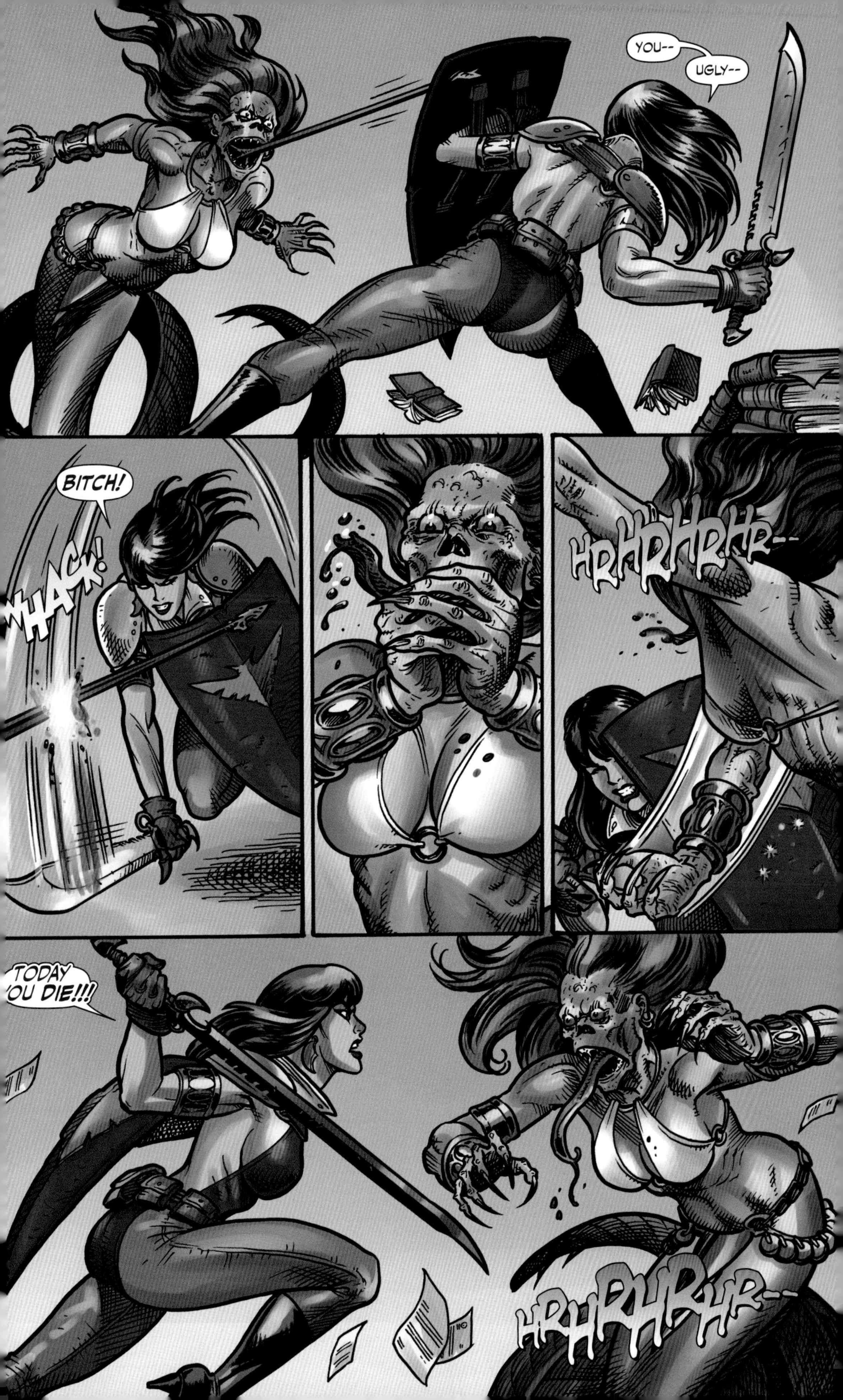
YOU--
UGLY--
BITCH!
WHACK!
HRHRHRHR--
TODAY
OU DIE!!!
HRHRHRHRHR--

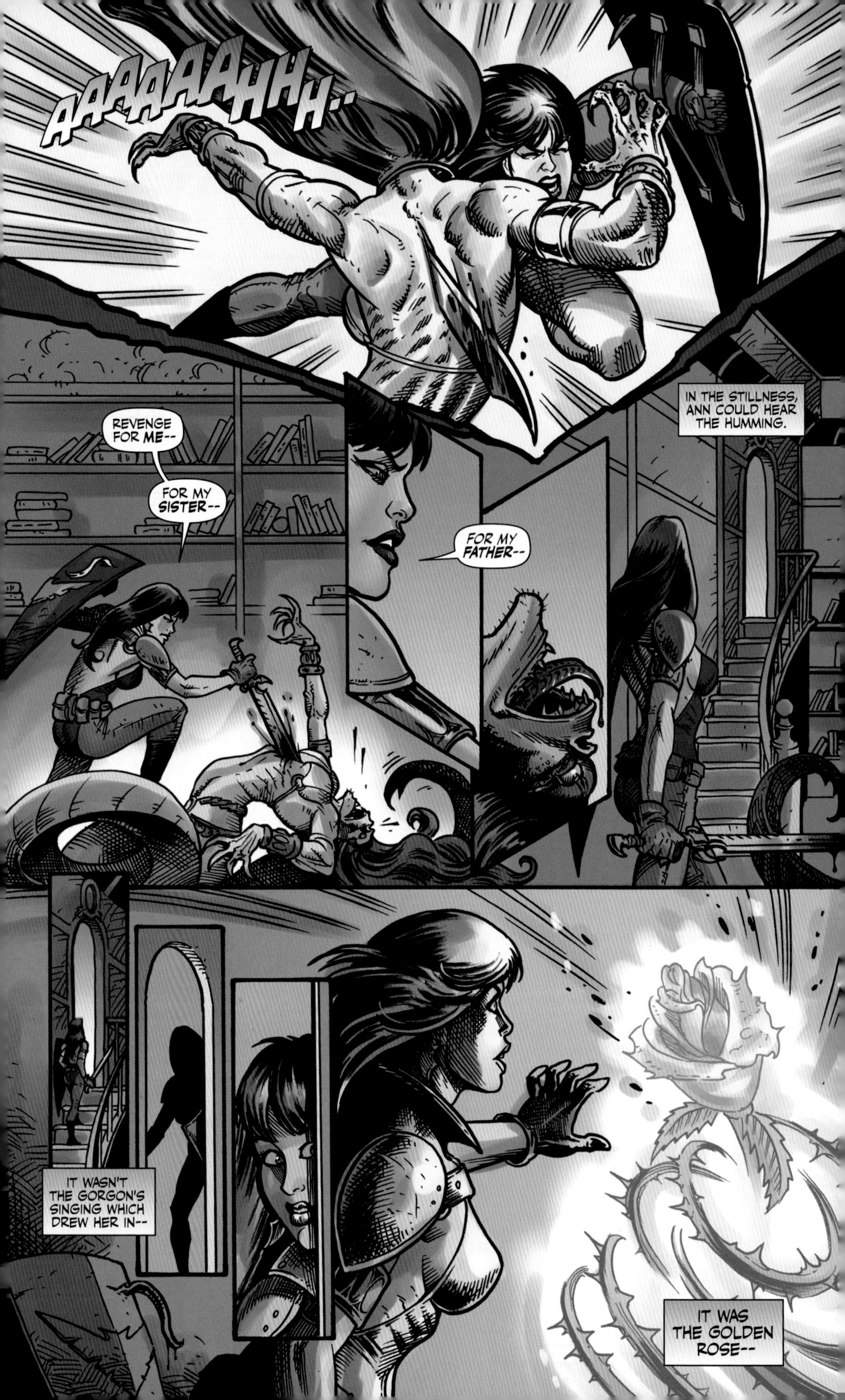
AAAAAAHHH..
IN THE STILLNESS, ANN COULD HEAR THE HUMMING.
REVENGE FOR ME--
FOR MY SISTER--
FOR MY FATHER--
IT WASN'T THE GORGON'S SINGING WHICH DREW HER IN--
IT WAS THE GOLDEN ROSE--

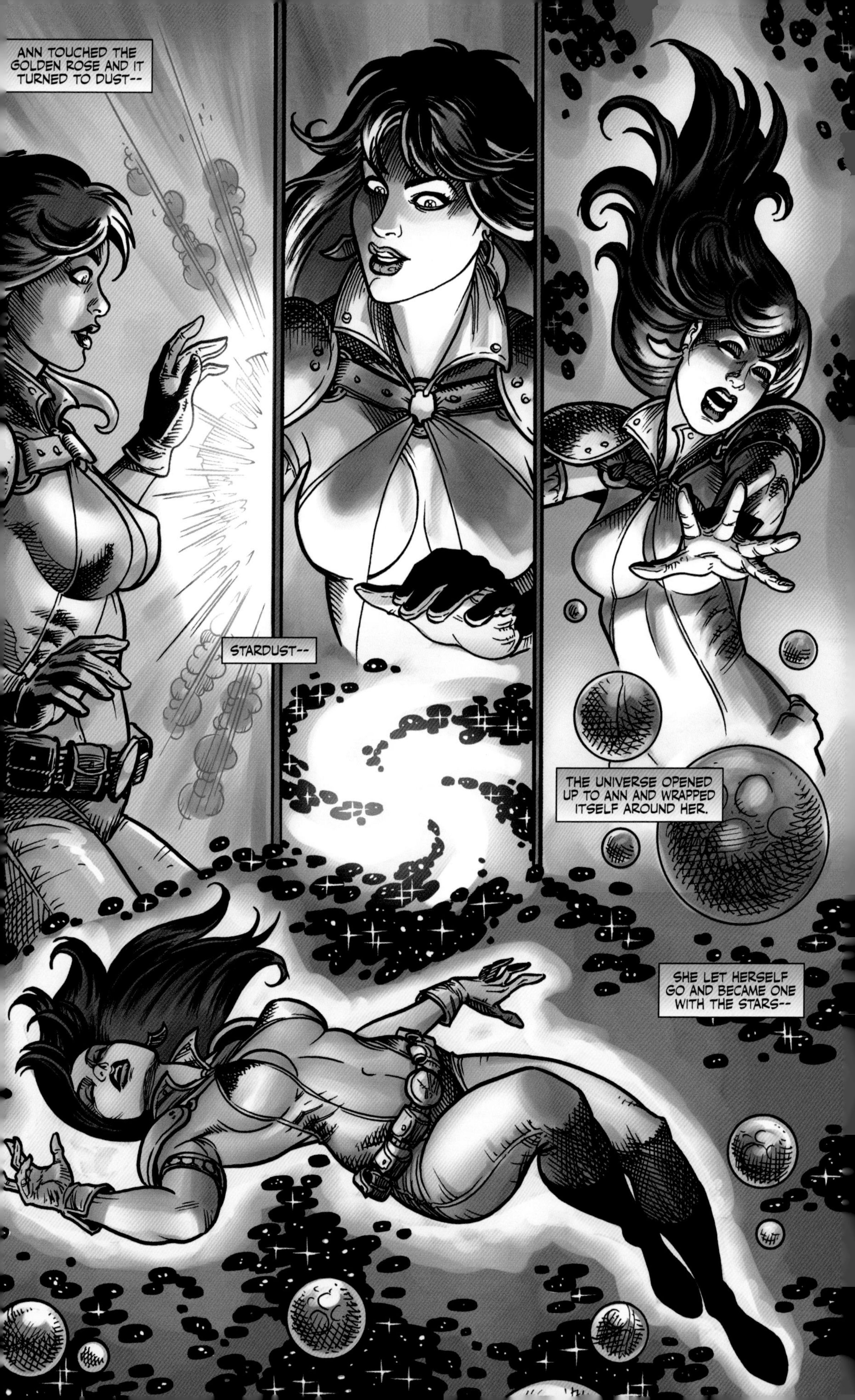
ANN TOUCHED THE GOLDEN ROSE AND IT TURNED TO DUST--
STARDUST--
THE UNIVERSE OPENED UP TO ANN AND WRAPPED ITSELF AROUND HER.
SHE LET HERSELF GO AND BECAME ONE WITH THE STARS--

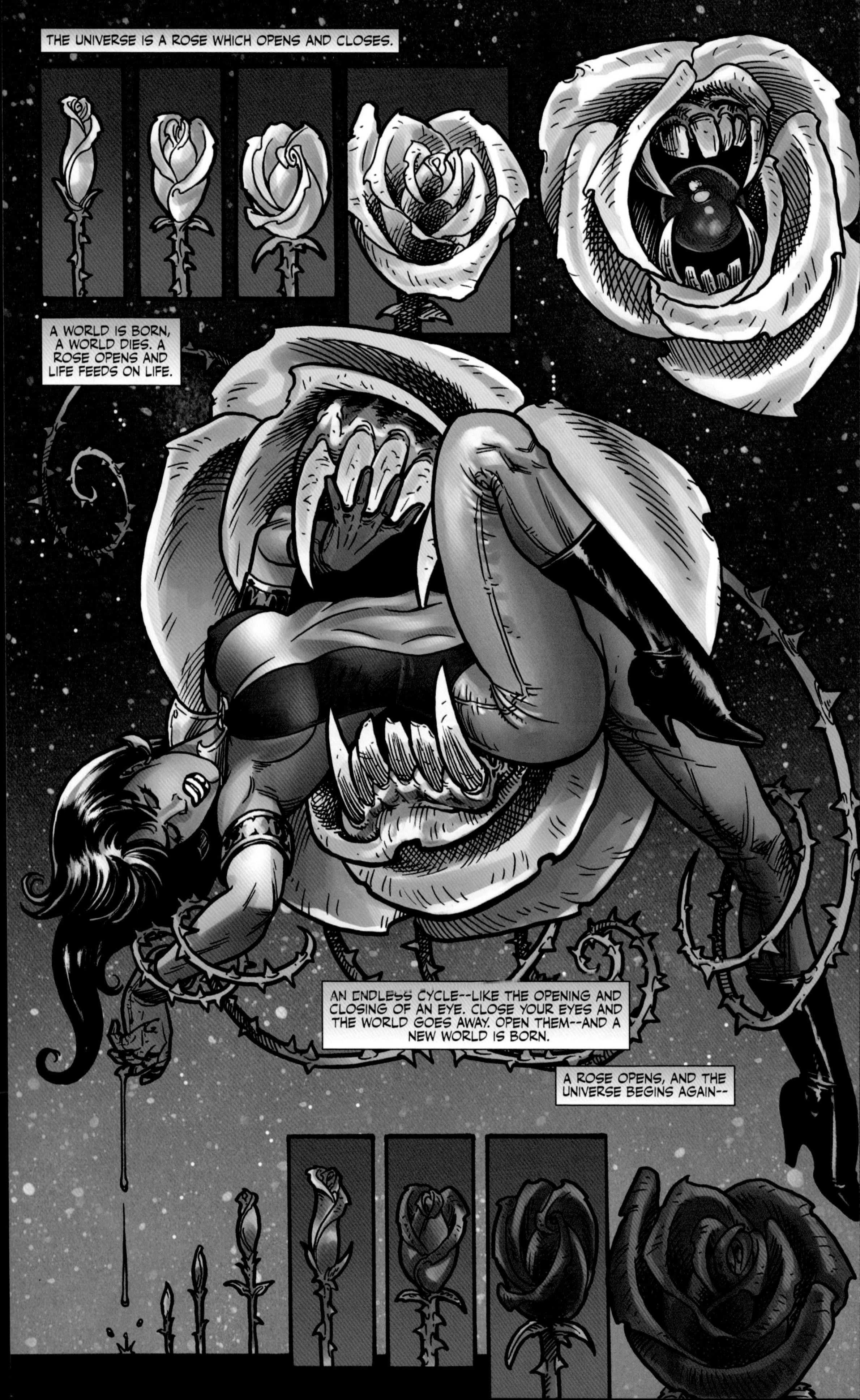
THE UNIVERSE IS A ROSE WHICH OPENS AND CLOSES.
A WORLD IS BORN, A WORLD DIES. A ROSE OPENS AND LIFE FEEDS ON LIFE.
AN ENDLESS CYCLE--LIKE THE OPENING AND CLOSING OF AN EYE. CLOSE YOUR EYES AND THE WORLD GOES AWAY. OPEN THEM--AND A NEW WORLD IS BORN.
A ROSE OPENS, AND THE UNIVERSE BEGINS AGAIN--

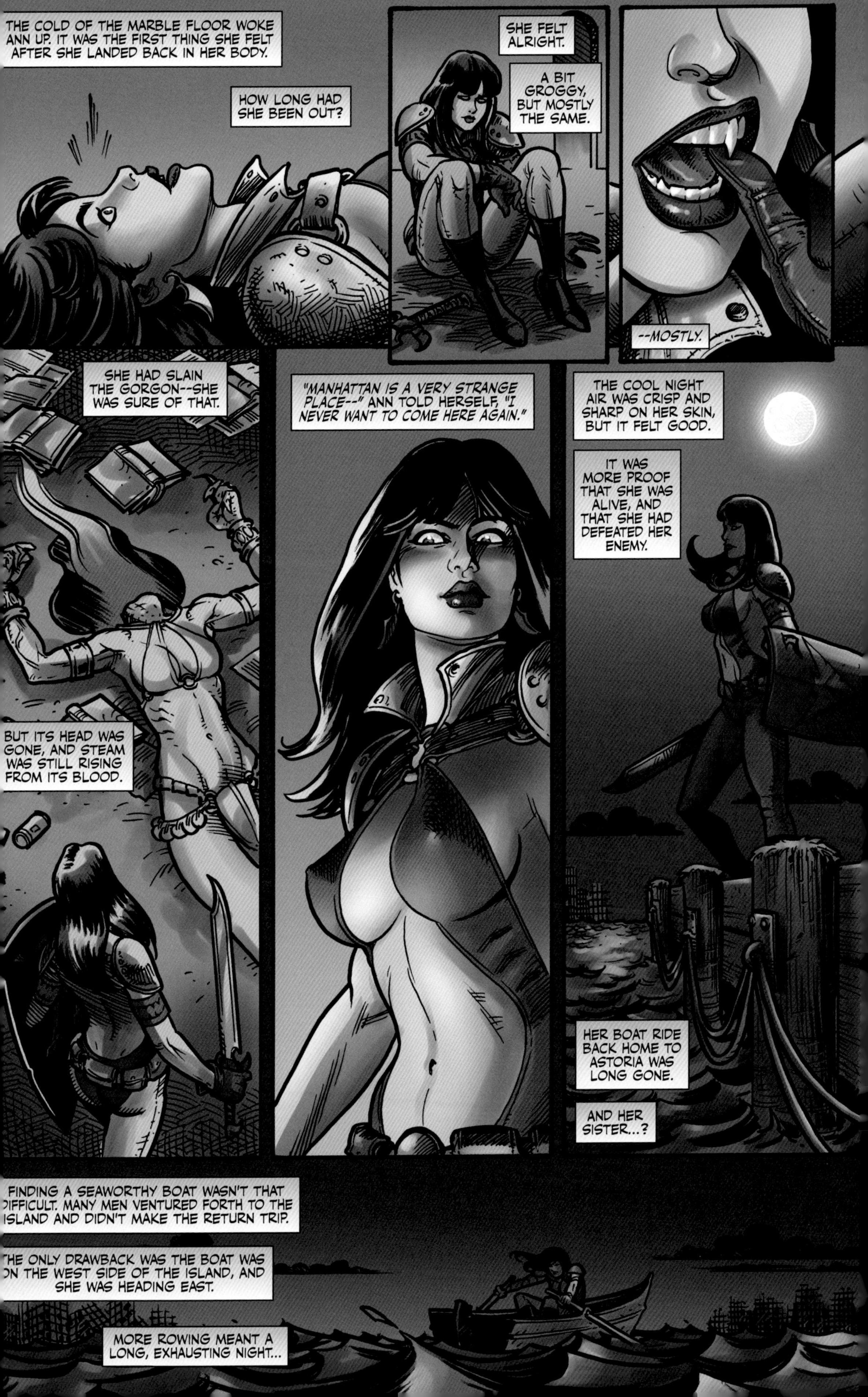

THE COLD OF THE MARBLE FLOOR WOKE ANN UP. IT WAS THE FIRST THING SHE FELT AFTER SHE LANDED BACK IN HER BODY.
HOW LONG HAD SHE BEEN OUT?
SHE FELT ALRIGHT.
A BIT GROGGY, BUT MOSTLY THE SAME.
--MOSTLY.
SHE HAD SLAIN THE GORGON--SHE WAS SURE OF THAT.
BUT ITS HEAD WAS GONE, AND STEAM WAS STILL RISING FROM ITS BLOOD.
"MANHATTAN IS A VERY STRANGE PLACE--" ANN TOLD HERSELF, "I NEVER WANT TO COME HERE AGAIN."
THE COOL NIGHT AIR WAS CRISP AND SHARP ON HER SKIN, BUT IT FELT GOOD.
IT WAS MORE PROOF THAT SHE WAS ALIVE, AND THAT SHE HAD DEFEATED HER ENEMY.
HER BOAT RIDE BACK HOME TO ASTORIA WAS LONG GONE.
AND HER SISTER...?
FINDING A SEAWORTHY BOAT WASN'T THAT DIFFICULT. MANY MEN VENTURED FORTH TO THE ISLAND AND DIDN'T MAKE THE RETURN TRIP.
THE ONLY DRAWBACK WAS THE BOAT WAS ON THE WEST SIDE OF THE ISLAND, AND SHE WAS HEADING EAST.
MORE ROWING MEANT A LONG, EXHAUSTING NIGHT...

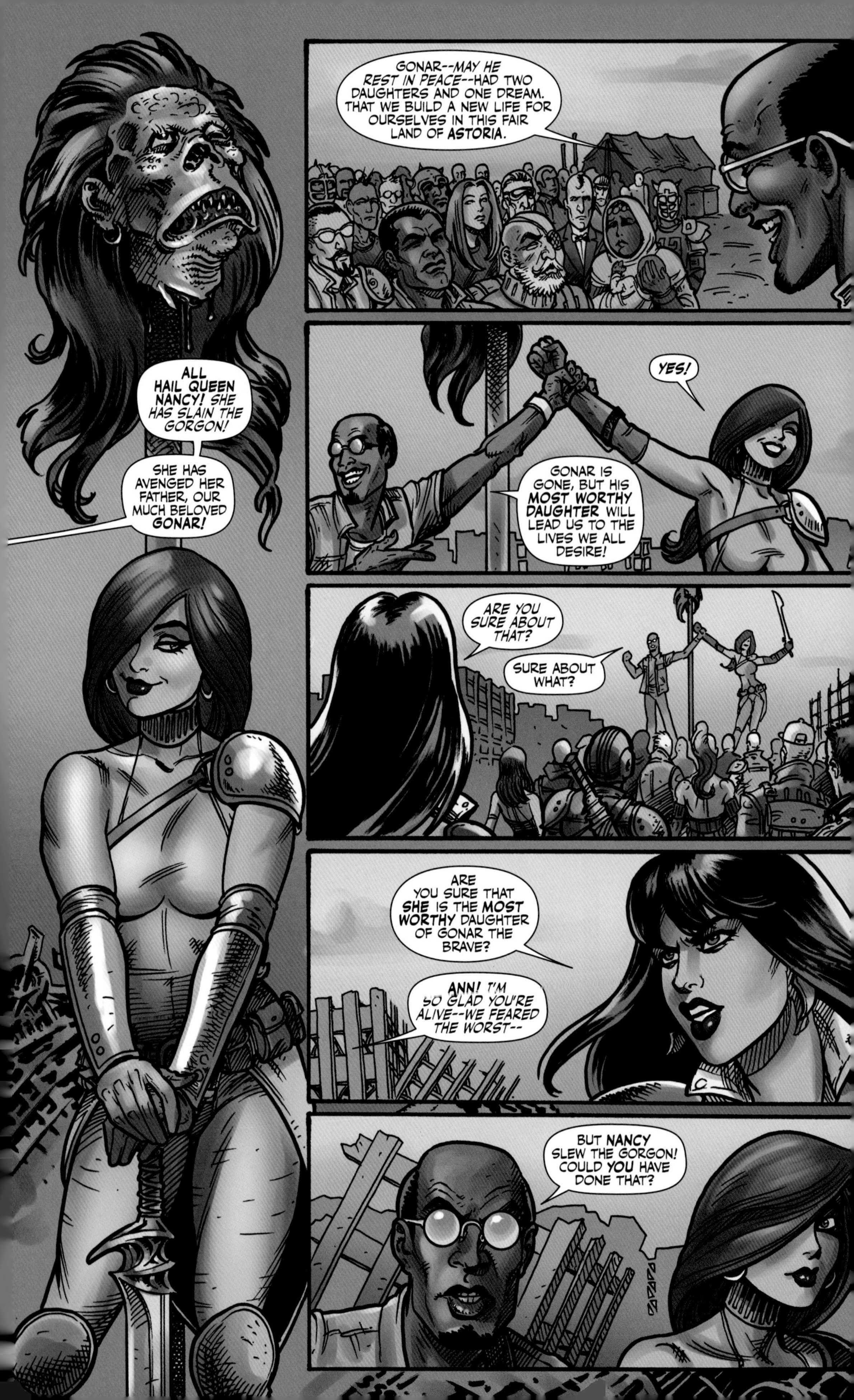

GONAR--MAY HE REST IN PEACE--HAD TWO DAUGHTERS AND ONE DREAM. THAT WE BUILD A NEW LIFE FOR OURSELVES IN THIS FAIR LAND OF ASTORIA.
ALL HAIL QUEEN NANCY! SHE HAS SLAIN THE GORGON!
SHE HAS AVENGED HER FATHER, OUR MUCH BELOVED GONAR!
YES!
GONAR IS GONE, BUT HIS MOST WORTHY DAUGHTER WILL LEAD US TO THE LIVES WE ALL DESIRE!
ARE YOU SURE ABOUT THAT?
SURE ABOUT WHAT?
ARE YOU SURE THAT SHE IS THE MOST WORTHY DAUGHTER OF GONAR THE BRAVE?
ANN! I'M SO GLAD YOU'RE ALIVE--WE FEARED THE WORST--
BUT NANCY SLEW THE GORGON! COULD YOU HAVE DONE THAT?

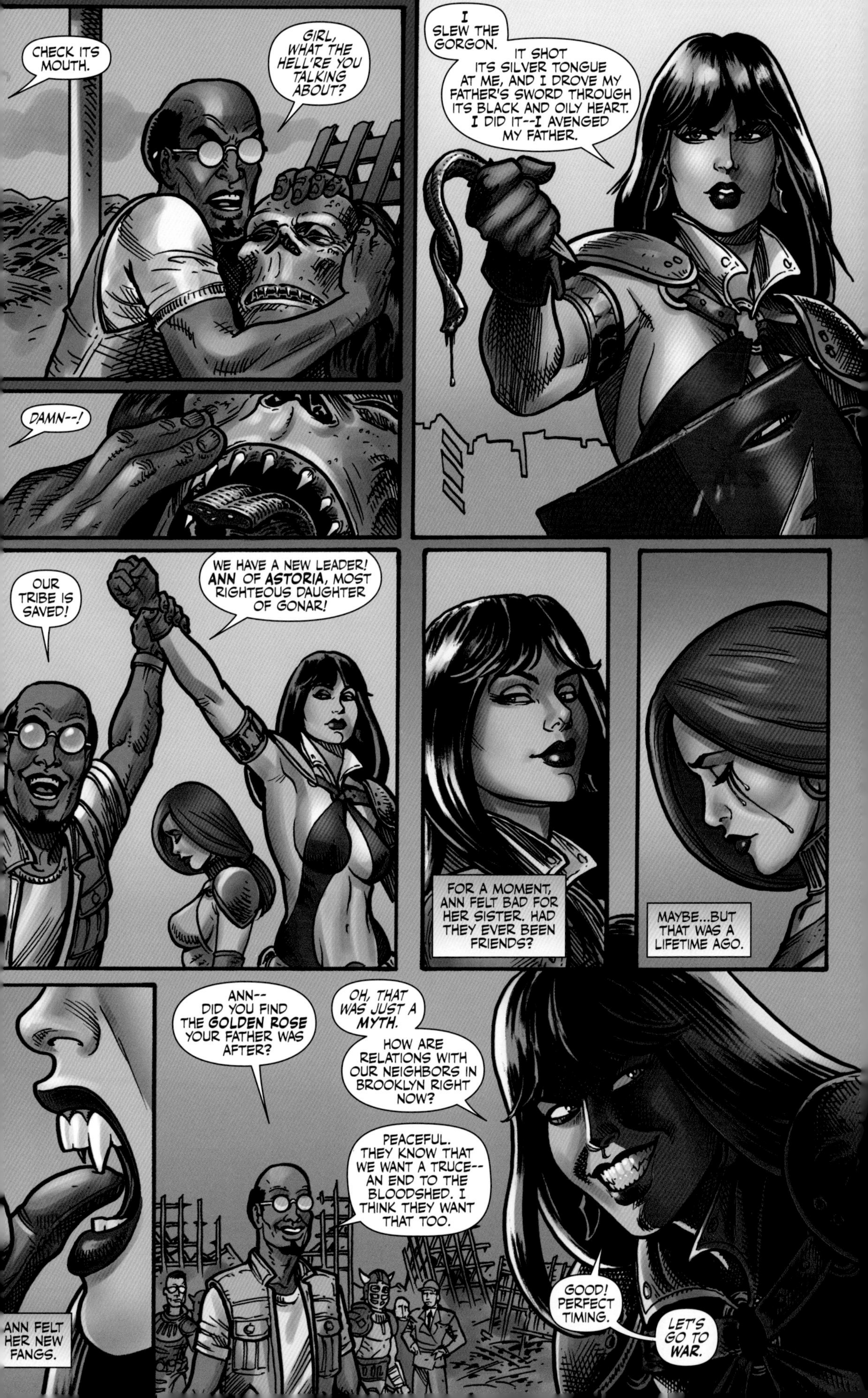
CHECK ITS MOUTH.
GIRL, WHAT THE HELL'RE YOU TALKING ABOUT?
DAMN--!
I SLEW THE GORGON.
IT SHOT ITS SILVER TONGUE AT ME, AND I DROVE MY FATHER'S SWORD THROUGH ITS BLACK AND OILY HEART. I DID IT--I AVENGED MY FATHER.
OUR TRIBE IS SAVED!
WE HAVE A NEW LEADER! ANN OF ASTORIA, MOST RIGHTEOUS DAUGHTER OF GONAR!
FOR A MOMENT, ANN FELT BAD FOR HER SISTER. HAD THEY EVER BEEN FRIENDS?
MAYBE...BUT THAT WAS A LIFETIME AGO.
ANN FELT HER NEW FANGS.
ANN-- DID YOU FIND THE GOLDEN ROSE YOUR FATHER WAS AFTER?
OH, THAT WAS JUST A MYTH.
HOW ARE RELATIONS WITH OUR NEIGHBORS IN BROOKLYN RIGHT NOW?
PEACEFUL. THEY KNOW THAT WE WANT A TRUCE-- AN END TO THE BLOODSHED. I THINK THEY WANT THAT TOO.
GOOD! PERFECT TIMING.
LET'S GO TO WAR.

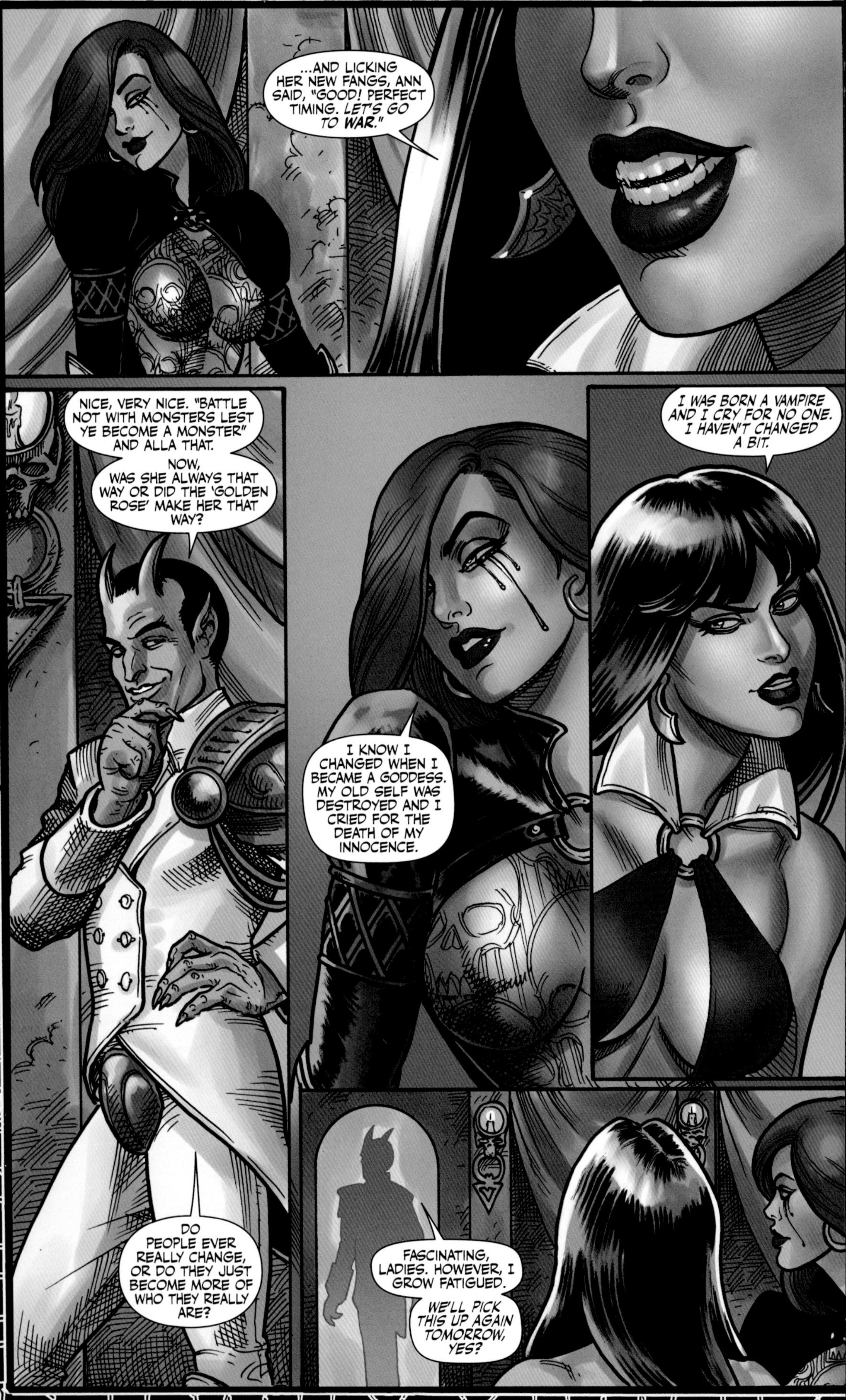
...AND LICKING HER NEW FANGS, ANN SAID, "GOOD! PERFECT TIMING. LET'S GO TO WAR."
NICE, VERY NICE. "BATTLE NOT WITH MONSTERS LEST YE BECOME A MONSTER" AND ALLA THAT.
NOW, WAS SHE ALWAYS THAT WAY OR DID THE 'GOLDEN ROSE' MAKE HER THAT WAY?
I KNOW I CHANGED WHEN I BECAME A GODDESS. MY OLD SELF WAS DESTROYED AND I CRIED FOR THE DEATH OF MY INNOCENCE.
I WAS BORN A VAMPIRE AND I CRY FOR NO ONE. I HAVEN'T CHANGED A BIT.
DO PEOPLE EVER REALLY CHANGE, OR DO THEY JUST BECOME MORE OF WHO THEY REALLY ARE?
FASCINATING, LADIES. HOWEVER, I GROW FATIGUED.
WE'LL PICK THIS UP AGAIN TOMORROW, YES?

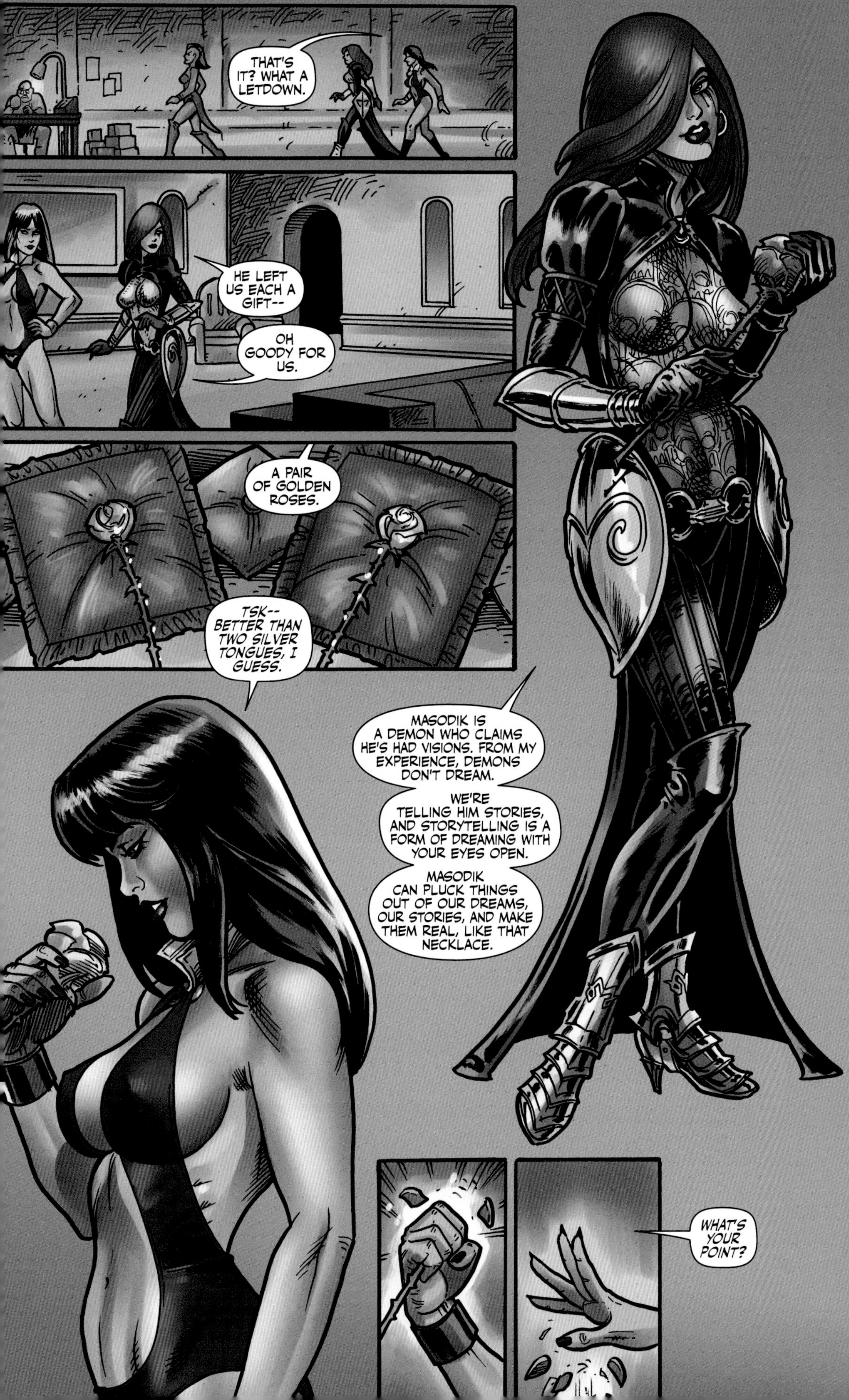
THAT'S IT? WHAT A LETDOWN.
HE LEFT US EACH A GIFT--
OH GOODY FOR US.
A PAIR OF GOLDEN ROSES.
TSK-- BETTER THAN TWO SILVER TONGUES, I GUESS.
MASODIK IS A DEMON WHO CLAIMS HE'S HAD VISIONS. FROM MY EXPERIENCE, DEMONS DON'T DREAM.
WE'RE TELLING HIM STORIES, AND STORYTELLING IS A FORM OF DREAMING WITH YOUR EYES OPEN.
MASODIK CAN PLUCK THINGS OUT OF OUR DREAMS, OUR STORIES, AND MAKE THEM REAL, LIKE THAT NECKLACE.
WHAT'S YOUR POINT?

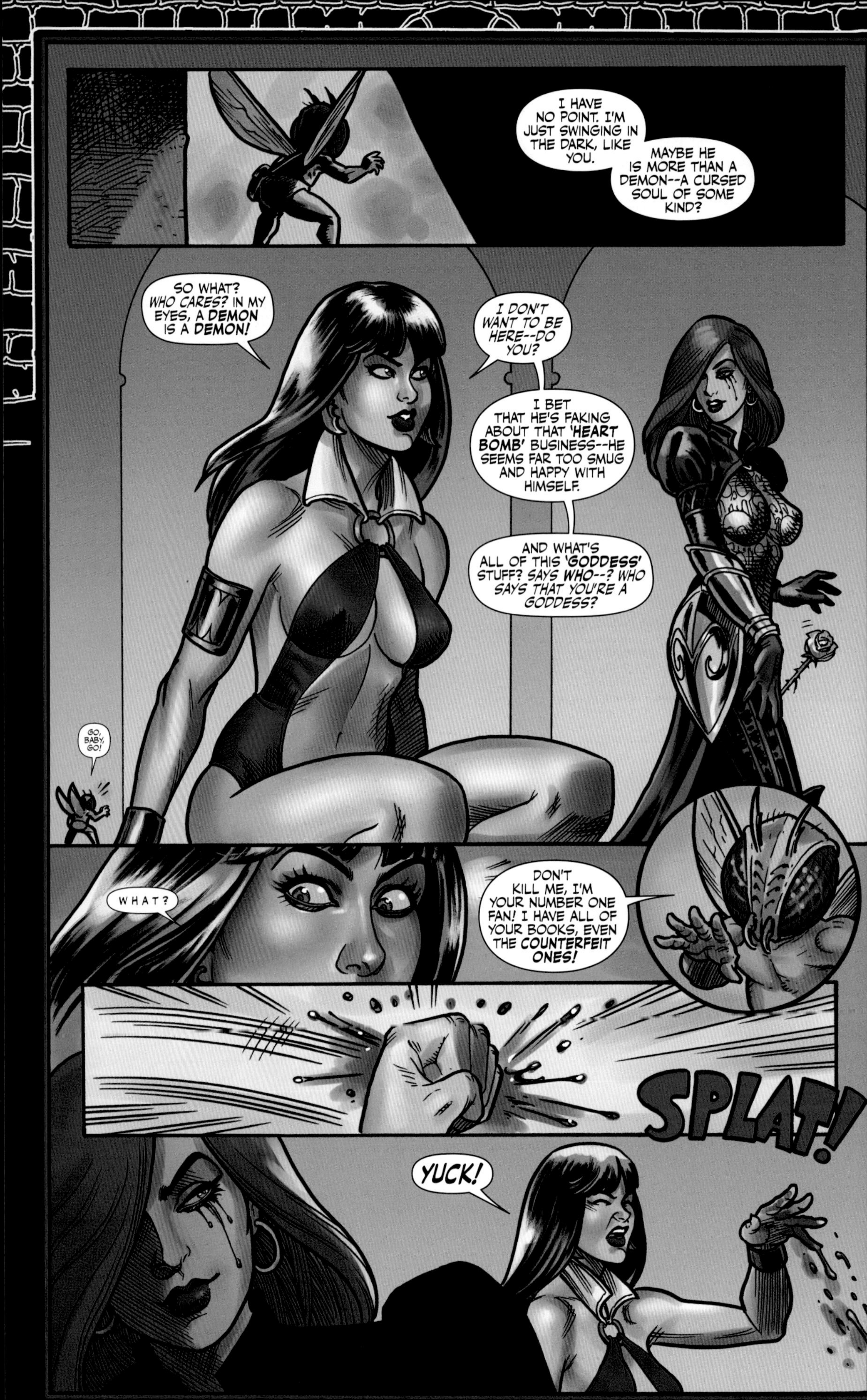
I HAVE NO POINT. I'M JUST SWINGING IN THE DARK, LIKE YOU.
MAYBE HE IS MORE THAN A DEMON--A CURSED SOUL OF SOME KIND?
SO WHAT? WHO CARES? IN MY EYES, A DEMON IS A DEMON!
I DON'T WANT TO BE HERE--DO YOU?
I BET THAT HE'S FAKING ABOUT THAT 'HEART BOMB' BUSINESS--HE SEEMS FAR TOO SMUG AND HAPPY WITH HIMSELF.
AND WHAT'S ALL OF THIS 'GODDESS' STUFF? SAYS WHO--? WHO SAYS THAT YOU'RE A GODDESS?
GO, BABY, GO!
WHAT?
DON'T KILL ME, I'M YOUR NUMBER ONE FAN! I HAVE ALL OF YOUR BOOKS, EVEN THE COUNTERFEIT ONES!
SPLAT!
YUCK!

CHAPTER • THREE

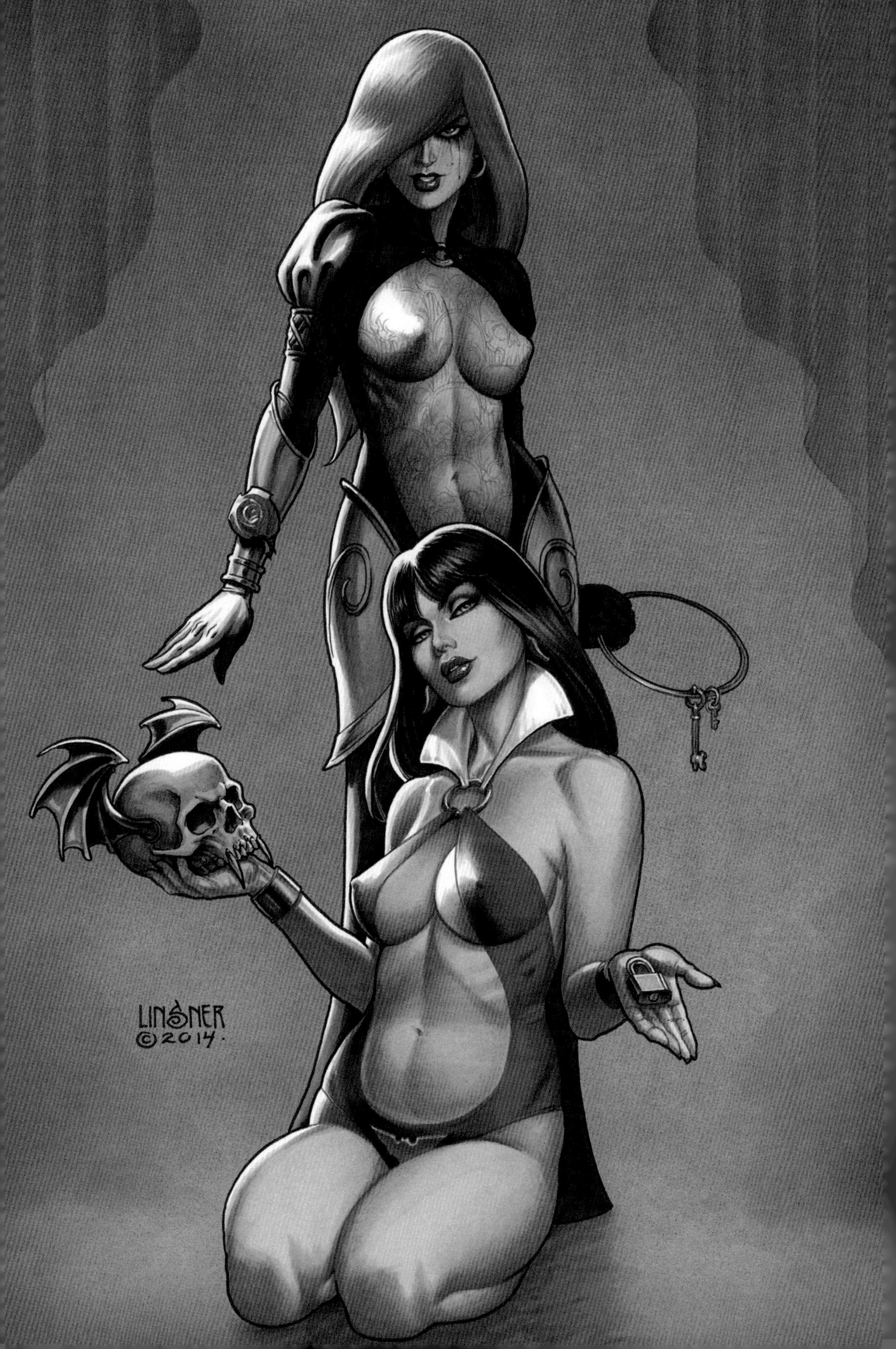
LINSNER
©2014.

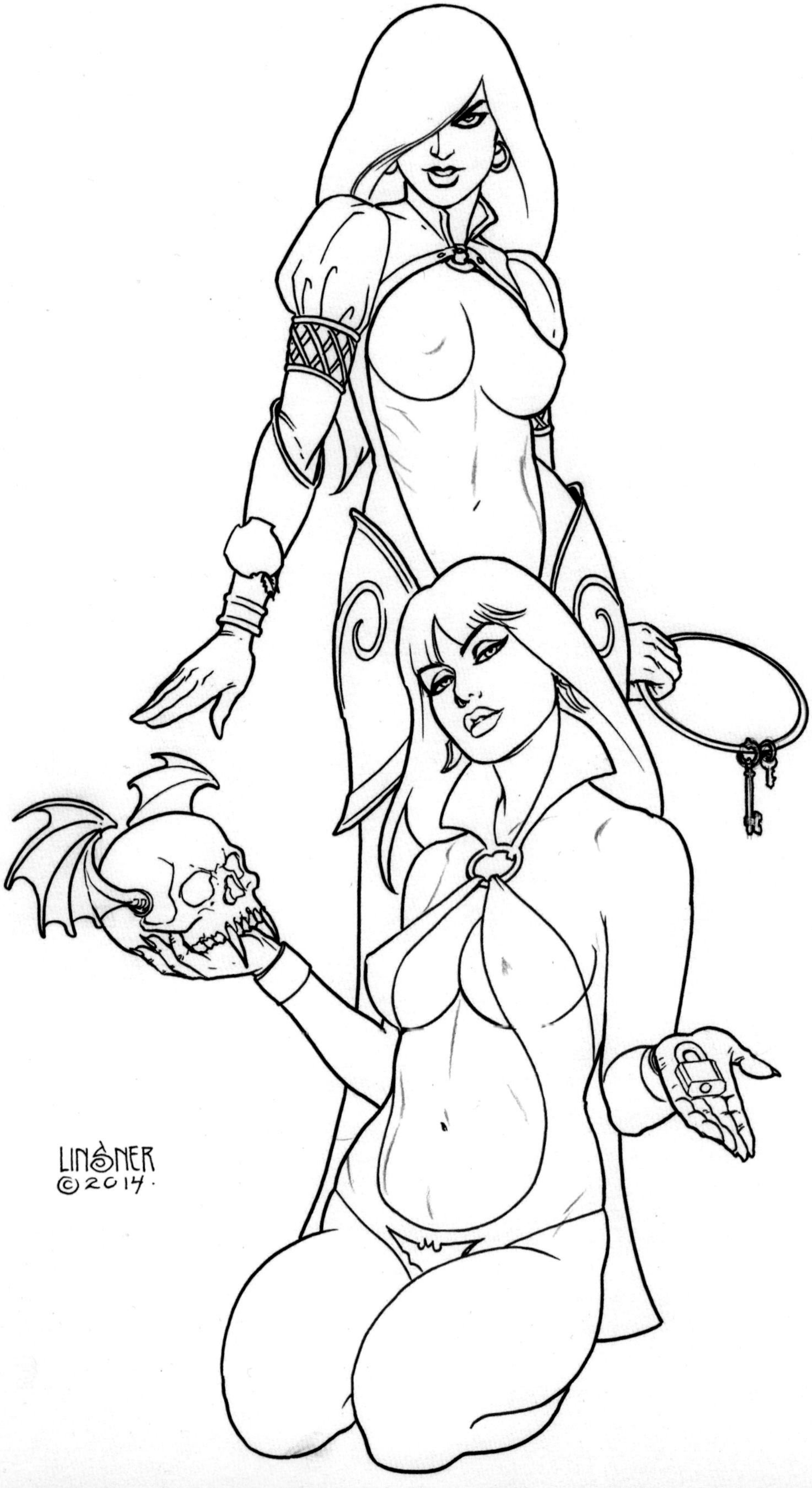
LINSNER
©2014.

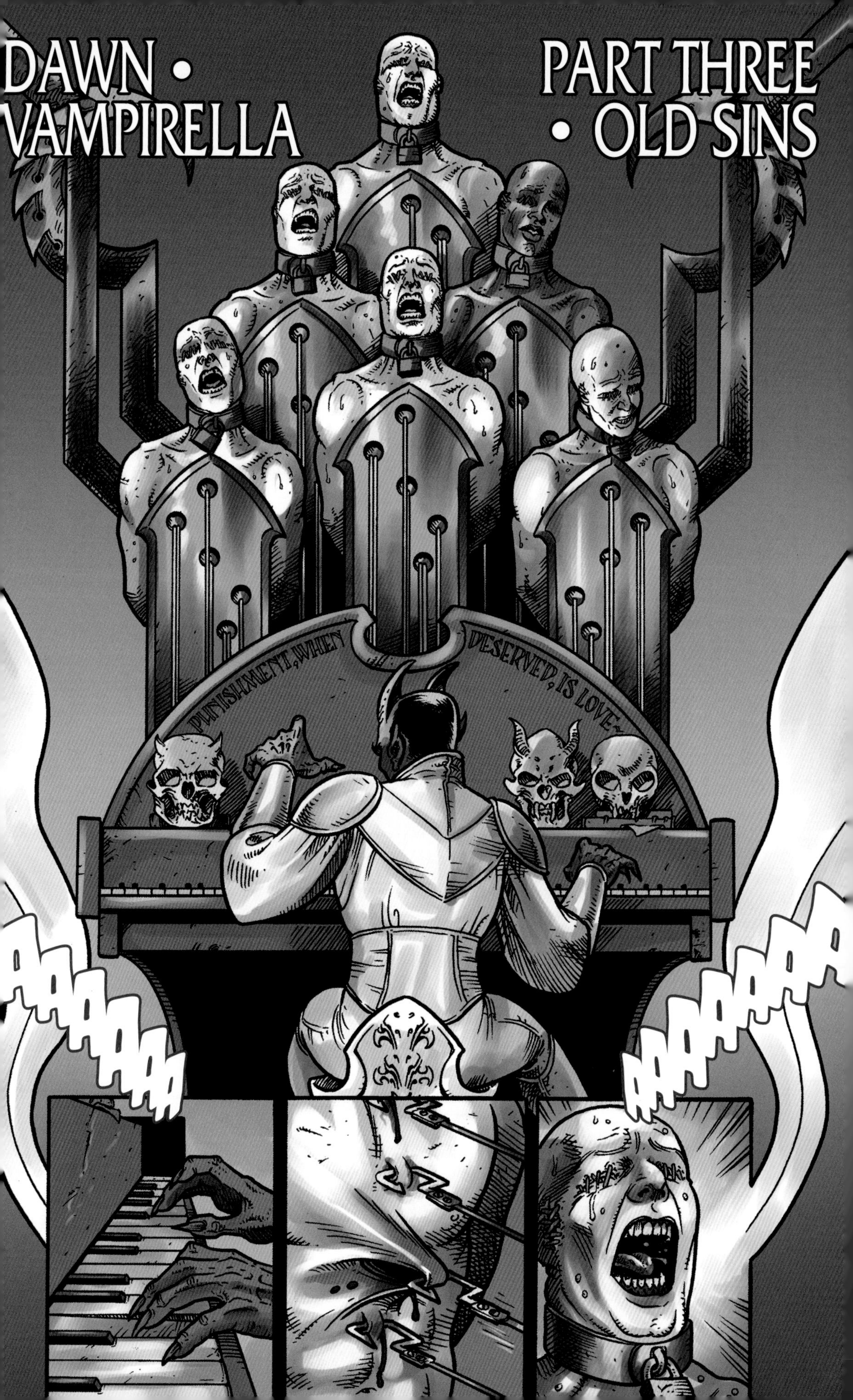
DAWN • VAMPIRELLA
PART THREE • OLD SINS
PUNISHMENT, WHEN DESERVED, IS LOVE.
AAAAAAAA
AAAAAAAAA

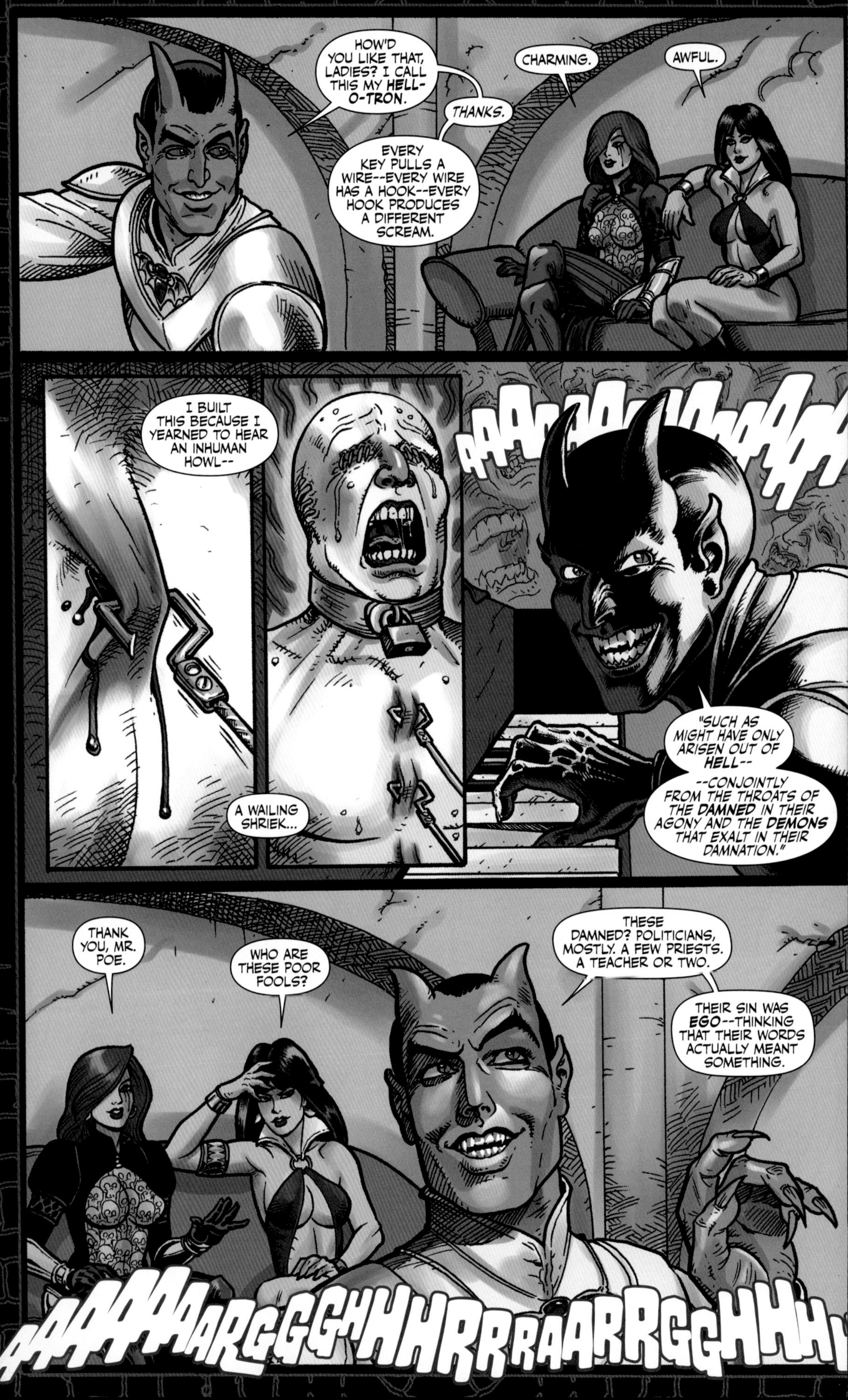
HOW'D YOU LIKE THAT, LADIES? I CALL THIS MY HELL-O-TRON.
CHARMING.
AWFUL.
THANKS.
EVERY KEY PULLS A WIRE--EVERY WIRE HAS A HOOK--EVERY HOOK PRODUCES A DIFFERENT SCREAM.
I BUILT THIS BECAUSE I YEARNED TO HEAR AN INHUMAN HOWL--
A WAILING SHRIEK...
"SUCH AS MIGHT HAVE ONLY ARISEN OUT OF HELL--
--CONJOINTLY FROM THE THROATS OF THE DAMNED IN THEIR AGONY AND THE DEMONS THAT EXALT IN THEIR DAMNATION."
THANK YOU, MR. POE.
WHO ARE THESE POOR FOOLS?
THESE DAMNED? POLITICIANS, MOSTLY. A FEW PRIESTS. A TEACHER OR TWO.
THEIR SIN WAS EGO--THINKING THAT THEIR WORDS ACTUALLY MEANT SOMETHING.
AAAAAARGGGHHHRRRAARRGGHHHH

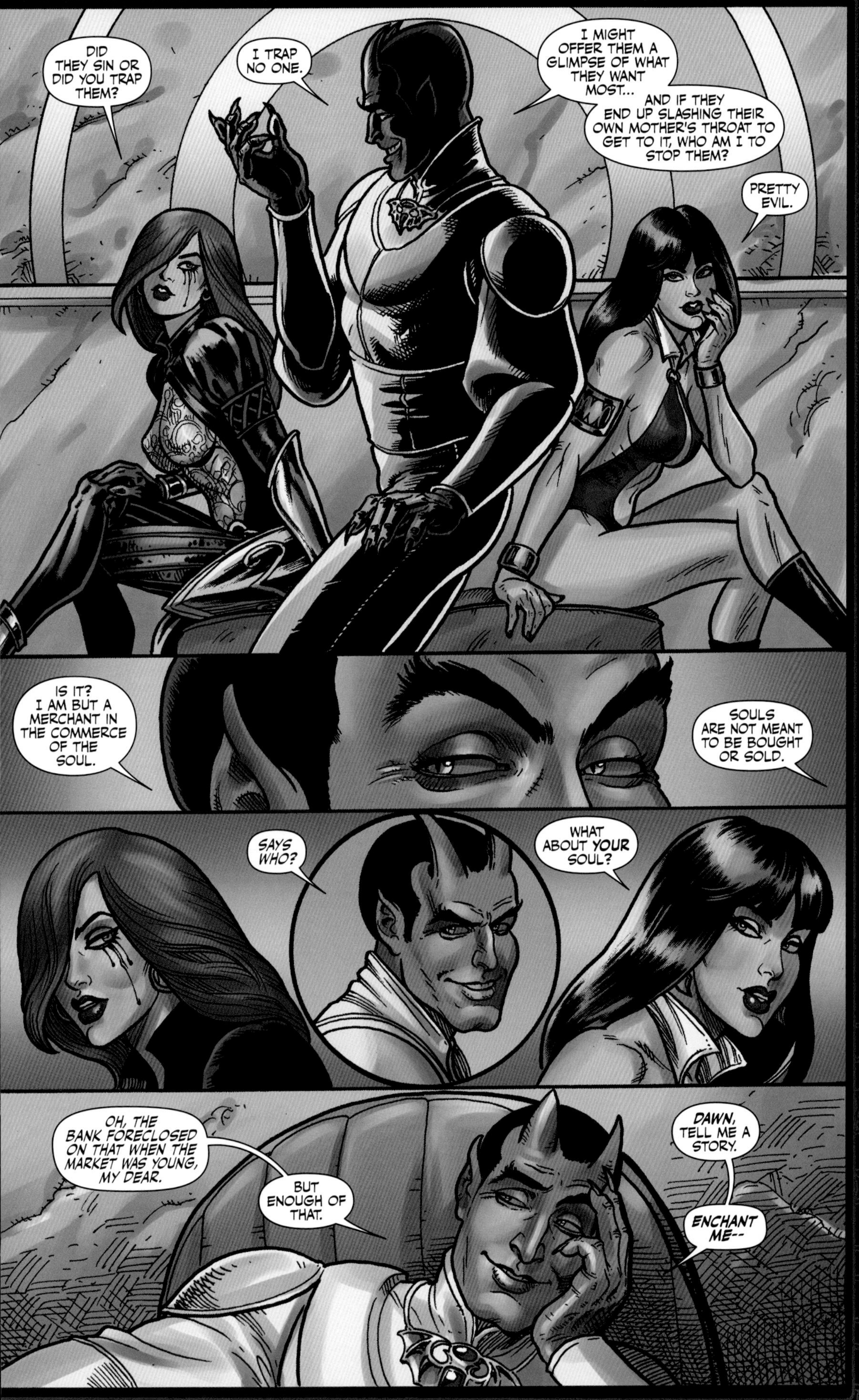
DID THEY SIN OR DID YOU TRAP THEM?
I TRAP NO ONE.
I MIGHT OFFER THEM A GLIMPSE OF WHAT THEY WANT MOST...
AND IF THEY END UP SLASHING THEIR OWN MOTHER'S THROAT TO GET TO IT, WHO AM I TO STOP THEM?
PRETTY EVIL.
IS IT? I AM BUT A MERCHANT IN THE COMMERCE OF THE SOUL.
SOULS ARE NOT MEANT TO BE BOUGHT OR SOLD.
SAYS WHO?
WHAT ABOUT YOUR SOUL?
OH, THE BANK FORECLOSED ON THAT WHEN THE MARKET WAS YOUNG, MY DEAR.
BUT ENOUGH OF THAT.
DAWN, TELL ME A STORY.
ENCHANT ME--

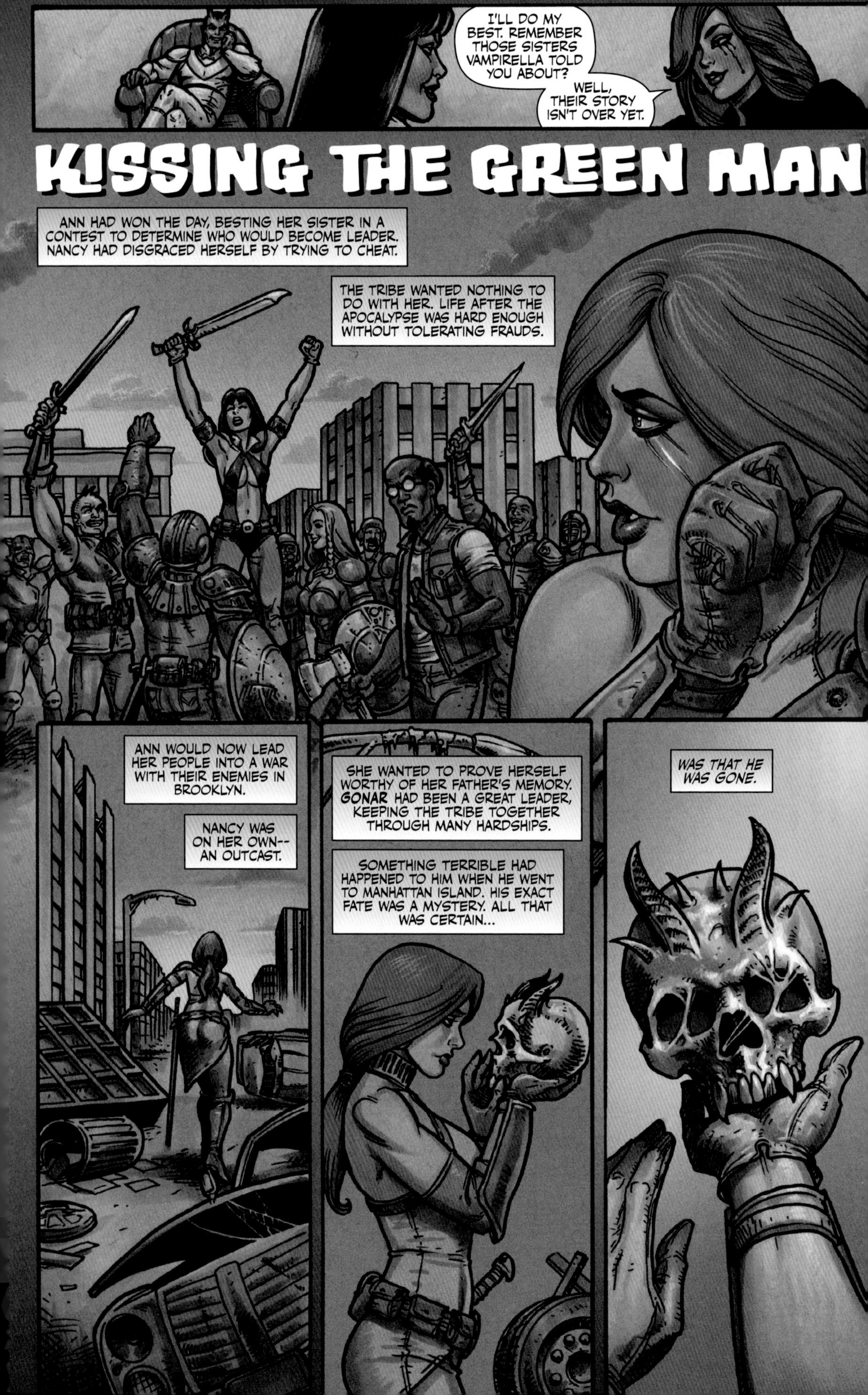
I'LL DO MY BEST. REMEMBER THOSE SISTERS VAMPIRELLA TOLD YOU ABOUT?
WELL, THEIR STORY ISN'T OVER YET.
KISSING THE GREEN MAN
ANN HAD WON THE DAY, BESTING HER SISTER IN A CONTEST TO DETERMINE WHO WOULD BECOME LEADER. NANCY HAD DISGRACED HERSELF BY TRYING TO CHEAT.
THE TRIBE WANTED NOTHING TO DO WITH HER. LIFE AFTER THE APOCALYPSE WAS HARD ENOUGH WITHOUT TOLERATING FRAUDS.
ANN WOULD NOW LEAD HER PEOPLE INTO A WAR WITH THEIR ENEMIES IN BROOKLYN.
NANCY WAS ON HER OWN-- AN OUTCAST.
SHE WANTED TO PROVE HERSELF WORTHY OF HER FATHER'S MEMORY. GONAR HAD BEEN A GREAT LEADER, KEEPING THE TRIBE TOGETHER THROUGH MANY HARDSHIPS.
SOMETHING TERRIBLE HAD HAPPENED TO HIM WHEN HE WENT TO MANHATTAN ISLAND. HIS EXACT FATE WAS A MYSTERY. ALL THAT WAS CERTAIN...
WAS THAT HE WAS GONE.

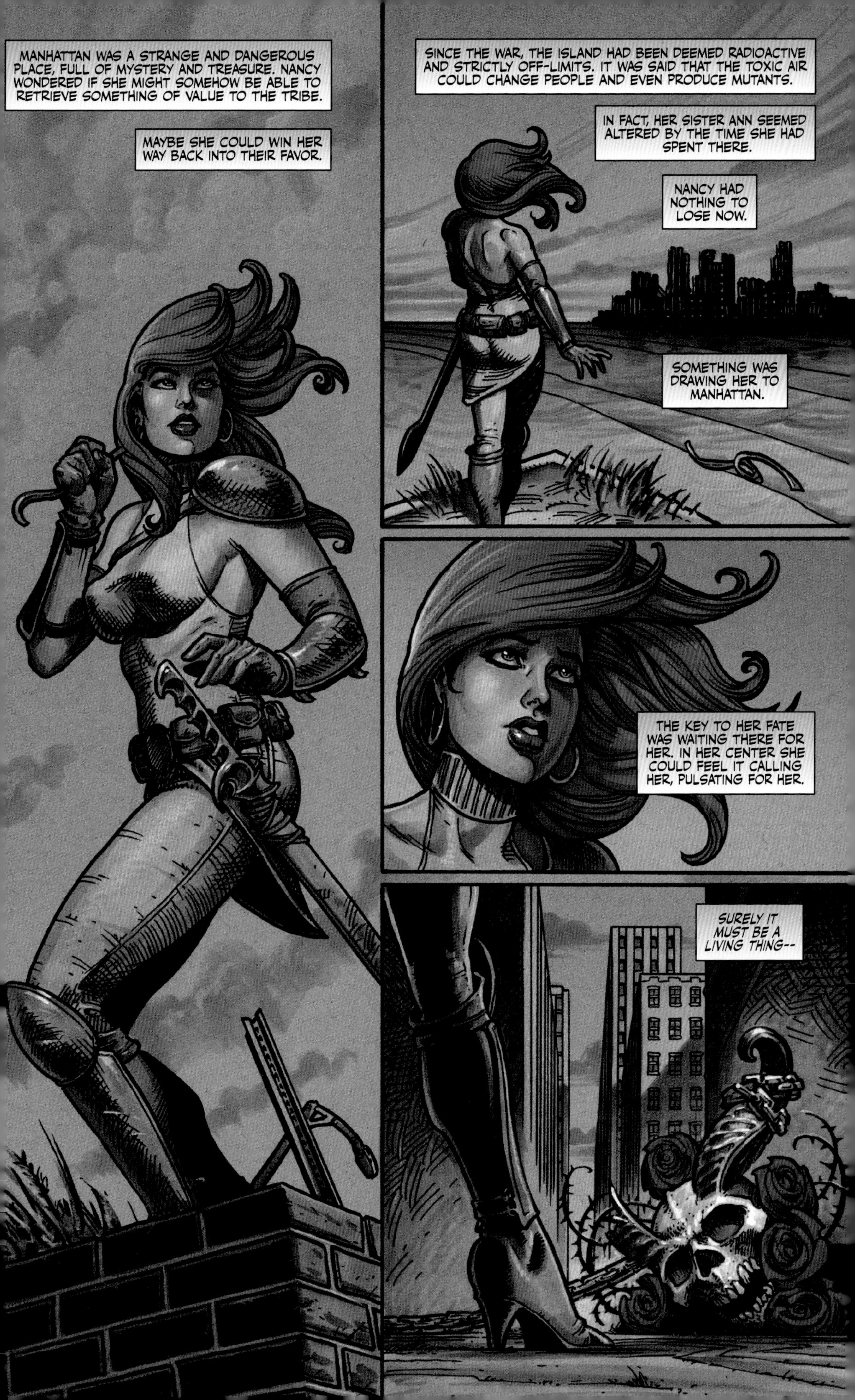
MANHATTAN WAS A STRANGE AND DANGEROUS PLACE, FULL OF MYSTERY AND TREASURE. NANCY WONDERED IF SHE MIGHT SOMEHOW BE ABLE TO RETRIEVE SOMETHING OF VALUE TO THE TRIBE.
MAYBE SHE COULD WIN HER WAY BACK INTO THEIR FAVOR.
SINCE THE WAR, THE ISLAND HAD BEEN DEEMED RADIOACTIVE AND STRICTLY OFF-LIMITS. IT WAS SAID THAT THE TOXIC AIR COULD CHANGE PEOPLE AND EVEN PRODUCE MUTANTS.
IN FACT, HER SISTER ANN SEEMED ALTERED BY THE TIME SHE HAD SPENT THERE.
NANCY HAD NOTHING TO LOSE NOW.
SOMETHING WAS DRAWING HER TO MANHATTAN.
THE KEY TO HER FATE WAS WAITING THERE FOR HER. IN HER CENTER SHE COULD FEEL IT CALLING HER, PULSATING FOR HER.
SURELY IT MUST BE A LIVING THING--

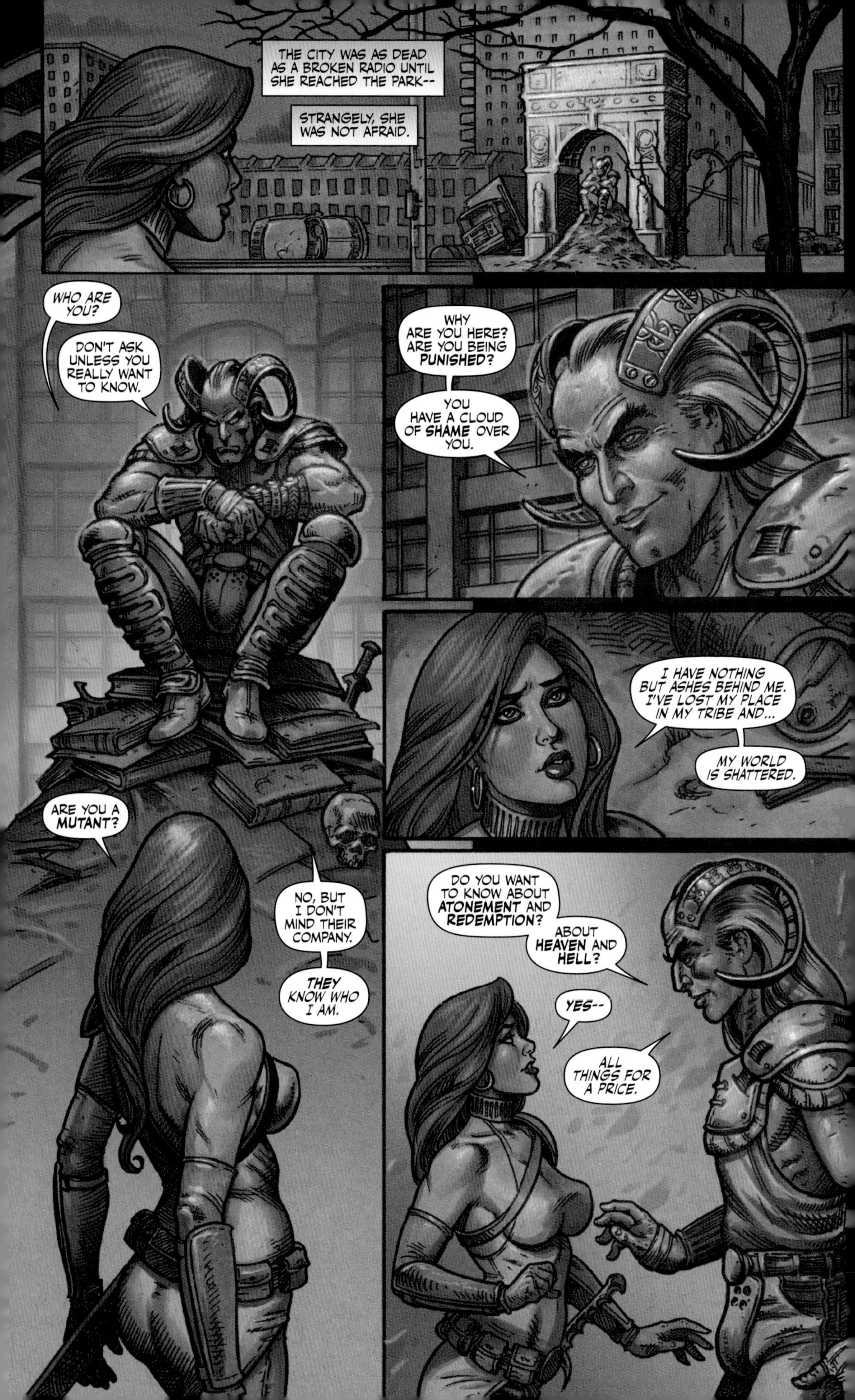
THE CITY WAS AS DEAD AS A BROKEN RADIO UNTIL SHE REACHED THE PARK--
STRANGELY, SHE WAS NOT AFRAID.
WHO ARE YOU?
DON'T ASK UNLESS YOU REALLY WANT TO KNOW.
ARE YOU A MUTANT?
NO, BUT I DON'T MIND THEIR COMPANY.
THEY KNOW WHO I AM.
WHY ARE YOU HERE? ARE YOU BEING PUNISHED?
YOU HAVE A CLOUD OF SHAME OVER YOU.
I HAVE NOTHING BUT ASHES BEHIND ME. I'VE LOST MY PLACE IN MY TRIBE AND...
MY WORLD IS SHATTERED.
DO YOU WANT TO KNOW ABOUT ATONEMENT AND REDEMPTION?
ABOUT HEAVEN AND HELL?
YES--
ALL THINGS FOR A PRICE.

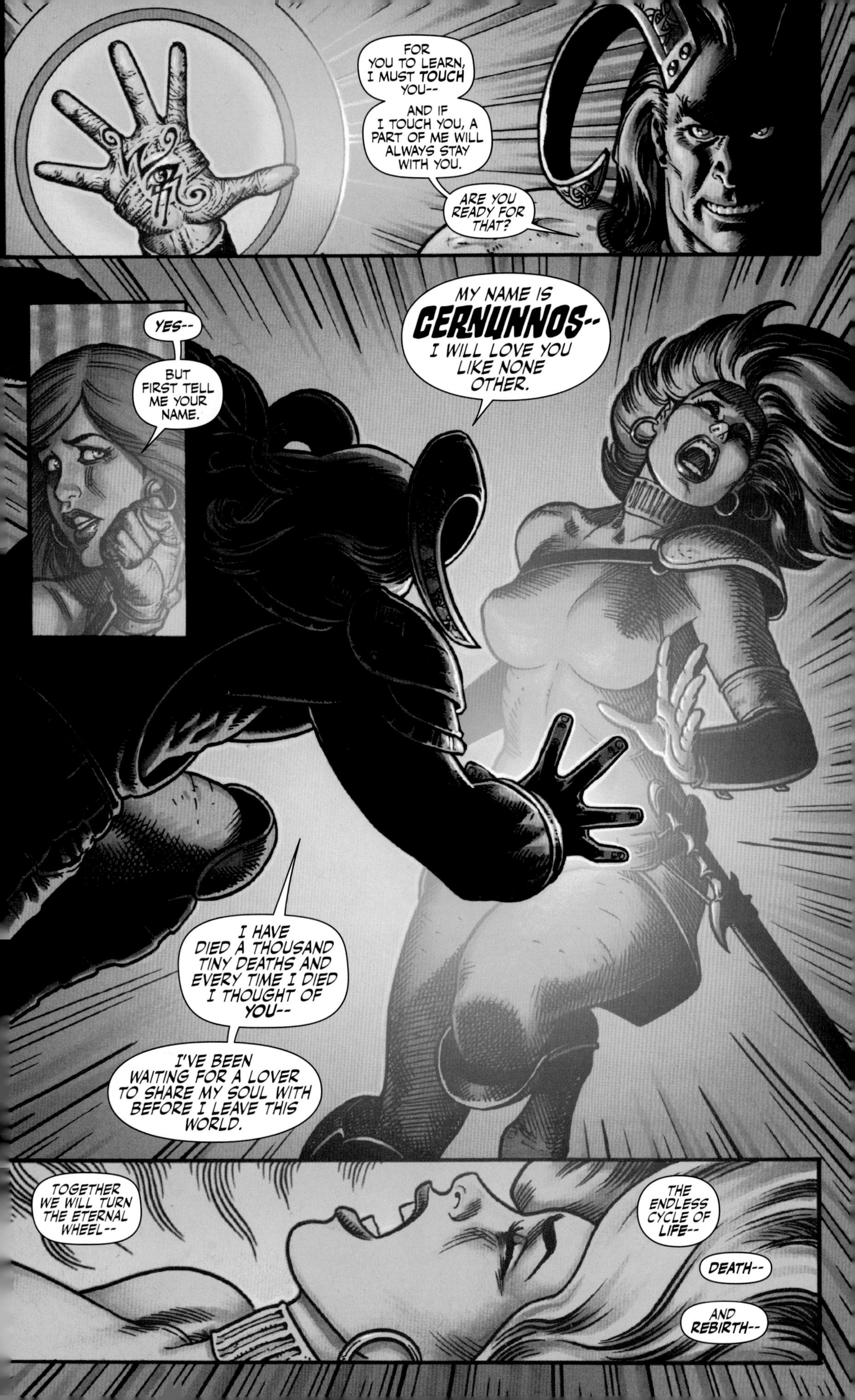
FOR YOU TO LEARN, I MUST TOUCH YOU--
AND IF I TOUCH YOU, A PART OF ME WILL ALWAYS STAY WITH YOU.
ARE YOU READY FOR THAT?
YES--
BUT FIRST TELL ME YOUR NAME.
MY NAME IS CERNUNNOS-- I WILL LOVE YOU LIKE NONE OTHER.
I HAVE DIED A THOUSAND TINY DEATHS AND EVERY TIME I DIED I THOUGHT OF YOU--
I'VE BEEN WAITING FOR A LOVER TO SHARE MY SOUL WITH BEFORE I LEAVE THIS WORLD.
TOGETHER WE WILL TURN THE ETERNAL WHEEL--
THE ENDLESS CYCLE OF LIFE--
DEATH--
AND REBIRTH--

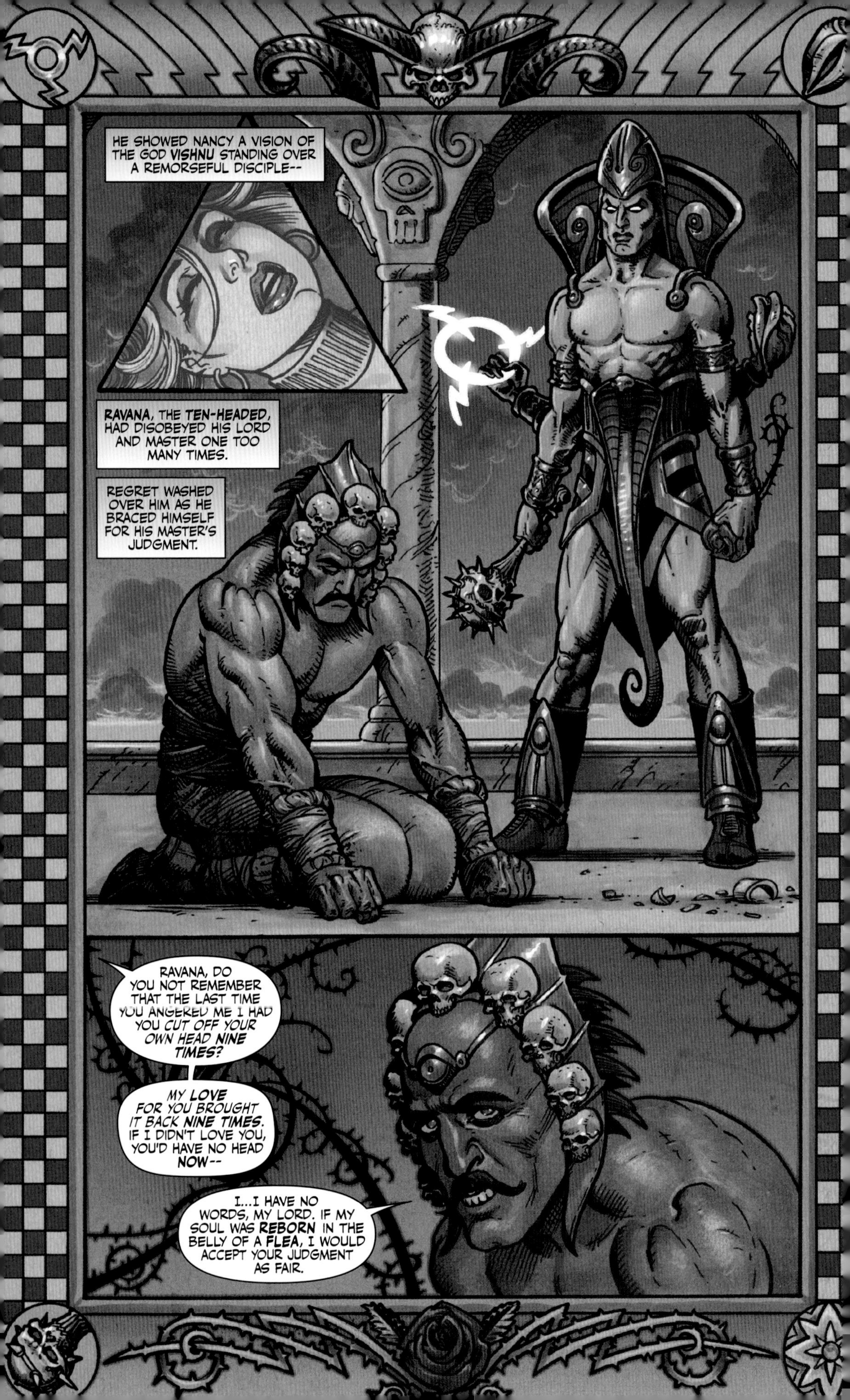
HE SHOWED NANCY A VISION OF THE GOD **VISHNU** STANDING OVER A REMORSEFUL DISCIPLE--
RAVANA, THE **TEN-HEADED**, HAD DISOBEYED HIS LORD AND MASTER ONE TOO MANY TIMES.
REGRET WASHED OVER HIM AS HE BRACED HIMSELF FOR HIS MASTER'S JUDGMENT.
RAVANA, DO YOU NOT REMEMBER THAT THE LAST TIME YOU ANGERED ME I HAD YOU *CUT OFF YOUR OWN HEAD* ***NINE TIMES?***
MY ***LOVE*** *FOR YOU BROUGHT IT BACK* ***NINE TIMES***. IF I DIDN'T LOVE YOU, YOU'D HAVE NO HEAD **NOW**--
I...I HAVE NO WORDS, MY LORD. IF MY SOUL WAS **REBORN** IN THE BELLY OF A **FLEA**, I WOULD ACCEPT YOUR JUDGMENT AS FAIR.

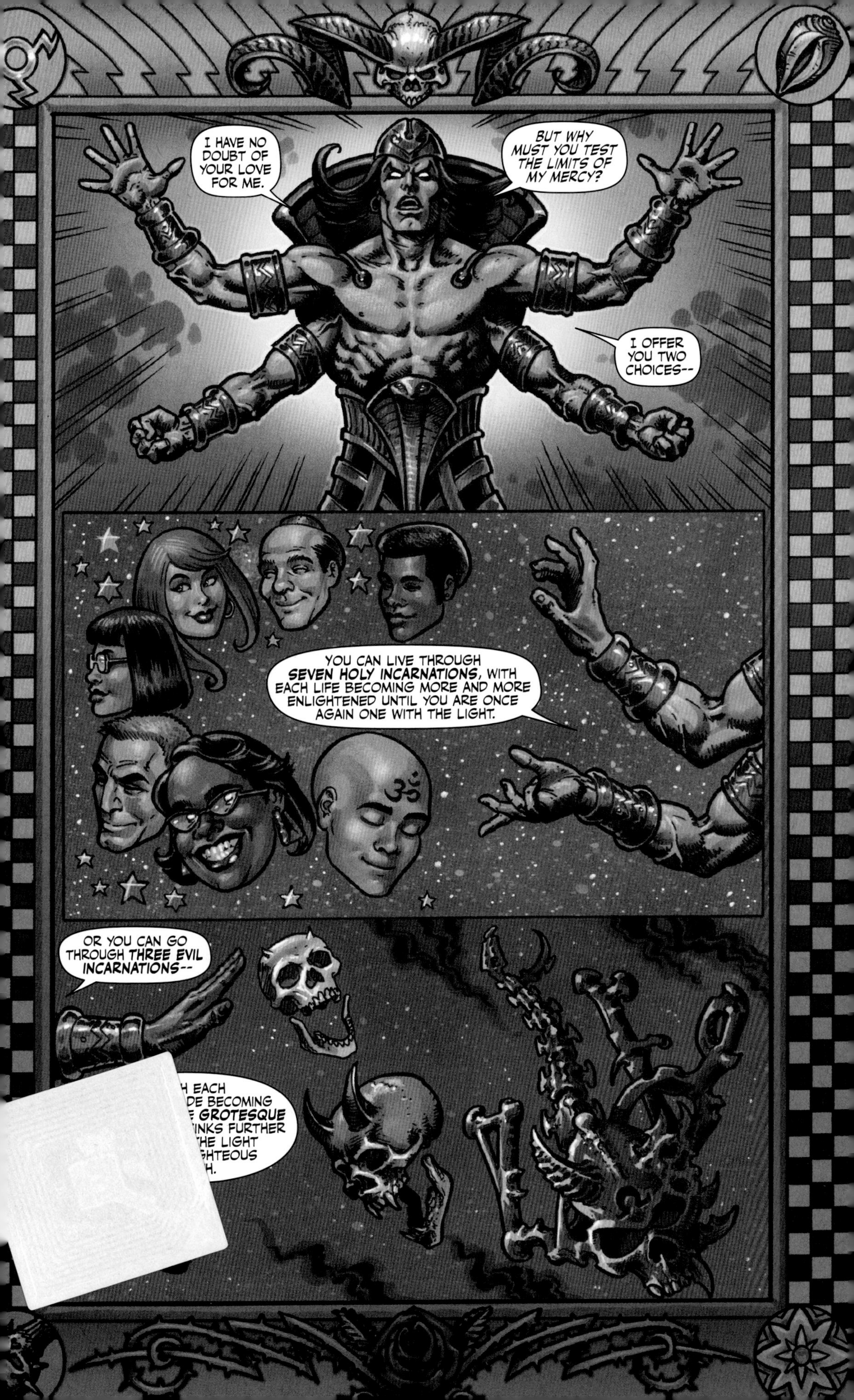
I HAVE NO DOUBT OF YOUR LOVE FOR ME.
BUT WHY MUST YOU TEST THE LIMITS OF MY MERCY?
I OFFER YOU TWO CHOICES--
YOU CAN LIVE THROUGH **SEVEN HOLY INCARNATIONS,** WITH EACH LIFE BECOMING MORE AND MORE ENLIGHTENED UNTIL YOU ARE ONCE AGAIN ONE WITH THE LIGHT.
OR YOU CAN GO THROUGH **THREE EVIL INCARNATIONS**--
H EACH
DE BECOMING
GROTESQUE
INKS FURTHER
THE LIGHT
GHTEOUS
H.

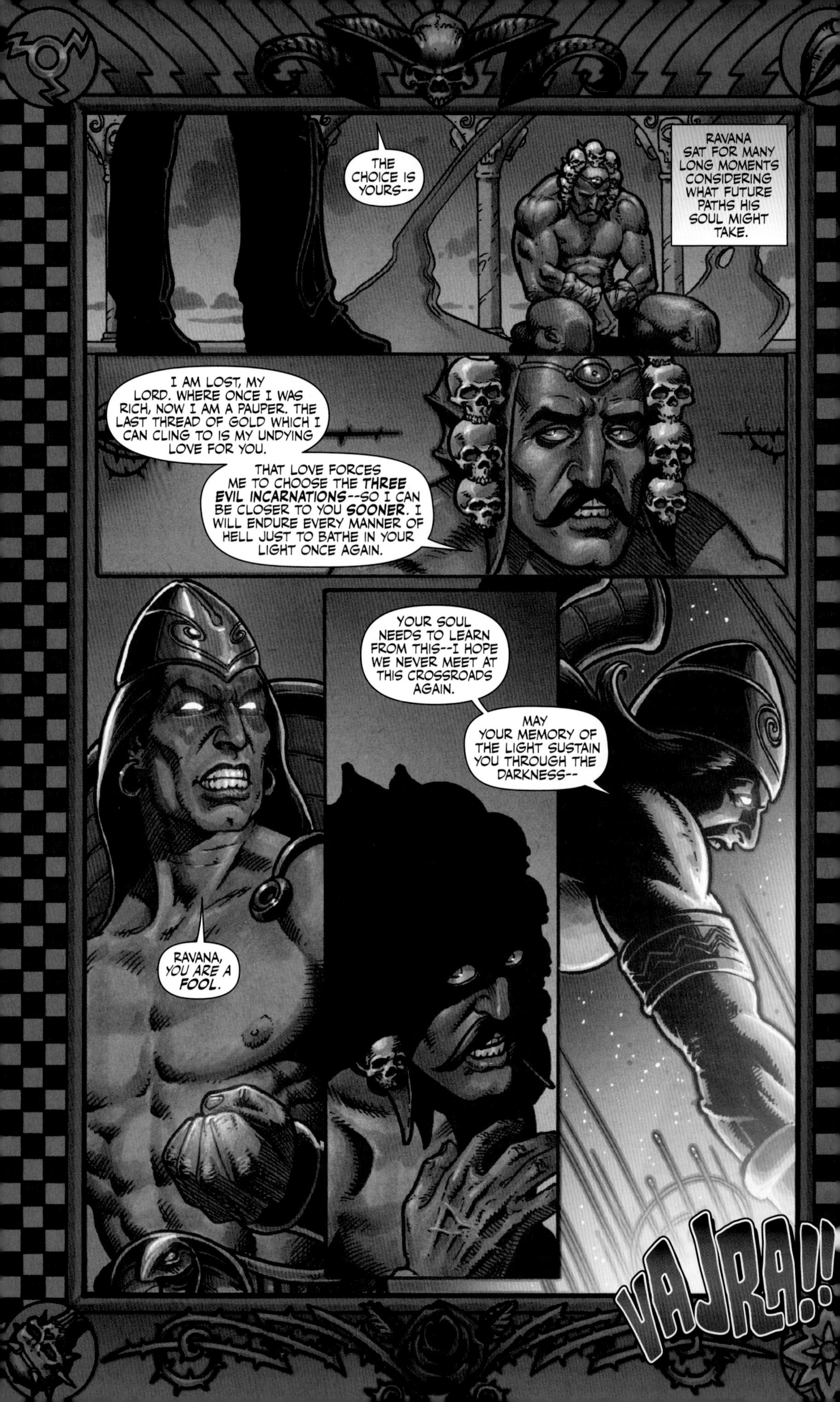
THE CHOICE IS YOURS--
RAVANA SAT FOR MANY LONG MOMENTS CONSIDERING WHAT FUTURE PATHS HIS SOUL MIGHT TAKE.
I AM LOST, MY LORD. WHERE ONCE I WAS RICH, NOW I AM A PAUPER. THE LAST THREAD OF GOLD WHICH I CAN CLING TO IS MY UNDYING LOVE FOR YOU.
THAT LOVE FORCES ME TO CHOOSE THE **THREE EVIL INCARNATIONS**--SO I CAN BE CLOSER TO YOU **SOONER**. I WILL ENDURE EVERY MANNER OF HELL JUST TO BATHE IN YOUR LIGHT ONCE AGAIN.
RAVANA, *YOU ARE A* ***FOOL***.
YOUR SOUL NEEDS TO LEARN FROM THIS--I HOPE WE NEVER MEET AT THIS CROSSROADS AGAIN.
MAY YOUR MEMORY OF THE LIGHT SUSTAIN YOU THROUGH THE DARKNESS--
VAJRA!!

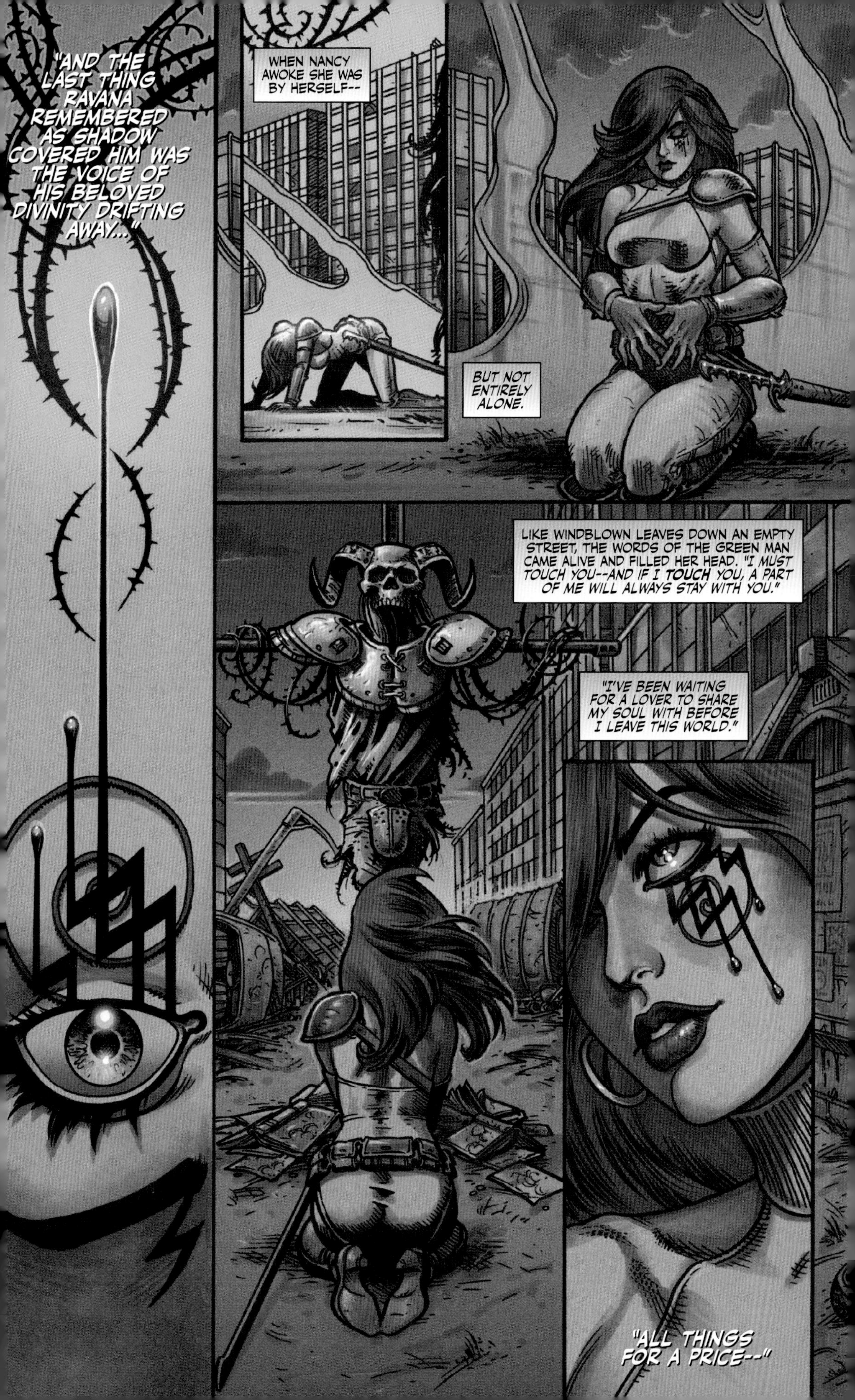
"AND THE LAST THING RAVANA REMEMBERED AS SHADOW COVERED HIM WAS THE VOICE OF HIS BELOVED DIVINITY DRIFTING AWAY..."
WHEN NANCY AWOKE SHE WAS BY HERSELF--
BUT NOT ENTIRELY ALONE.
LIKE WINDBLOWN LEAVES DOWN AN EMPTY STREET, THE WORDS OF THE GREEN MAN CAME ALIVE AND FILLED HER HEAD. "I MUST TOUCH YOU--AND IF I TOUCH YOU, A PART OF ME WILL ALWAYS STAY WITH YOU."
"I'VE BEEN WAITING FOR A LOVER TO SHARE MY SOUL WITH BEFORE I LEAVE THIS WORLD."
"ALL THINGS FOR A PRICE--"

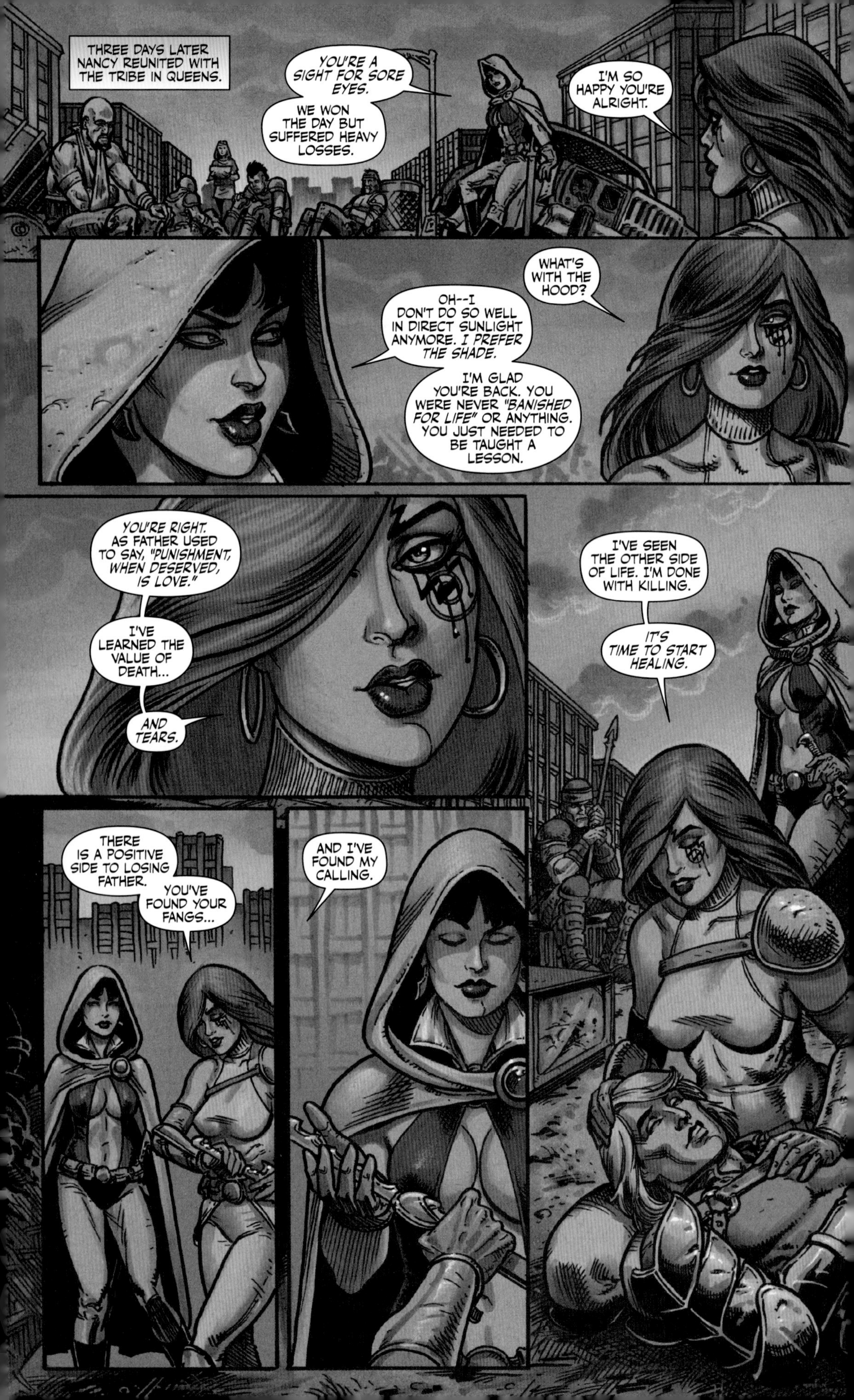
THREE DAYS LATER NANCY REUNITED WITH THE TRIBE IN QUEENS.
YOU'RE A SIGHT FOR SORE EYES.
WE WON THE DAY BUT SUFFERED HEAVY LOSSES.
I'M SO HAPPY YOU'RE ALRIGHT.
WHAT'S WITH THE HOOD?
OH--I DON'T DO SO WELL IN DIRECT SUNLIGHT ANYMORE. I PREFER THE SHADE.
I'M GLAD YOU'RE BACK. YOU WERE NEVER "BANISHED FOR LIFE" OR ANYTHING. YOU JUST NEEDED TO BE TAUGHT A LESSON.
YOU'RE RIGHT. AS FATHER USED TO SAY, "PUNISHMENT, WHEN DESERVED, IS LOVE."
I'VE LEARNED THE VALUE OF DEATH...
AND TEARS.
I'VE SEEN THE OTHER SIDE OF LIFE. I'M DONE WITH KILLING.
IT'S TIME TO START HEALING.
THERE IS A POSITIVE SIDE TO LOSING FATHER.
YOU'VE FOUND YOUR FANGS...
AND I'VE FOUND MY CALLING.

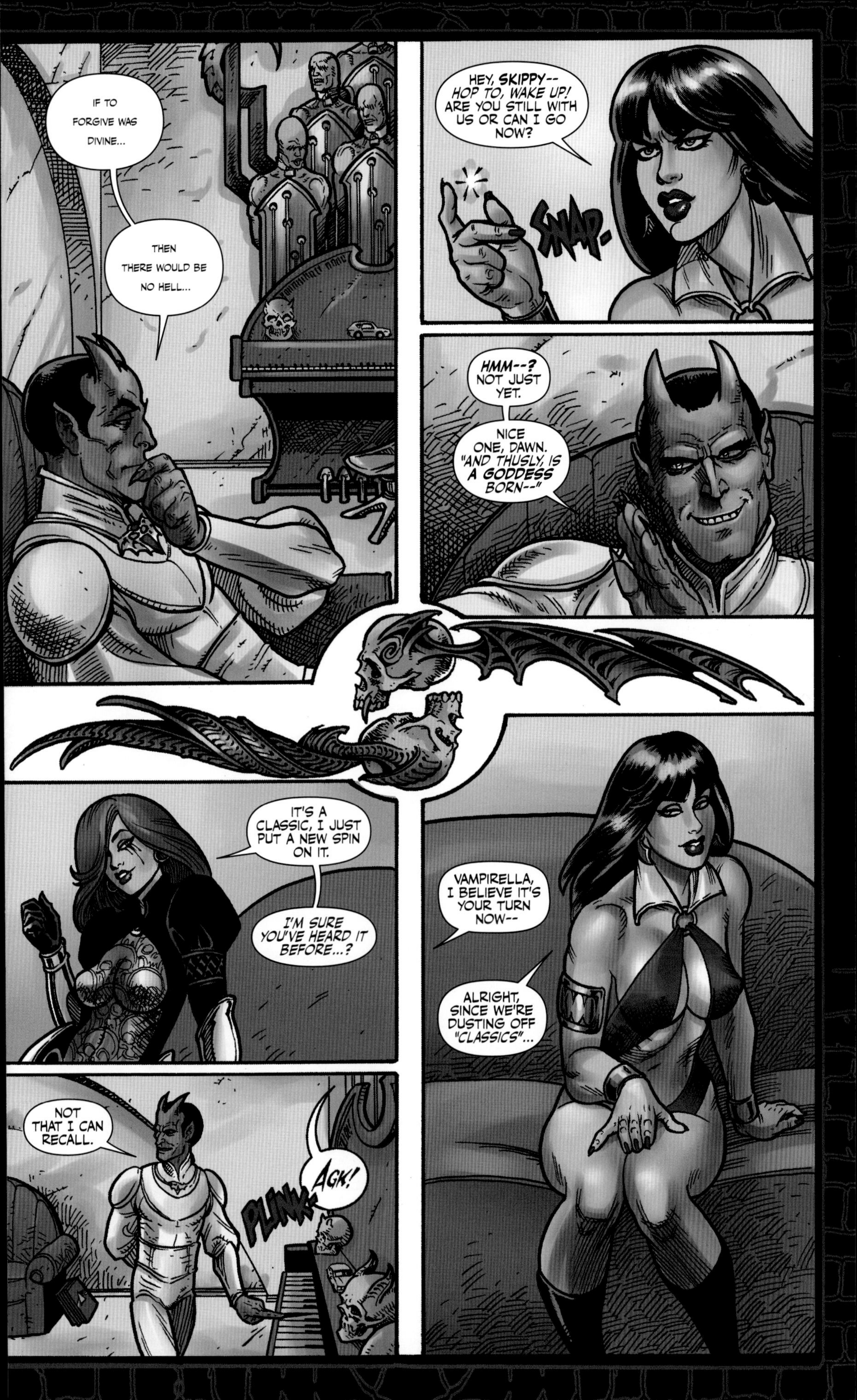
IF TO FORGIVE WAS DIVINE...
THEN THERE WOULD BE NO HELL...
HEY, SKIPPY-- HOP TO, WAKE UP! ARE YOU STILL WITH US OR CAN I GO NOW?
SNAP-
HMM--? NOT JUST YET.
NICE ONE, DAWN. "AND THUSLY, IS A GODDESS BORN--"
IT'S A CLASSIC, I JUST PUT A NEW SPIN ON IT.
I'M SURE YOU'VE HEARD IT BEFORE...?
VAMPIRELLA, I BELIEVE IT'S YOUR TURN NOW--
ALRIGHT, SINCE WE'RE DUSTING OFF "CLASSICS"...
NOT THAT I CAN RECALL.
PLINK-
AGK!

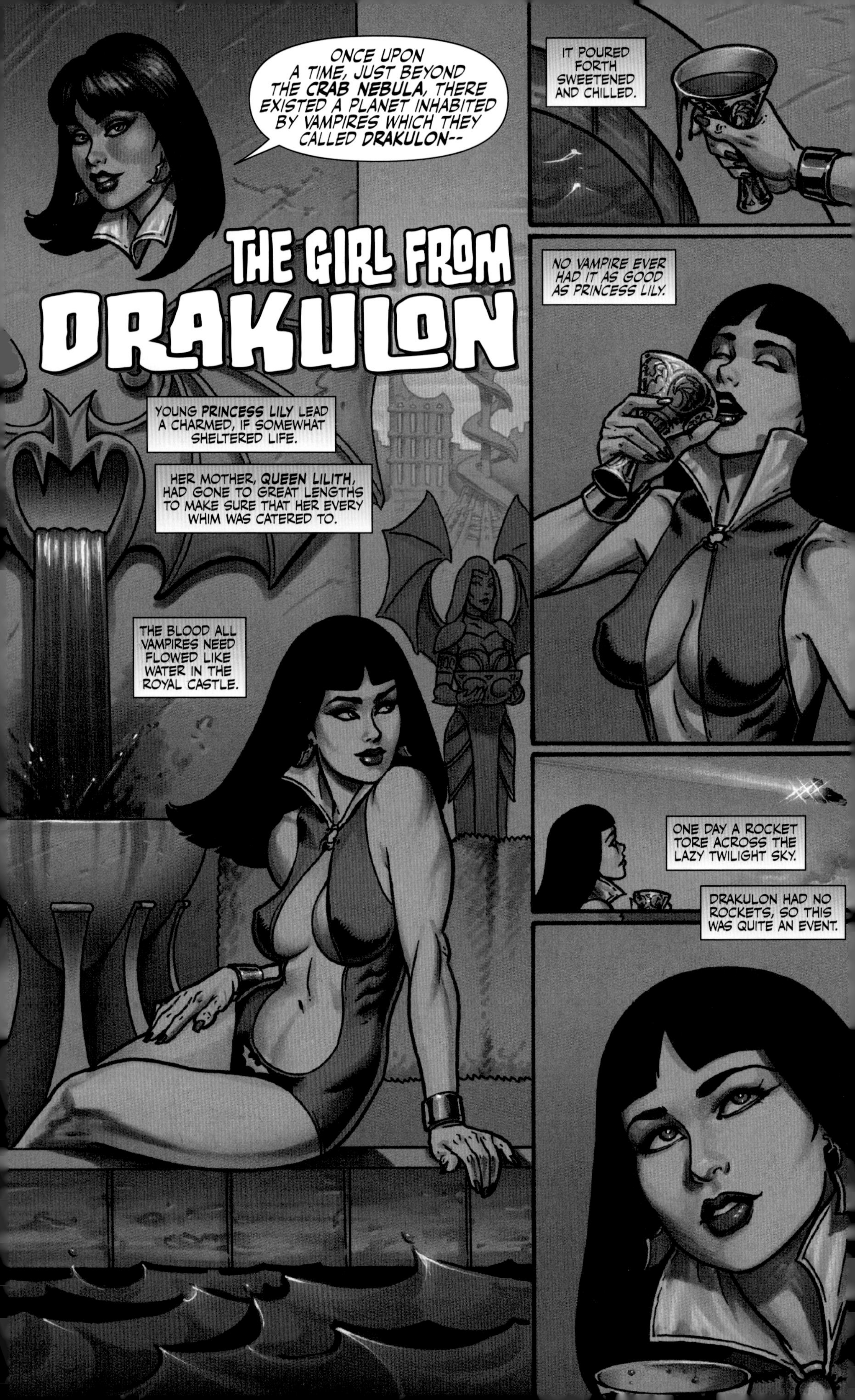
ONCE UPON A TIME, JUST BEYOND THE CRAB NEBULA, THERE EXISTED A PLANET INHABITED BY VAMPIRES WHICH THEY CALLED DRAKULON--
THE GIRL FROM DRAKULON
YOUNG PRINCESS LILY LEAD A CHARMED, IF SOMEWHAT SHELTERED LIFE.
HER MOTHER, QUEEN LILITH, HAD GONE TO GREAT LENGTHS TO MAKE SURE THAT HER EVERY WHIM WAS CATERED TO.
THE BLOOD ALL VAMPIRES NEED FLOWED LIKE WATER IN THE ROYAL CASTLE.
IT POURED FORTH SWEETENED AND CHILLED.
NO VAMPIRE EVER HAD IT AS GOOD AS PRINCESS LILY.
ONE DAY A ROCKET TORE ACROSS THE LAZY TWILIGHT SKY.
DRAKULON HAD NO ROCKETS, SO THIS WAS QUITE AN EVENT.

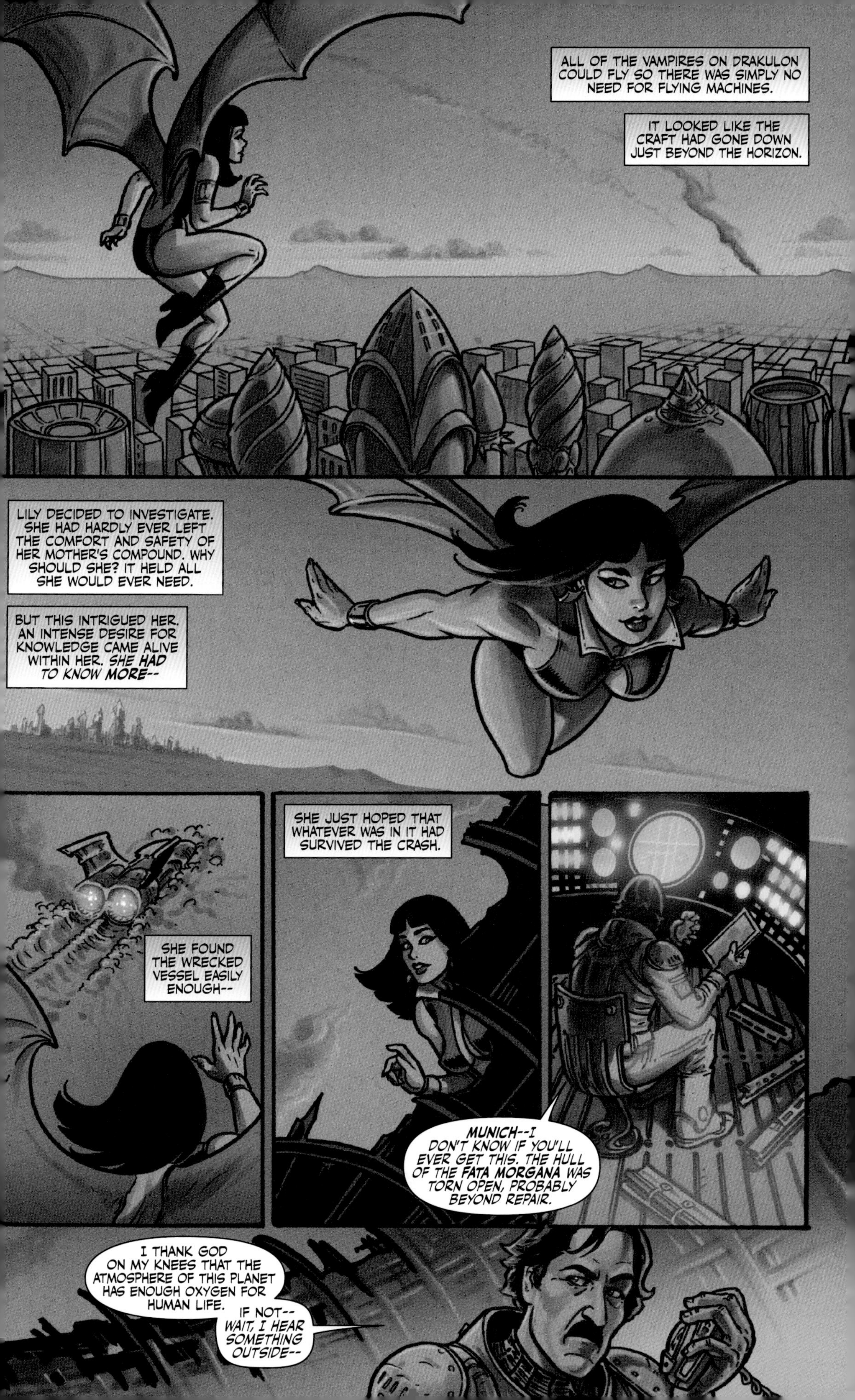
ALL OF THE VAMPIRES ON DRAKULON COULD FLY SO THERE WAS SIMPLY NO NEED FOR FLYING MACHINES.
IT LOOKED LIKE THE CRAFT HAD GONE DOWN JUST BEYOND THE HORIZON.
LILY DECIDED TO INVESTIGATE. SHE HAD HARDLY EVER LEFT THE COMFORT AND SAFETY OF HER MOTHER'S COMPOUND. WHY SHOULD SHE? IT HELD ALL SHE WOULD EVER NEED.
BUT THIS INTRIGUED HER. AN INTENSE DESIRE FOR KNOWLEDGE CAME ALIVE WITHIN HER. SHE HAD TO KNOW MORE--
SHE FOUND THE WRECKED VESSEL EASILY ENOUGH--
SHE JUST HOPED THAT WHATEVER WAS IN IT HAD SURVIVED THE CRASH.
MUNICH--I DON'T KNOW IF YOU'LL EVER GET THIS. THE HULL OF THE FATA MORGANA WAS TORN OPEN, PROBABLY BEYOND REPAIR.
I THANK GOD ON MY KNEES THAT THE ATMOSPHERE OF THIS PLANET HAS ENOUGH OXYGEN FOR HUMAN LIFE.
IF NOT-- WAIT, I HEAR SOMETHING OUTSIDE--

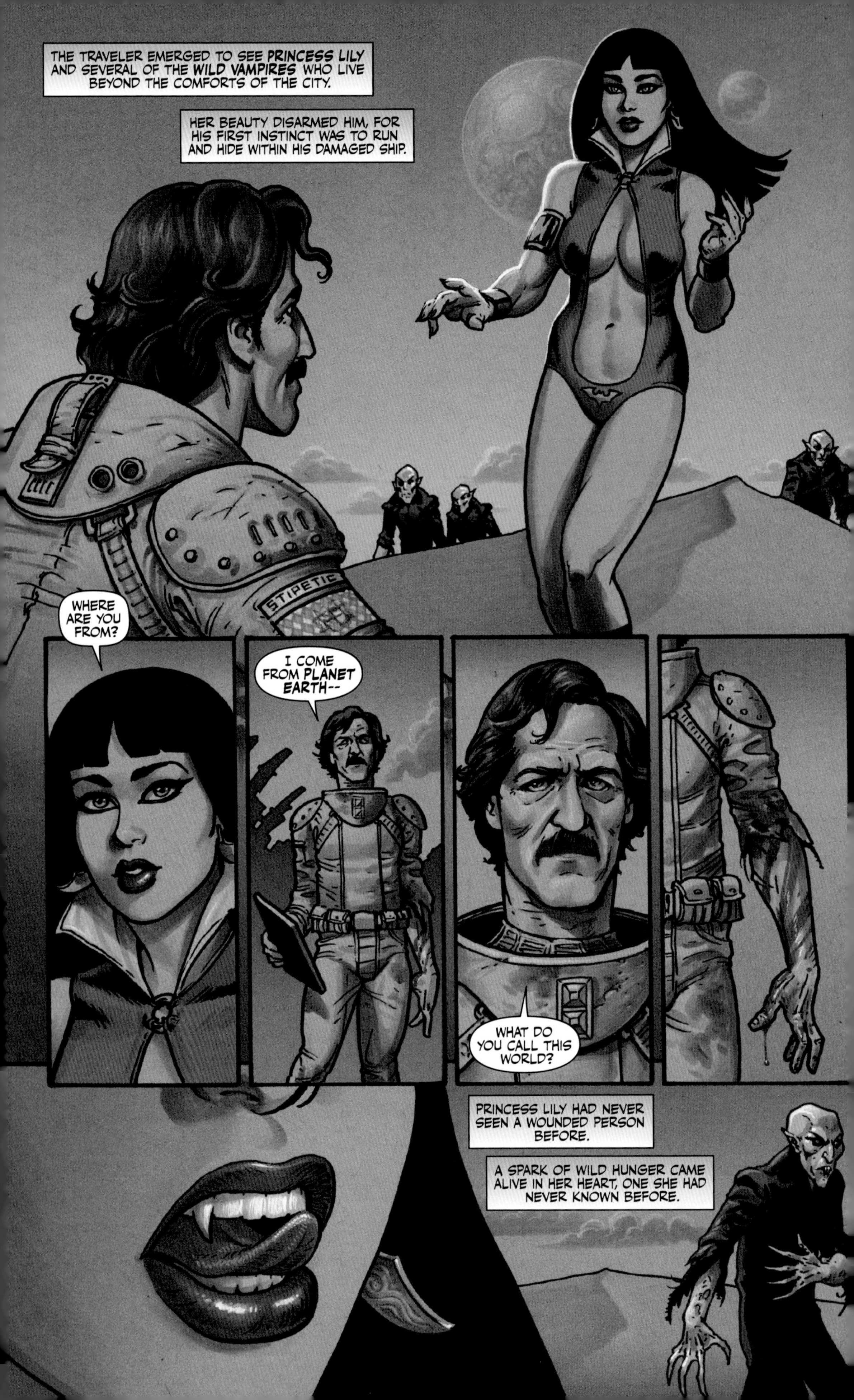
THE TRAVELER EMERGED TO SEE PRINCESS LILY AND SEVERAL OF THE WILD VAMPIRES WHO LIVE BEYOND THE COMFORTS OF THE CITY.
HER BEAUTY DISARMED HIM, FOR HIS FIRST INSTINCT WAS TO RUN AND HIDE WITHIN HIS DAMAGED SHIP.
STIPETIC
WHERE ARE YOU FROM?
I COME FROM PLANET EARTH--
WHAT DO YOU CALL THIS WORLD?
PRINCESS LILY HAD NEVER SEEN A WOUNDED PERSON BEFORE.
A SPARK OF WILD HUNGER CAME ALIVE IN HER HEART, ONE SHE HAD NEVER KNOWN BEFORE.

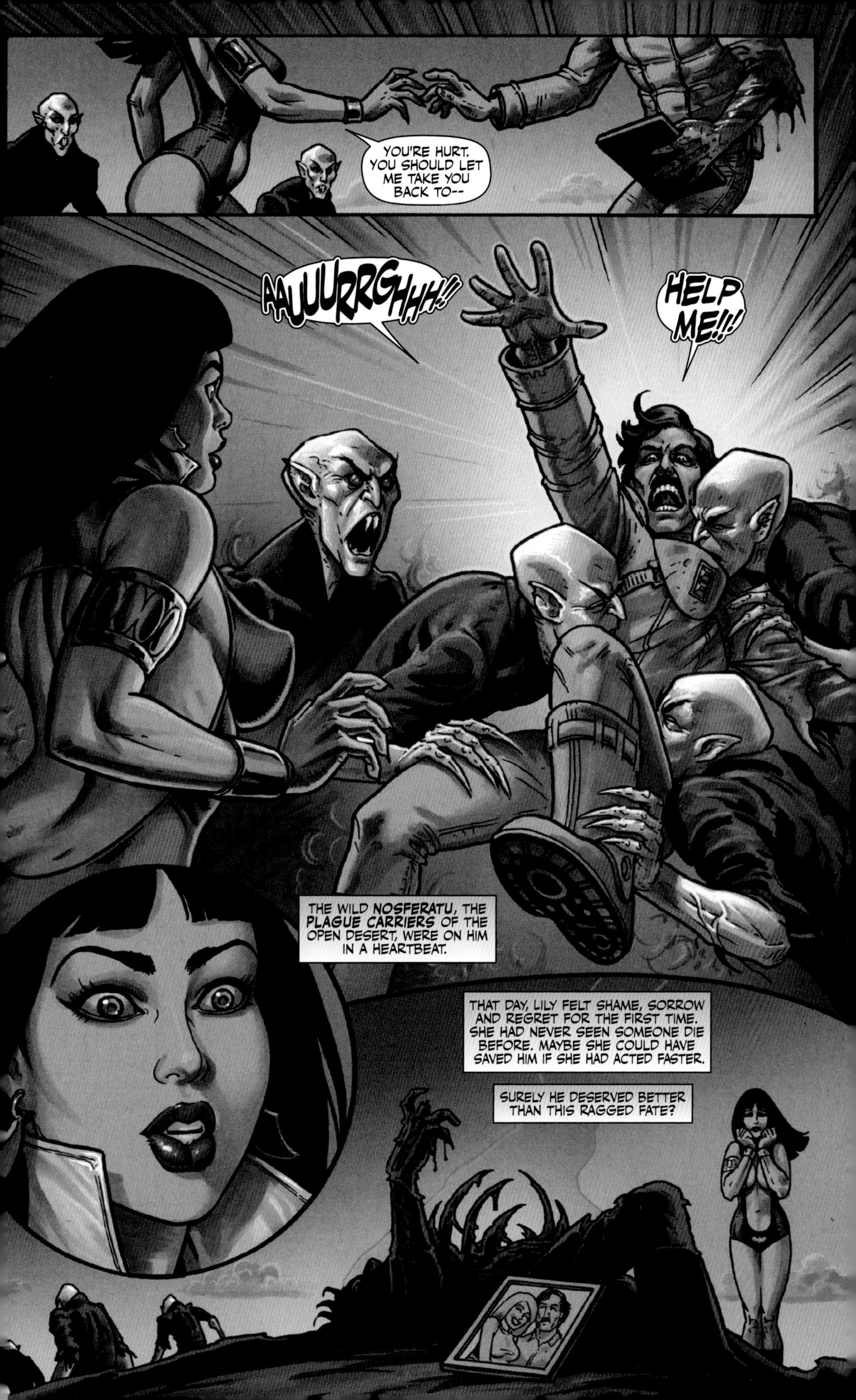
YOU'RE HURT. YOU SHOULD LET ME TAKE YOU BACK TO--
AAUUURRGHHH!!
HELP ME!!!
THE WILD NOSFERATU, THE PLAGUE CARRIERS OF THE OPEN DESERT, WERE ON HIM IN A HEARTBEAT.
THAT DAY, LILY FELT SHAME, SORROW AND REGRET FOR THE FIRST TIME. SHE HAD NEVER SEEN SOMEONE DIE BEFORE. MAYBE SHE COULD HAVE SAVED HIM IF SHE HAD ACTED FASTER.
SURELY HE DESERVED BETTER THAN THIS RAGGED FATE?

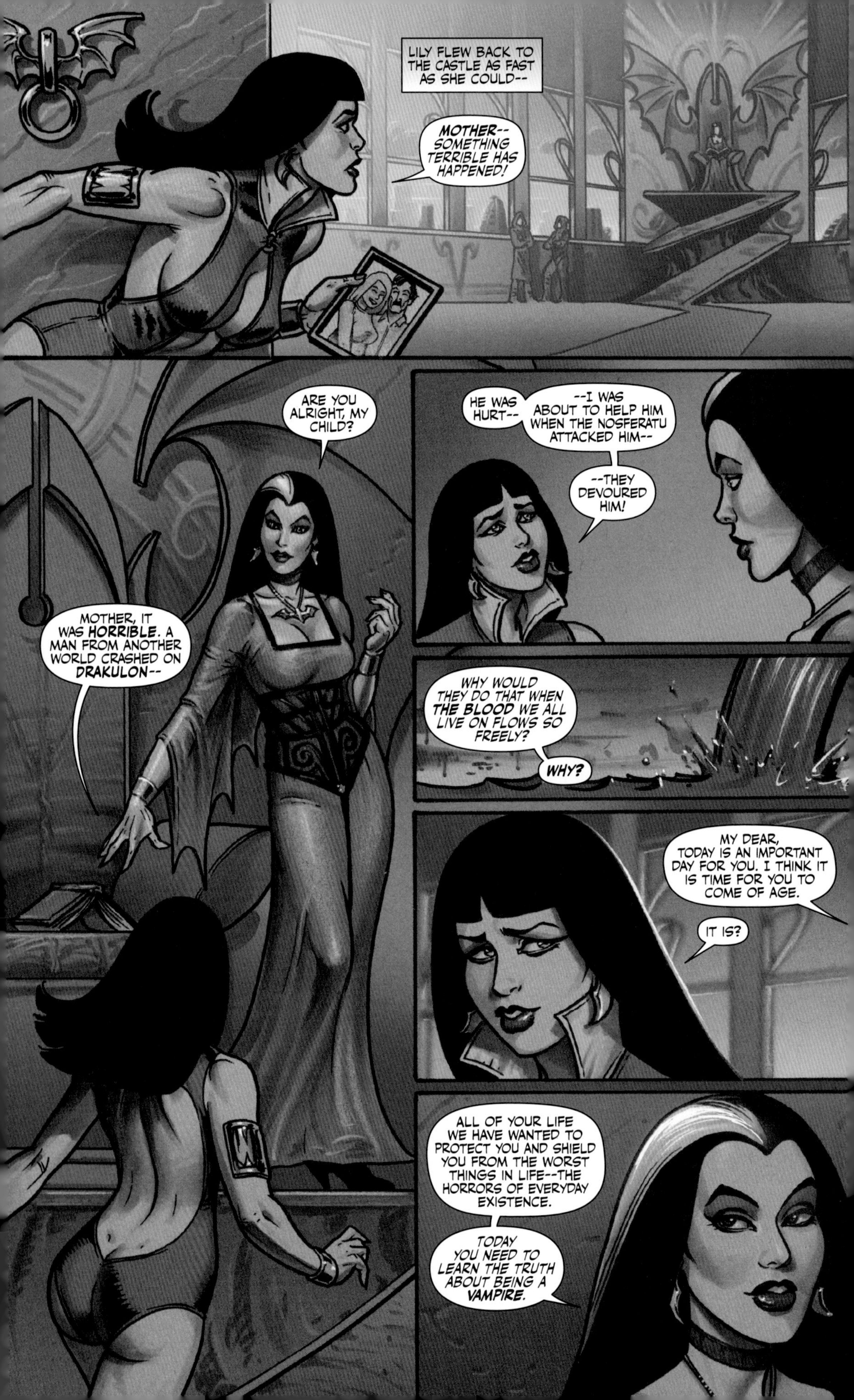
LILY FLEW BACK TO THE CASTLE AS FAST AS SHE COULD--
MOTHER-- SOMETHING TERRIBLE HAS HAPPENED!
ARE YOU ALRIGHT, MY CHILD?
MOTHER, IT WAS HORRIBLE. A MAN FROM ANOTHER WORLD CRASHED ON DRAKULON--
HE WAS HURT--
--I WAS ABOUT TO HELP HIM WHEN THE NOSFERATU ATTACKED HIM--
--THEY DEVOURED HIM!
WHY WOULD THEY DO THAT WHEN THE BLOOD WE ALL LIVE ON FLOWS SO FREELY?
WHY?
MY DEAR, TODAY IS AN IMPORTANT DAY FOR YOU. I THINK IT IS TIME FOR YOU TO COME OF AGE.
IT IS?
ALL OF YOUR LIFE WE HAVE WANTED TO PROTECT YOU AND SHIELD YOU FROM THE WORST THINGS IN LIFE--THE HORRORS OF EVERYDAY EXISTENCE.
TODAY YOU NEED TO LEARN THE TRUTH ABOUT BEING A VAMPIRE.

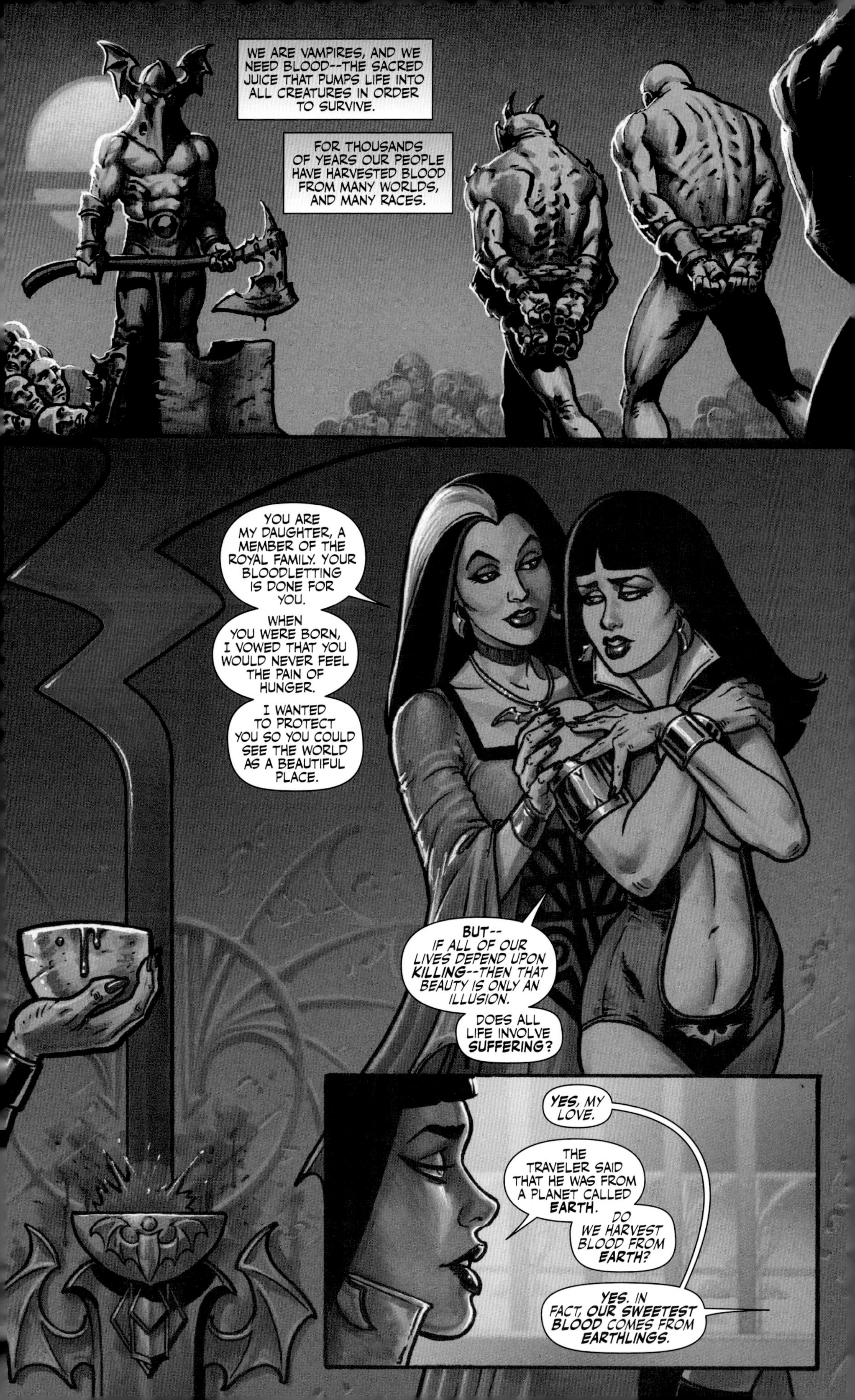
WE ARE VAMPIRES, AND WE NEED BLOOD--THE SACRED JUICE THAT PUMPS LIFE INTO ALL CREATURES IN ORDER TO SURVIVE.
FOR THOUSANDS OF YEARS OUR PEOPLE HAVE HARVESTED BLOOD FROM MANY WORLDS, AND MANY RACES.
YOU ARE MY DAUGHTER, A MEMBER OF THE ROYAL FAMILY. YOUR BLOODLETTING IS DONE FOR YOU.
WHEN YOU WERE BORN, I VOWED THAT YOU WOULD NEVER FEEL THE PAIN OF HUNGER.
I WANTED TO PROTECT YOU SO YOU COULD SEE THE WORLD AS A BEAUTIFUL PLACE.
BUT-- IF ALL OF OUR LIVES DEPEND UPON KILLING--THEN THAT BEAUTY IS ONLY AN ILLUSION.
DOES ALL LIFE INVOLVE SUFFERING?
YES, MY LOVE.
THE TRAVELER SAID THAT HE WAS FROM A PLANET CALLED EARTH.
DO WE HARVEST BLOOD FROM EARTH?
YES. IN FACT, OUR SWEETEST BLOOD COMES FROM EARTHLINGS.

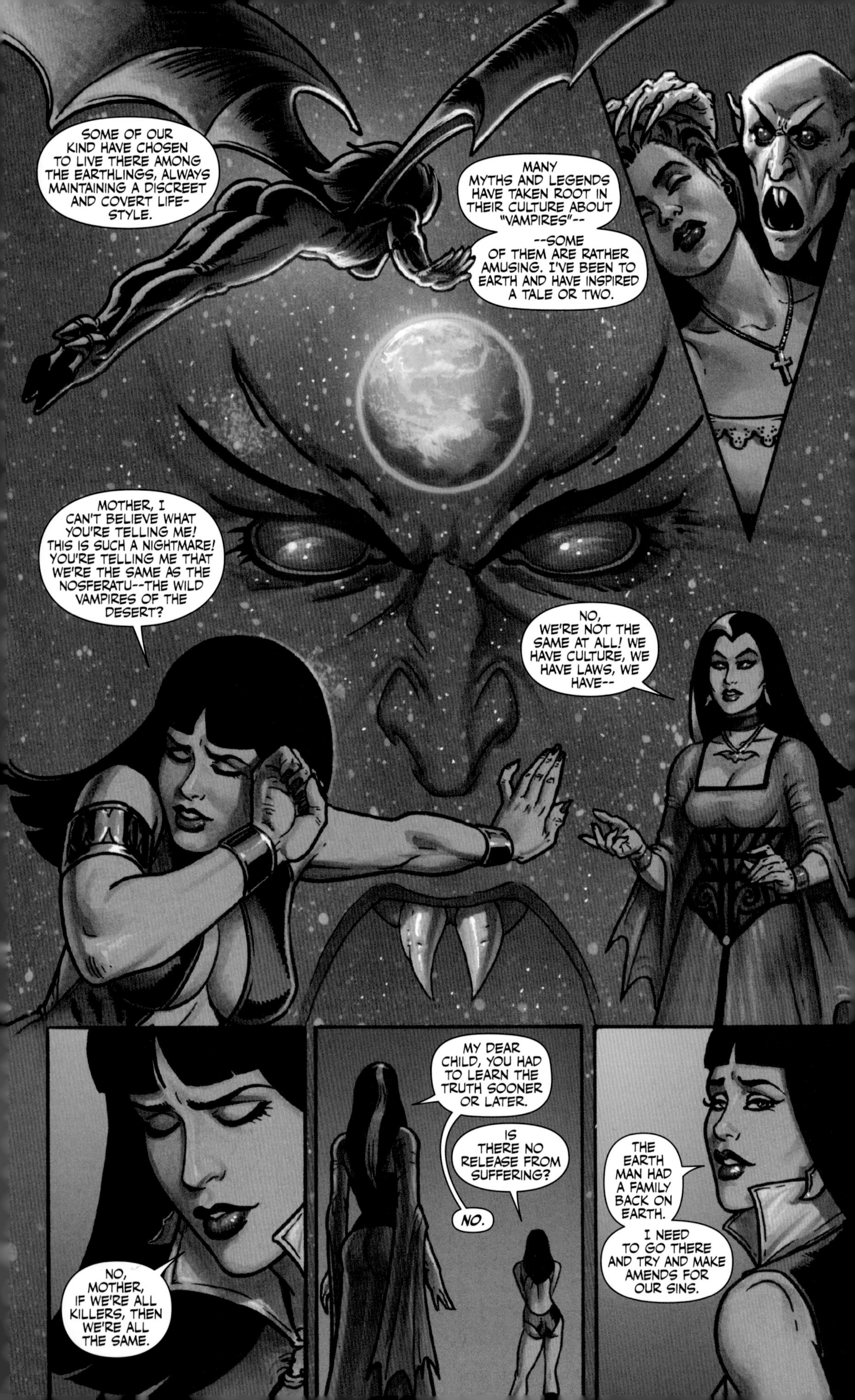
SOME OF OUR KIND HAVE CHOSEN TO LIVE THERE AMONG THE EARTHLINGS, ALWAYS MAINTAINING A DISCREET AND COVERT LIFE-STYLE.
MANY MYTHS AND LEGENDS HAVE TAKEN ROOT IN THEIR CULTURE ABOUT "VAMPIRES"--
--SOME OF THEM ARE RATHER AMUSING. I'VE BEEN TO EARTH AND HAVE INSPIRED A TALE OR TWO.
MOTHER, I CAN'T BELIEVE WHAT YOU'RE TELLING ME! THIS IS SUCH A NIGHTMARE! YOU'RE TELLING ME THAT WE'RE THE SAME AS THE NOSFERATU--THE WILD VAMPIRES OF THE DESERT?
NO, WE'RE NOT THE SAME AT ALL! WE HAVE CULTURE, WE HAVE LAWS, WE HAVE--
NO, MOTHER, IF WE'RE ALL KILLERS, THEN WE'RE ALL THE SAME.
MY DEAR CHILD, YOU HAD TO LEARN THE TRUTH SOONER OR LATER.
IS THERE NO RELEASE FROM SUFFERING?
NO.
THE EARTH MAN HAD A FAMILY BACK ON EARTH.
I NEED TO GO THERE AND TRY AND MAKE AMENDS FOR OUR SINS.

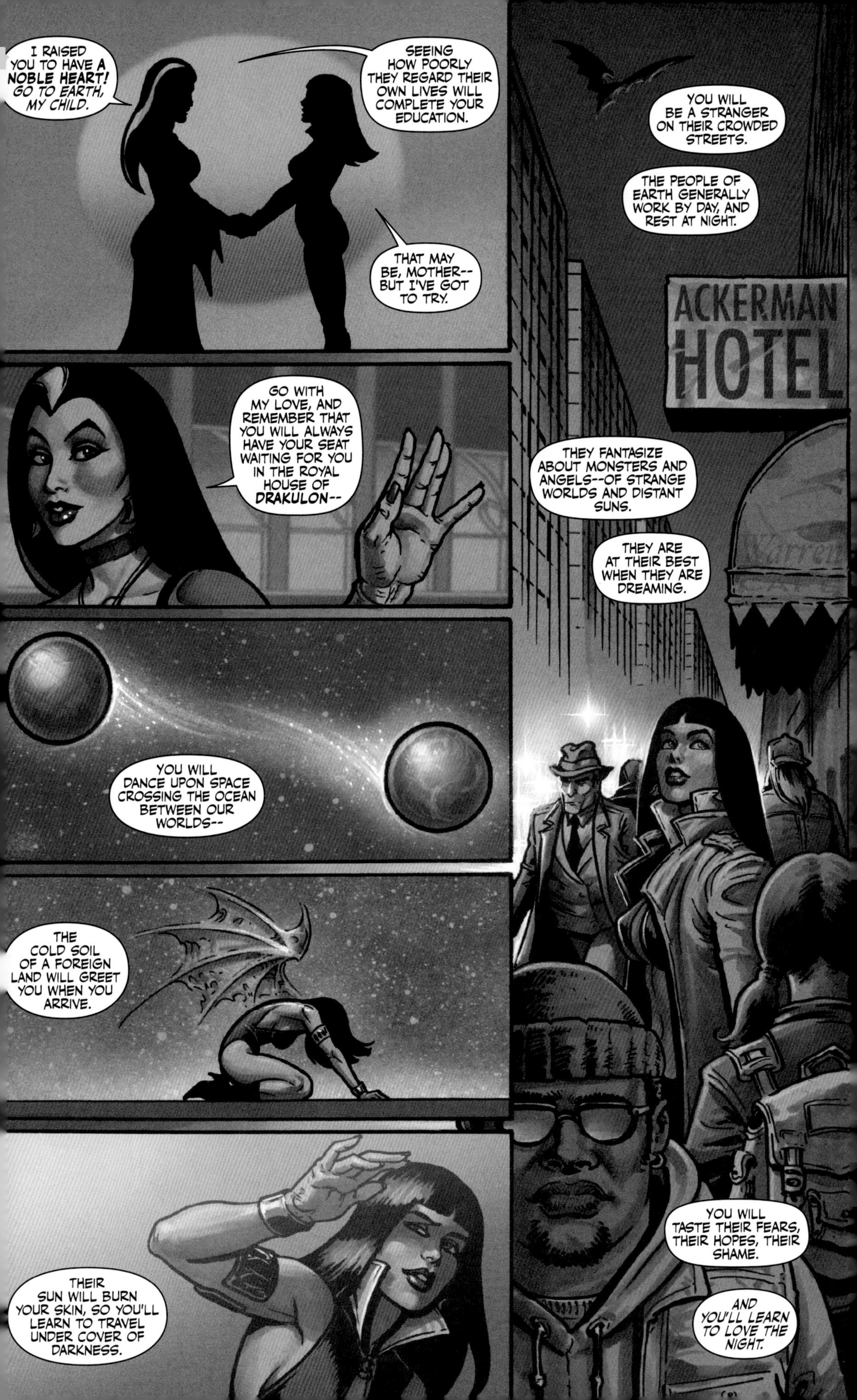

I RAISED YOU TO HAVE A **NOBLE HEART!** *GO TO EARTH, MY CHILD.*
SEEING HOW POORLY THEY REGARD THEIR OWN LIVES WILL COMPLETE YOUR EDUCATION.
THAT MAY BE, MOTHER-- BUT I'VE GOT TO TRY.
GO WITH MY LOVE, AND REMEMBER THAT YOU WILL ALWAYS HAVE YOUR SEAT WAITING FOR YOU IN THE ROYAL HOUSE OF **DRAKULON**--
YOU WILL DANCE UPON SPACE CROSSING THE OCEAN BETWEEN OUR WORLDS--
THE COLD SOIL OF A FOREIGN LAND WILL GREET YOU WHEN YOU ARRIVE.
THEIR SUN WILL BURN YOUR SKIN, SO YOU'LL LEARN TO TRAVEL UNDER COVER OF DARKNESS.
YOU WILL BE A STRANGER ON THEIR CROWDED STREETS.
THE PEOPLE OF EARTH GENERALLY WORK BY DAY, AND REST AT NIGHT.
ACKERMAN HOTEL
THEY FANTASIZE ABOUT MONSTERS AND ANGELS--OF STRANGE WORLDS AND DISTANT SUNS.
THEY ARE AT THEIR BEST WHEN THEY ARE DREAMING.
YOU WILL TASTE THEIR FEARS, THEIR HOPES, THEIR SHAME.
AND YOU'LL LEARN TO LOVE THE NIGHT.

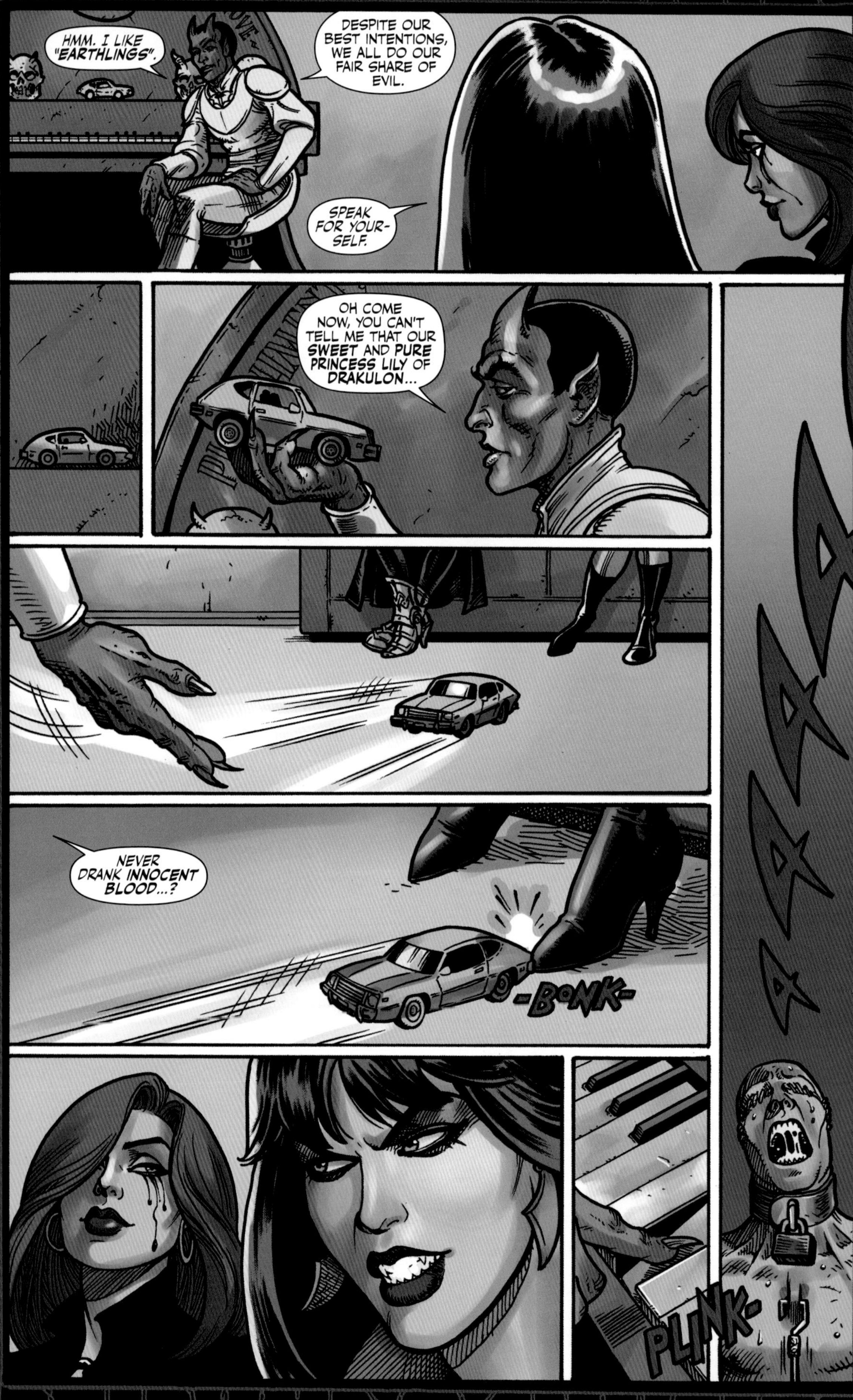
HMM. I LIKE "EARTHLINGS".
DESPITE OUR BEST INTENTIONS, WE ALL DO OUR FAIR SHARE OF EVIL.
SPEAK FOR YOUR-SELF.
OH COME NOW, YOU CAN'T TELL ME THAT OUR SWEET AND PURE PRINCESS LILY OF DRAKULON...
NEVER DRANK INNOCENT BLOOD...?
-BONK-
PLINK-

CHAPTER • FOUR

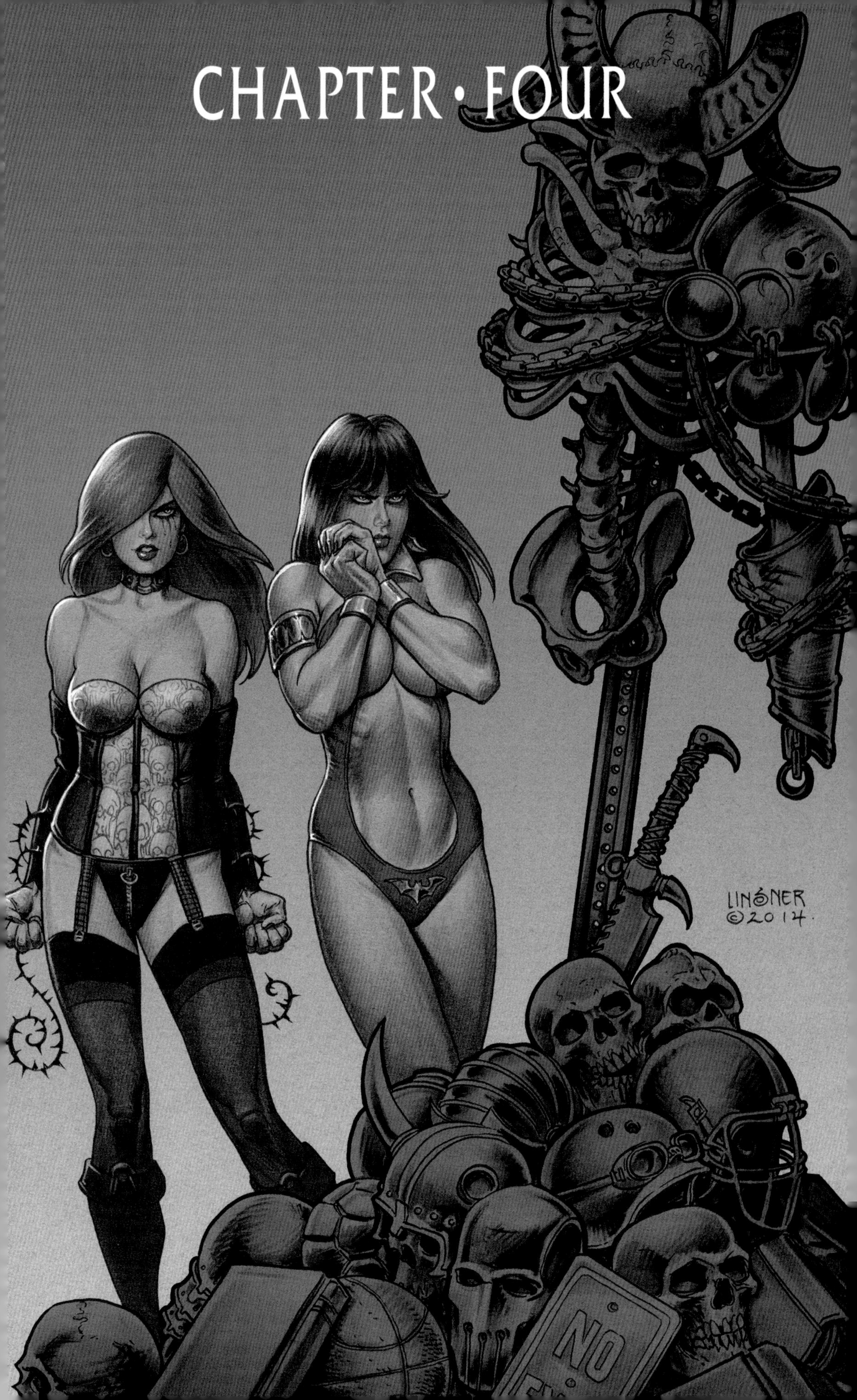
LINSNER ©2014.
NO

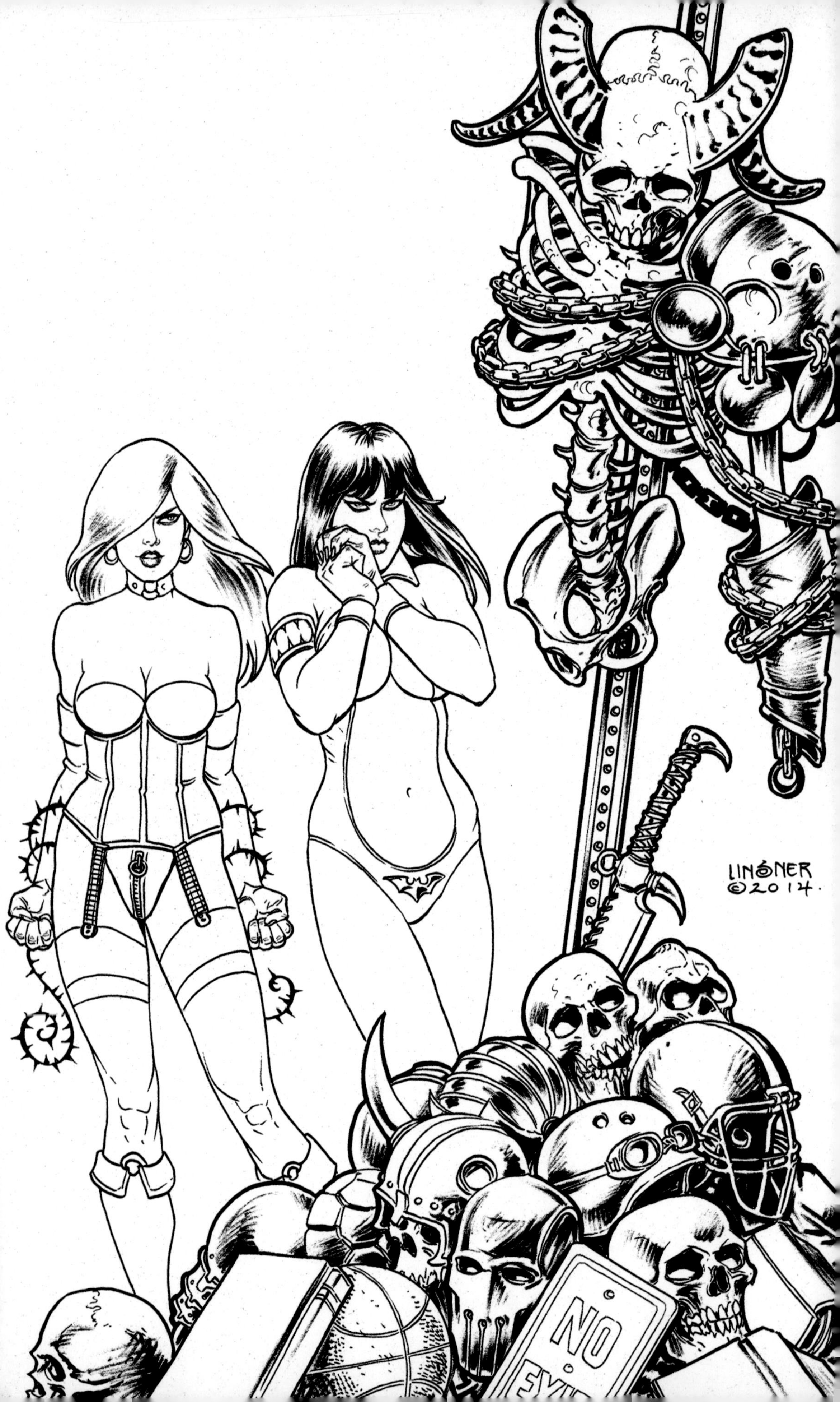
LINSNER
©2014.
NO

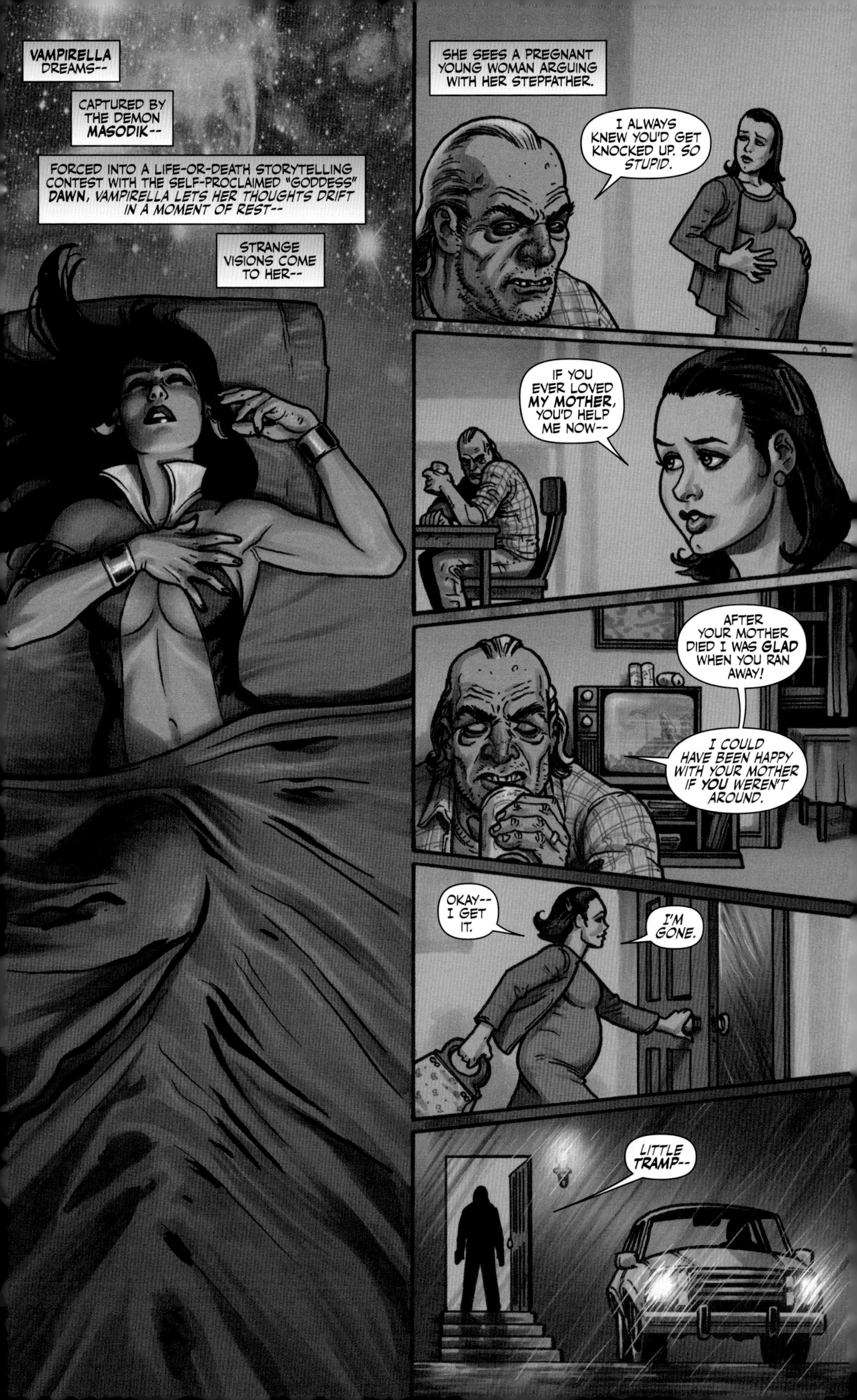
VAMPIRELLA DREAMS--
CAPTURED BY THE DEMON MASODIK--
FORCED INTO A LIFE-OR-DEATH STORYTELLING CONTEST WITH THE SELF-PROCLAIMED "GODDESS" DAWN, VAMPIRELLA LETS HER THOUGHTS DRIFT IN A MOMENT OF REST--
STRANGE VISIONS COME TO HER--
SHE SEES A PREGNANT YOUNG WOMAN ARGUING WITH HER STEPFATHER.
I ALWAYS KNEW YOU'D GET KNOCKED UP. SO STUPID.
IF YOU EVER LOVED MY MOTHER, YOU'D HELP ME NOW--
AFTER YOUR MOTHER DIED I WAS GLAD WHEN YOU RAN AWAY!
I COULD HAVE BEEN HAPPY WITH YOUR MOTHER IF YOU WEREN'T AROUND.
OKAY-- I GET IT.
I'M GONE.
LITTLE TRAMP--

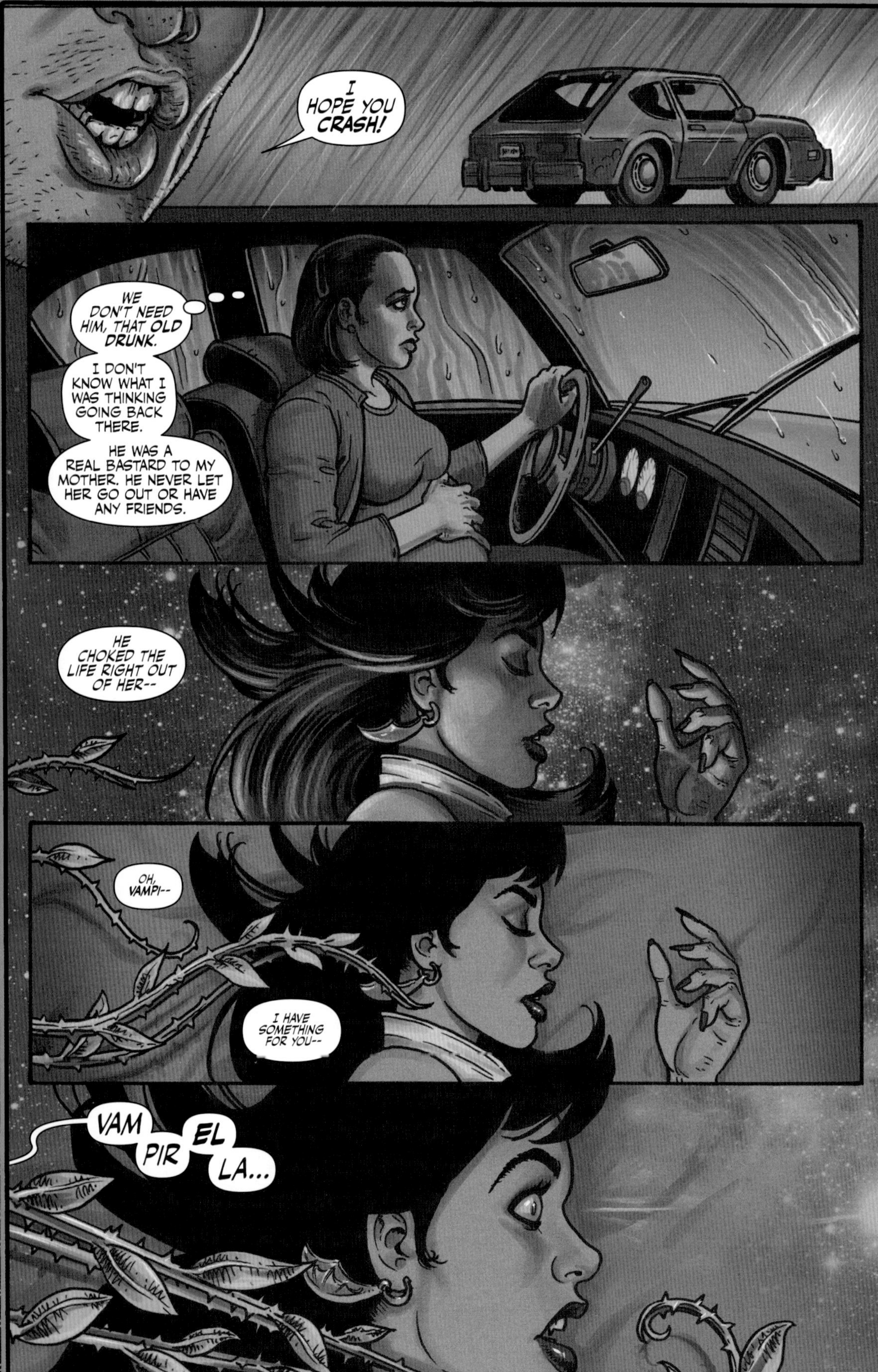
I HOPE YOU CRASH!
WE DON'T NEED HIM, THAT OLD DRUNK.
I DON'T KNOW WHAT I WAS THINKING GOING BACK THERE.
HE WAS A REAL BASTARD TO MY MOTHER. HE NEVER LET HER GO OUT OR HAVE ANY FRIENDS.
HE CHOKED THE LIFE RIGHT OUT OF HER--
OH, VAMPI--
I HAVE SOMETHING FOR YOU--
VAM PIR EL LA...

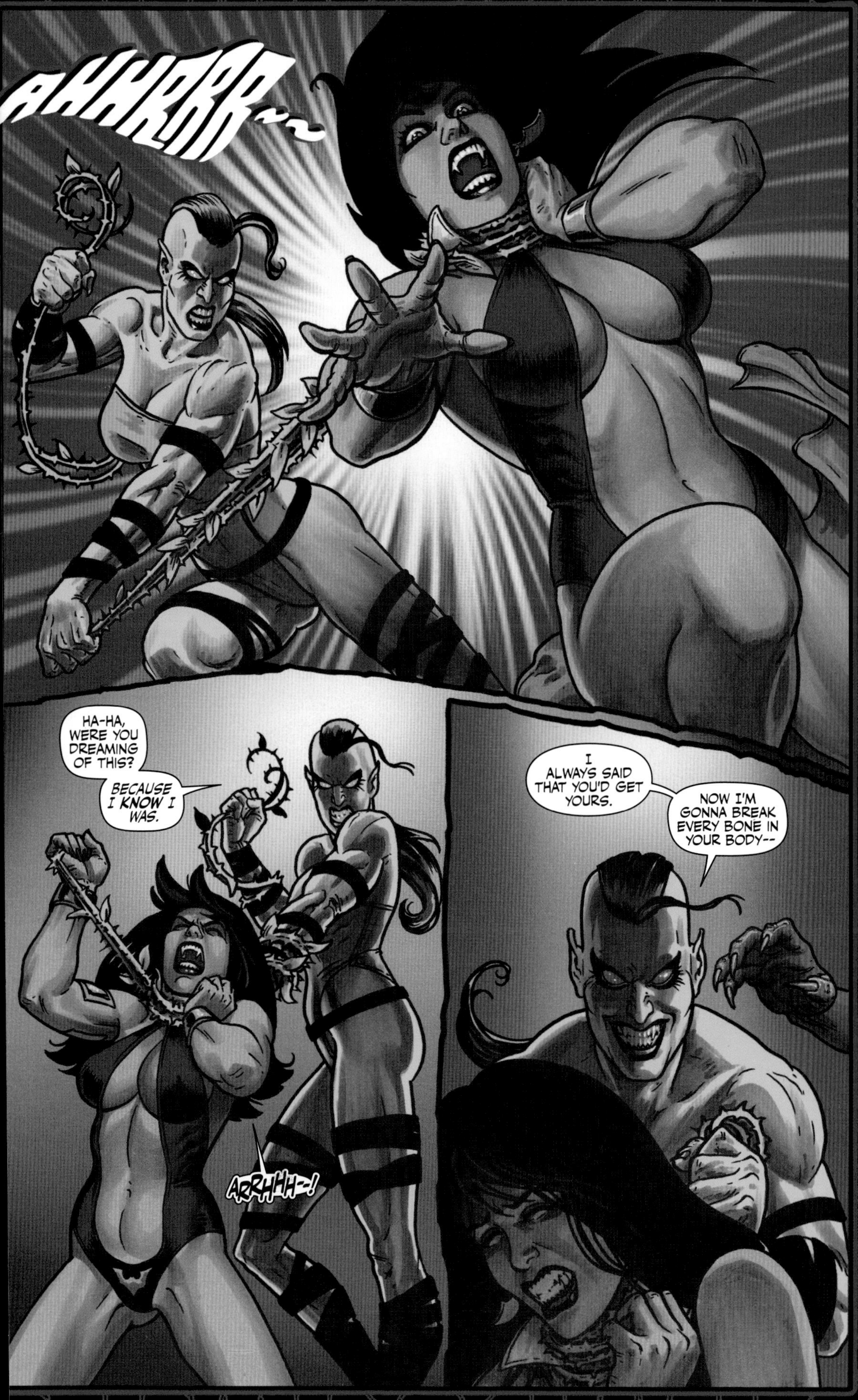
AHHRRR~~
HA-HA, WERE YOU DREAMING OF THIS?
BECAUSE I KNOW I WAS.
ARRHHH--!
I ALWAYS SAID THAT YOU'D GET YOURS.
NOW I'M GONNA BREAK EVERY BONE IN YOUR BODY--

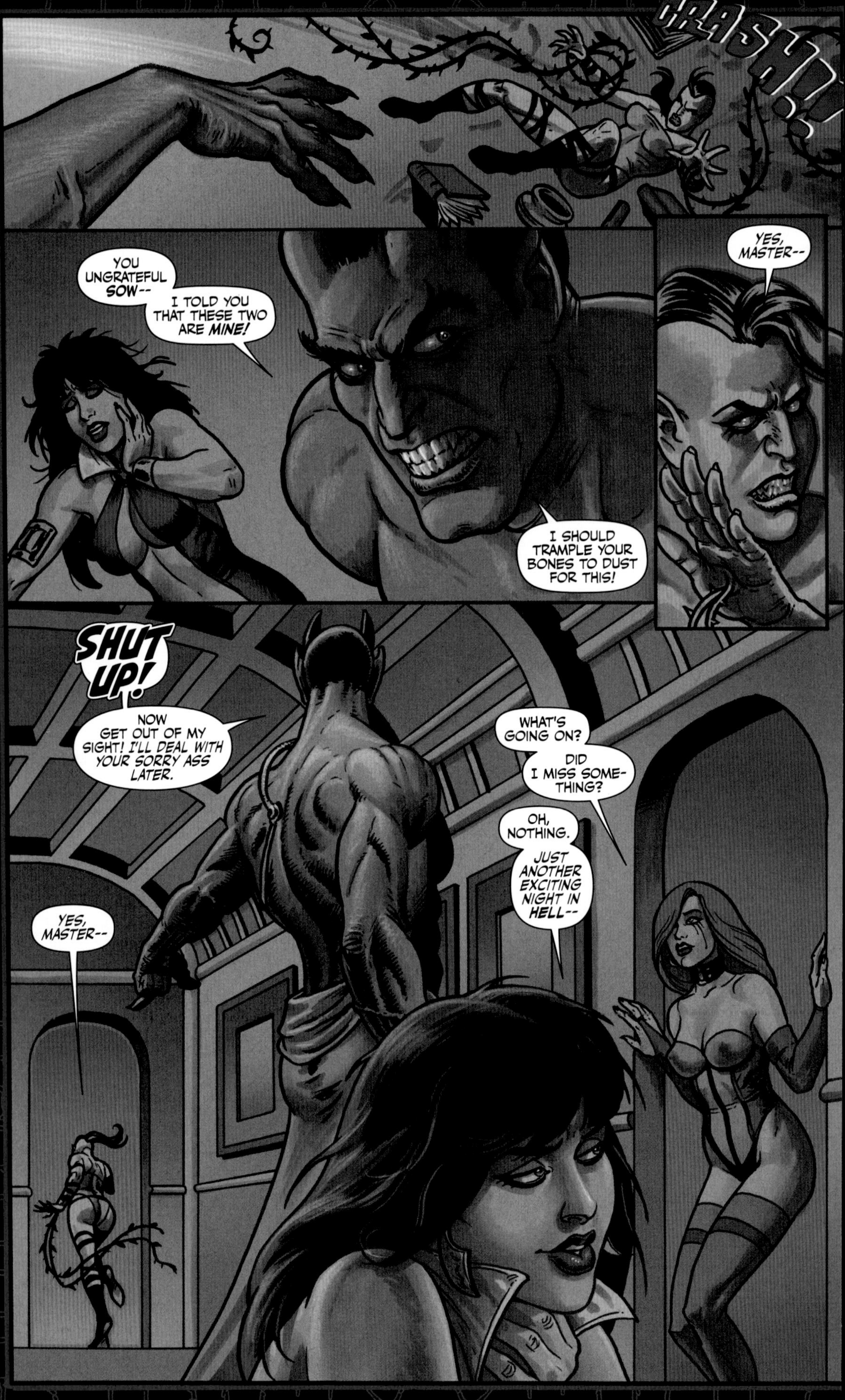
CRASH!!
YOU UNGRATEFUL SOW--
I TOLD YOU THAT THESE TWO ARE MINE!
I SHOULD TRAMPLE YOUR BONES TO DUST FOR THIS!
YES, MASTER--
SHUT UP!
NOW GET OUT OF MY SIGHT! I'LL DEAL WITH YOUR SORRY ASS LATER.
YES, MASTER--
WHAT'S GOING ON?
DID I MISS SOME-THING?
OH, NOTHING.
JUST ANOTHER EXCITING NIGHT IN HELL--

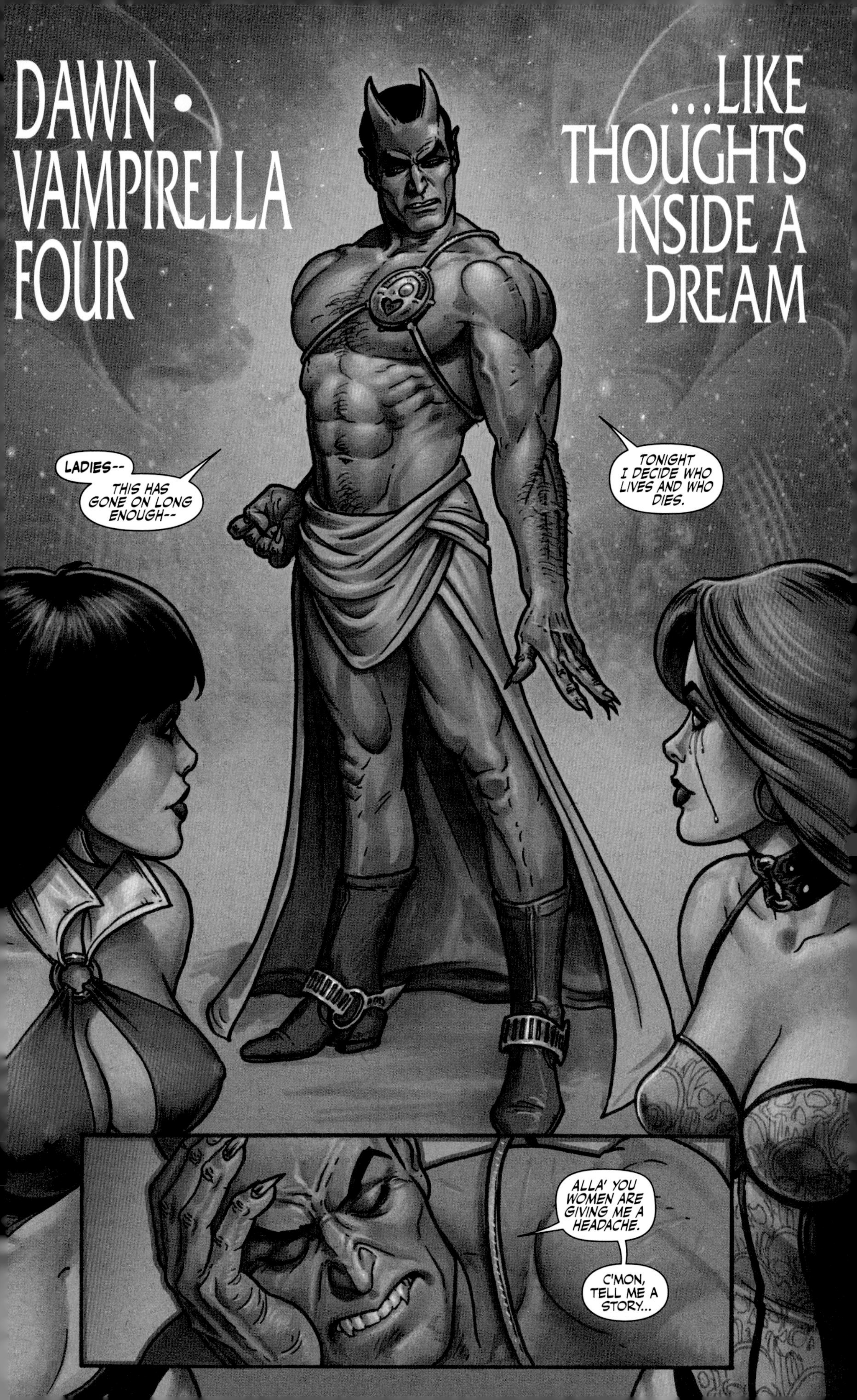
DAWN • VAMPIRELLA FOUR
...LIKE THOUGHTS INSIDE A DREAM
LADIES--
THIS HAS GONE ON LONG ENOUGH--
TONIGHT I DECIDE WHO LIVES AND WHO DIES.
ALLA' YOU WOMEN ARE GIVING ME A HEADACHE.
C'MON, TELL ME A STORY...

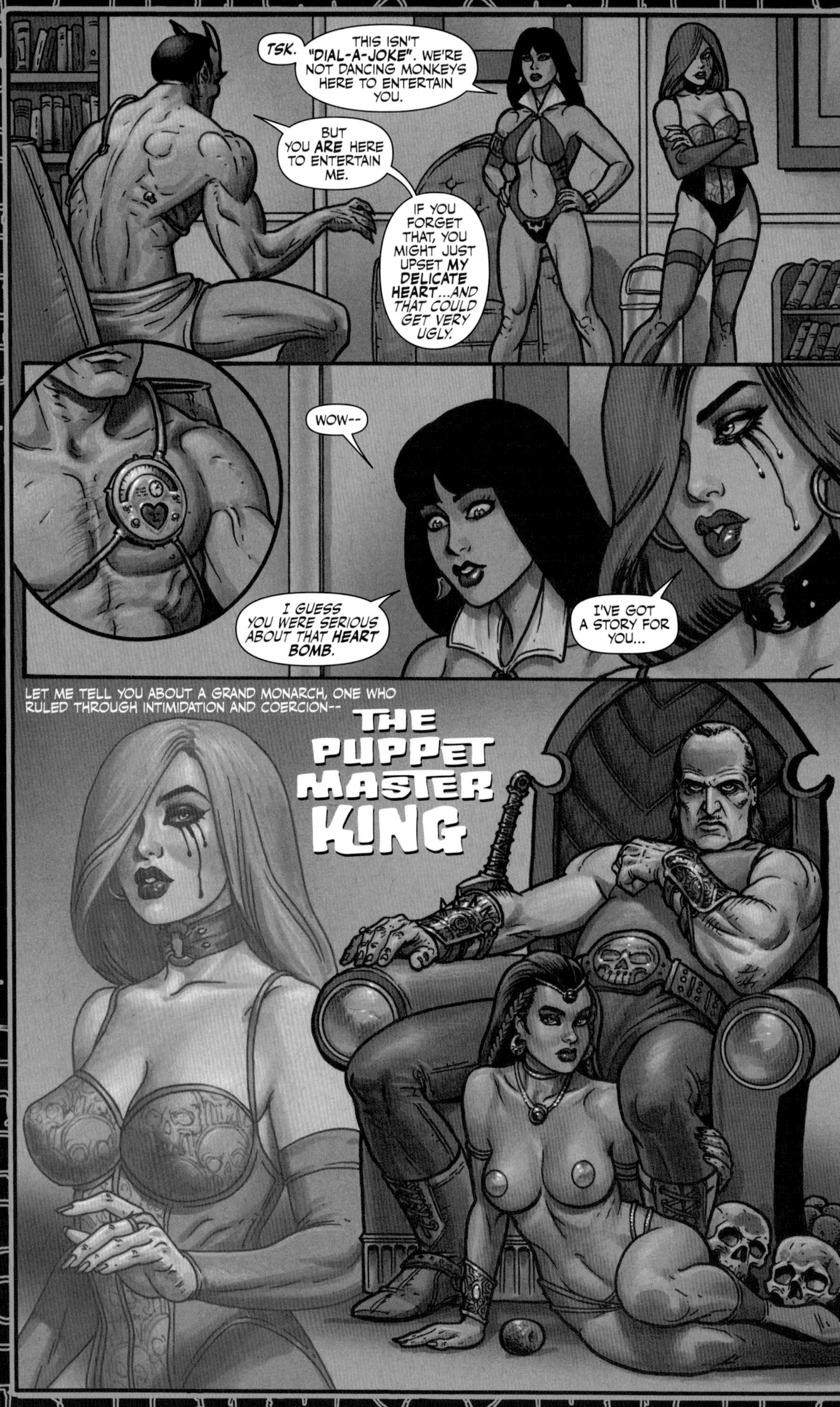
TSK.
THIS ISN'T "DIAL-A-JOKE". WE'RE NOT DANCING MONKEYS HERE TO ENTERTAIN YOU.
BUT YOU ARE HERE TO ENTERTAIN ME.
IF YOU FORGET THAT, YOU MIGHT JUST UPSET MY DELICATE HEART...AND THAT COULD GET VERY UGLY.
WOW--
I GUESS YOU WERE SERIOUS ABOUT THAT HEART BOMB.
I'VE GOT A STORY FOR YOU...
LET ME TELL YOU ABOUT A GRAND MONARCH, ONE WHO RULED THROUGH INTIMIDATION AND COERCION--
THE PUPPET MASTER KING

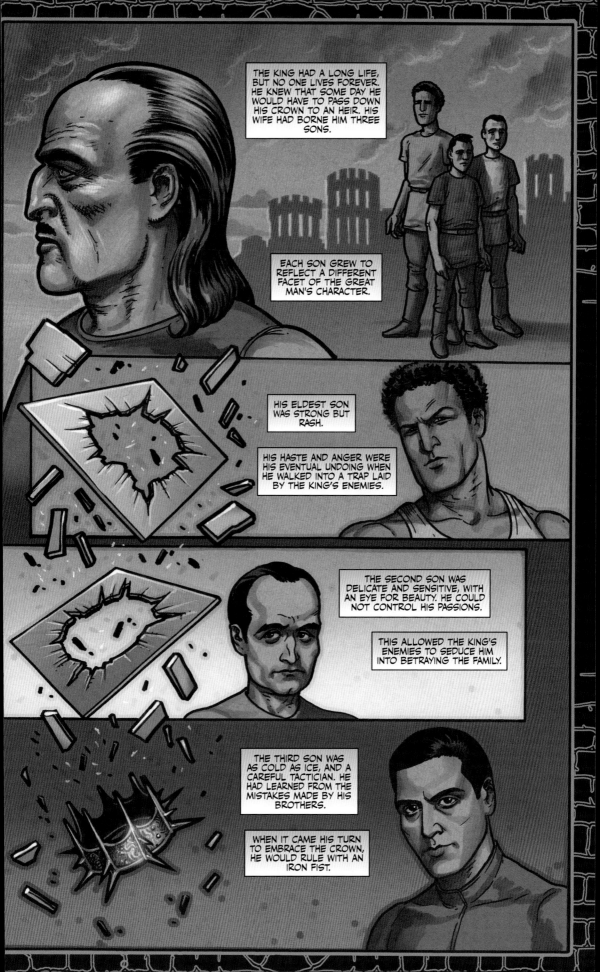

THE KING HAD A LONG LIFE, BUT NO ONE LIVES FOREVER. HE KNEW THAT SOME DAY HE WOULD HAVE TO PASS DOWN HIS CROWN TO AN HEIR. HIS WIFE HAD BORNE HIM THREE SONS.

EACH SON GREW TO REFLECT A DIFFERENT FACET OF THE GREAT MAN'S CHARACTER.

HIS ELDEST SON WAS STRONG BUT RASH.

HIS HASTE AND ANGER WERE HIS EVENTUAL UNDOING WHEN HE WALKED INTO A TRAP LAID BY THE KING'S ENEMIES.

THE SECOND SON WAS DELICATE AND SENSITIVE, WITH AN EYE FOR BEAUTY. HE COULD NOT CONTROL HIS PASSIONS.

THIS ALLOWED THE KING'S ENEMIES TO SEDUCE HIM INTO BETRAYING THE FAMILY.

THE THIRD SON WAS AS COLD AS ICE, AND A CAREFUL TACTICIAN. HE HAD LEARNED FROM THE MISTAKES MADE BY HIS BROTHERS.

WHEN IT CAME HIS TURN TO EMBRACE THE CROWN, HE WOULD RULE WITH AN IRON FIST.

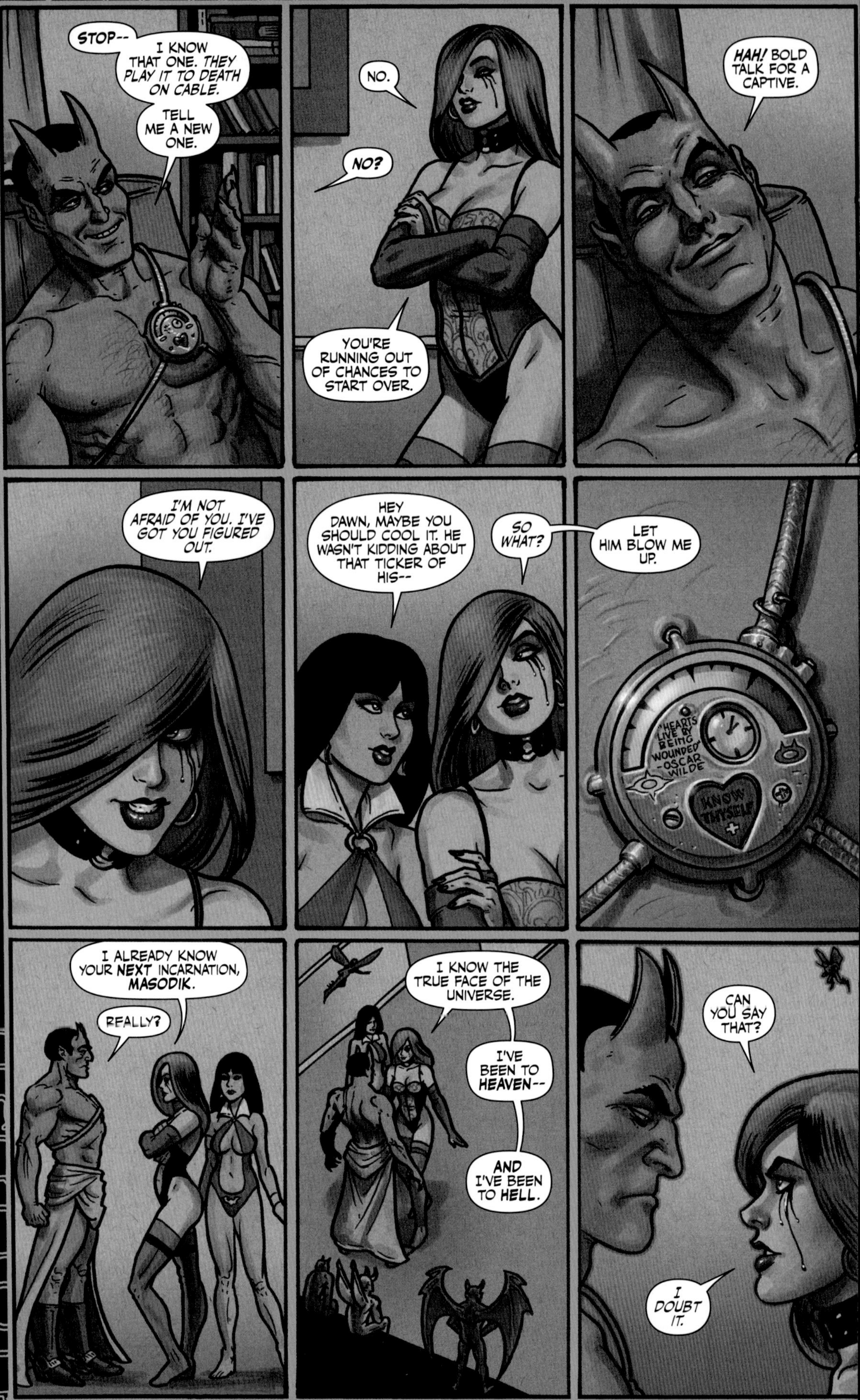
STOP--
I KNOW THAT ONE. THEY PLAY IT TO DEATH ON CABLE.
TELL ME A NEW ONE.
NO.
NO?
YOU'RE RUNNING OUT OF CHANCES TO START OVER.
HAH! BOLD TALK FOR A CAPTIVE.
I'M NOT AFRAID OF YOU. I'VE GOT YOU FIGURED OUT.
HEY DAWN, MAYBE YOU SHOULD COOL IT. HE WASN'T KIDDING ABOUT THAT TICKER OF HIS--
SO WHAT?
LET HIM BLOW ME UP.
"HEARTS LIVE BY BEING WOUNDED" -OSCAR WILDE
KNOW THYSELF
I ALREADY KNOW YOUR NEXT INCARNATION, MASODIK.
REALLY?
I KNOW THE TRUE FACE OF THE UNIVERSE.
I'VE BEEN TO HEAVEN--
AND I'VE BEEN TO HELL.
CAN YOU SAY THAT?
I DOUBT IT.

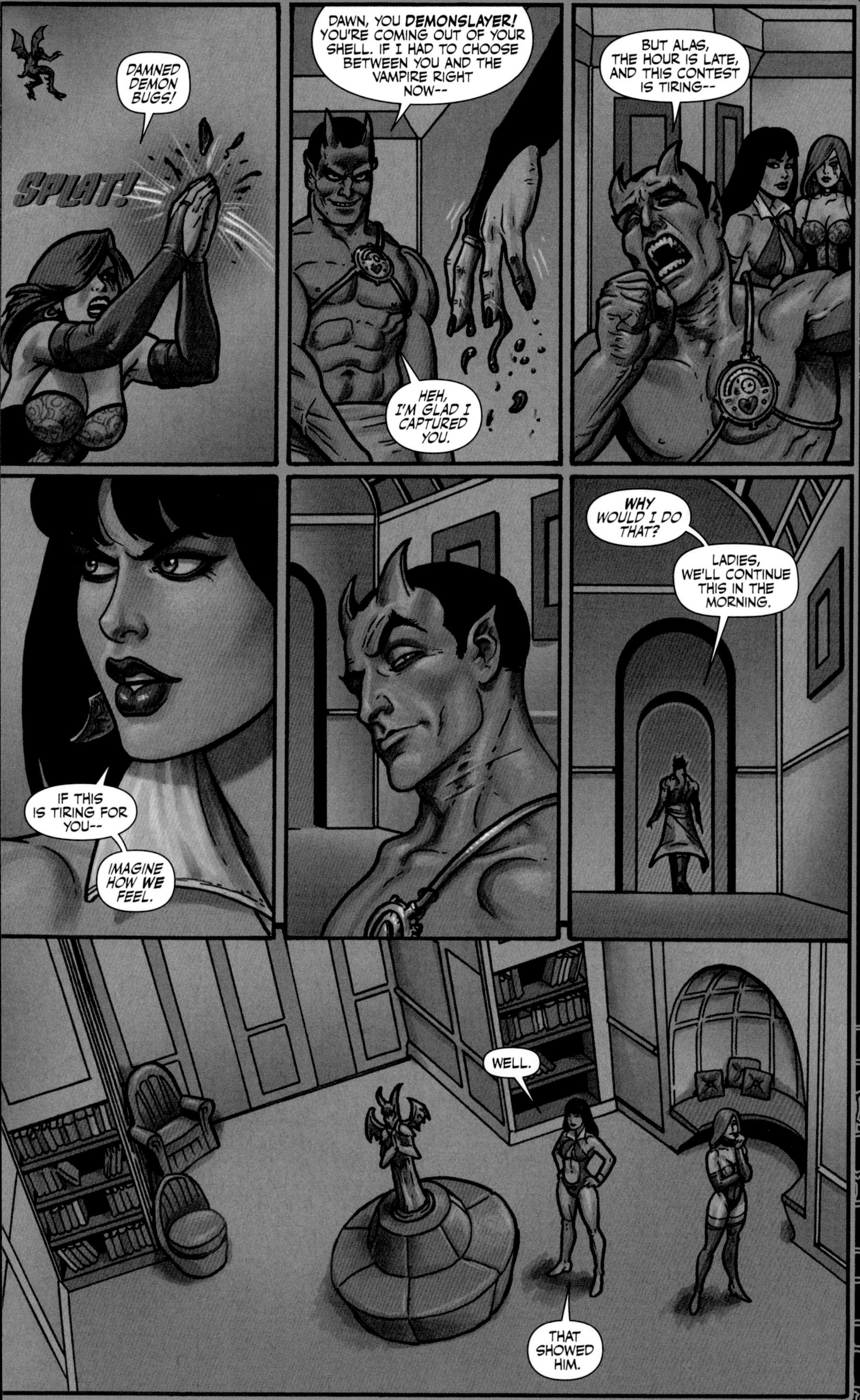

DAMNED DEMON BUGS!
SPLAT!
DAWN, YOU DEMONSLAYER! YOU'RE COMING OUT OF YOUR SHELL. IF I HAD TO CHOOSE BETWEEN YOU AND THE VAMPIRE RIGHT NOW--
HEH, I'M GLAD I CAPTURED YOU.
BUT ALAS, THE HOUR IS LATE, AND THIS CONTEST IS TIRING--
IF THIS IS TIRING FOR YOU--
IMAGINE HOW WE FEEL.
WHY WOULD I DO THAT?
LADIES, WE'LL CONTINUE THIS IN THE MORNING.
WELL.
THAT SHOWED HIM.

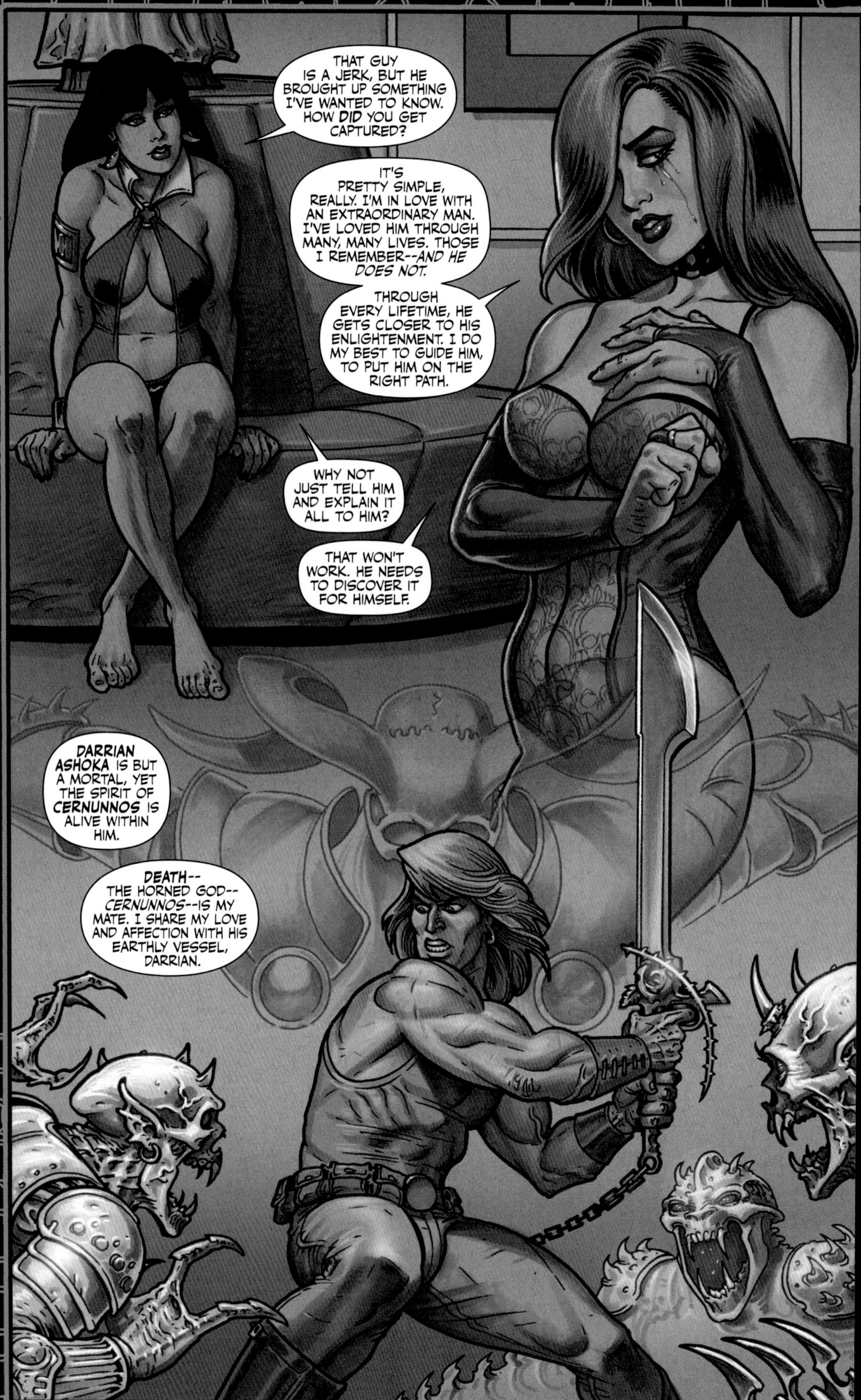
THAT GUY IS A JERK, BUT HE BROUGHT UP SOMETHING I'VE WANTED TO KNOW. HOW **DID** YOU GET CAPTURED?
IT'S PRETTY SIMPLE, REALLY. I'M IN LOVE WITH AN EXTRAORDINARY MAN. I'VE LOVED HIM THROUGH MANY, MANY LIVES. THOSE I REMEMBER--*AND HE DOES NOT.*
THROUGH EVERY LIFETIME, HE GETS CLOSER TO HIS ENLIGHTENMENT. I DO MY BEST TO GUIDE HIM, TO PUT HIM ON THE RIGHT PATH.
WHY NOT JUST TELL HIM AND EXPLAIN IT ALL TO HIM?
THAT WON'T WORK. HE NEEDS TO DISCOVER IT FOR HIMSELF.
DARRIAN ASHOKA IS BUT A MORTAL, YET THE SPIRIT OF **CERNUNNOS** IS ALIVE WITHIN HIM.
DEATH-- THE HORNED GOD-- *CERNUNNOS*--IS MY MATE. I SHARE MY LOVE AND AFFECTION WITH HIS EARTHLY VESSEL, DARRIAN.

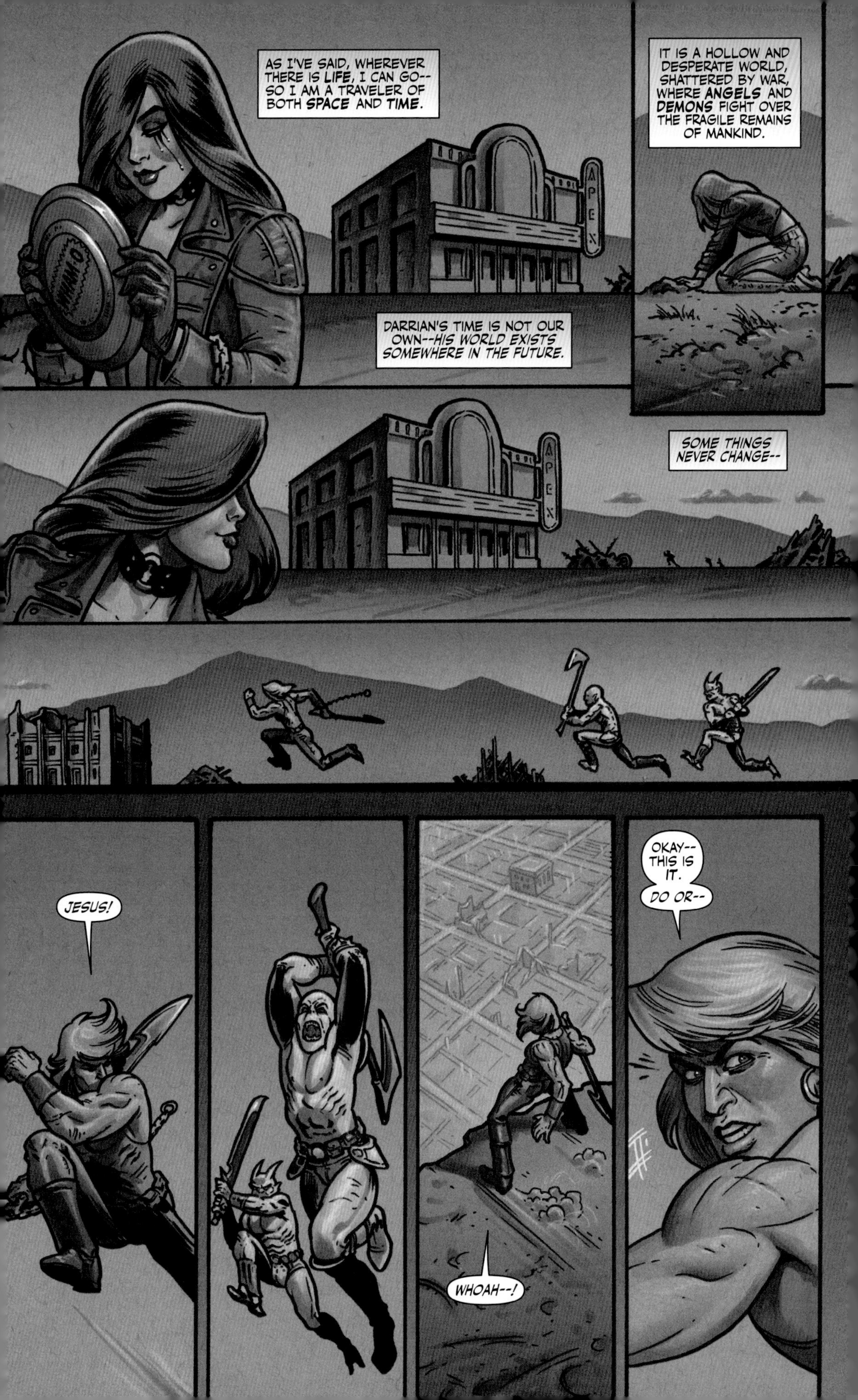
AS I'VE SAID, WHEREVER THERE IS LIFE, I CAN GO--SO I AM A TRAVELER OF BOTH SPACE AND TIME.
DARRIAN'S TIME IS NOT OUR OWN--HIS WORLD EXISTS SOMEWHERE IN THE FUTURE.
APEX
IT IS A HOLLOW AND DESPERATE WORLD, SHATTERED BY WAR, WHERE ANGELS AND DEMONS FIGHT OVER THE FRAGILE REMAINS OF MANKIND.
SOME THINGS NEVER CHANGE--
JESUS!
WHOAH--!
OKAY-- THIS IS IT.
DO OR--

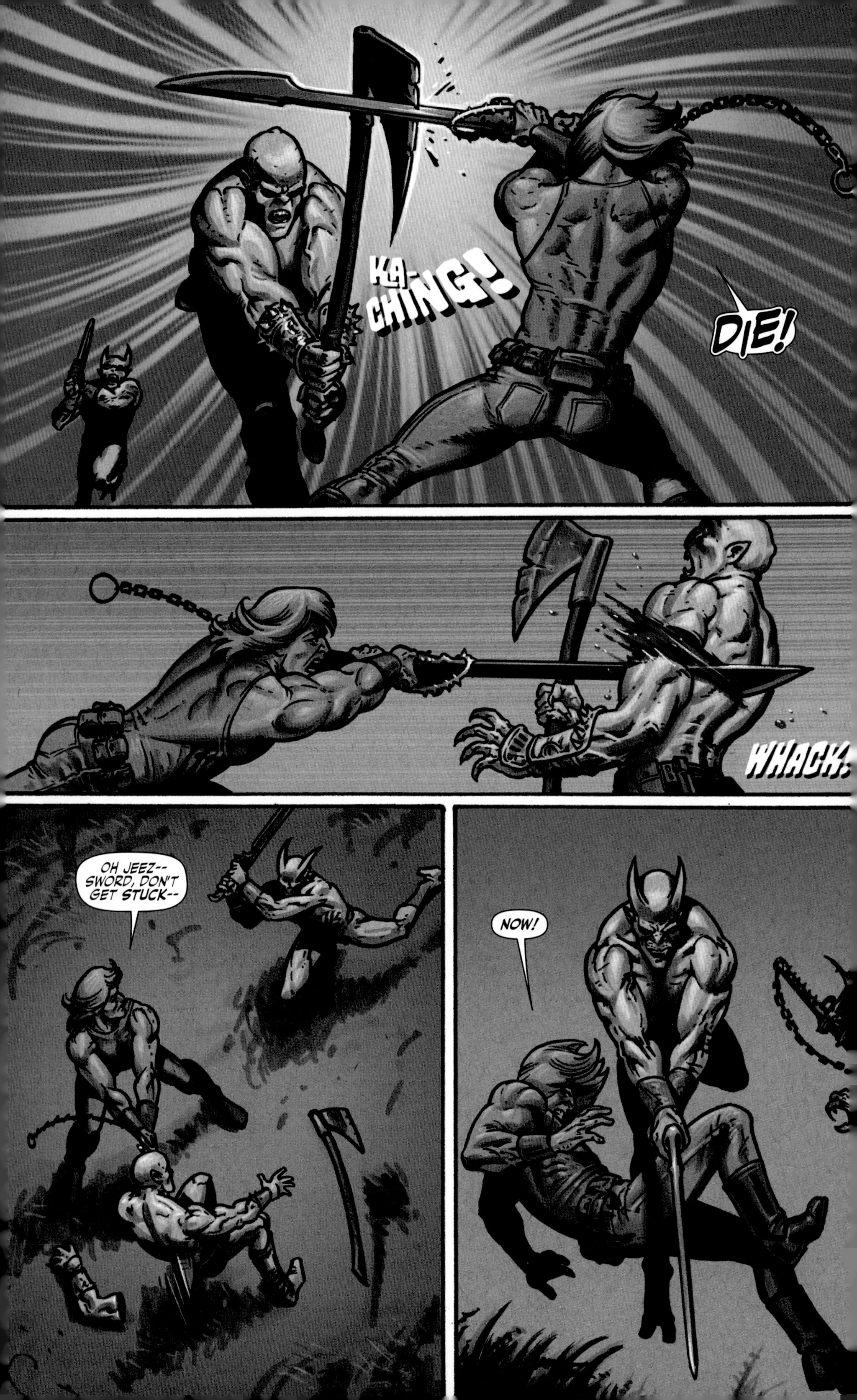
KA-CHING!
DIE!
WHACK!
OH JEEZ-- SWORD, DON'T GET STUCK--
NOW!

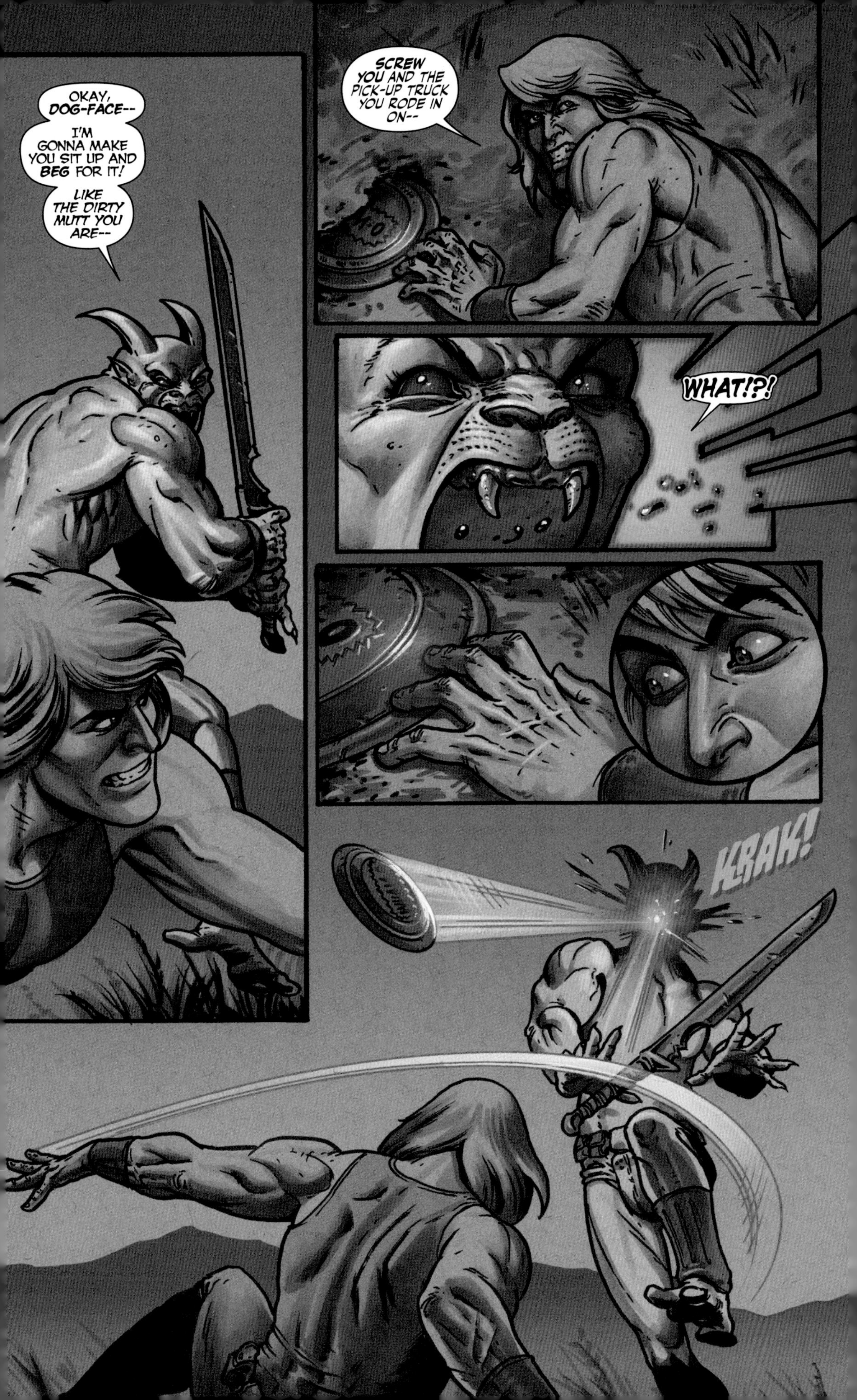
OKAY, DOG-FACE--
I'M GONNA MAKE YOU SIT UP AND BEG FOR IT!
LIKE THE DIRTY MUTT YOU ARE--
SCREW YOU AND THE PICK-UP TRUCK YOU RODE IN ON--
WHAT!?!
KRAK!

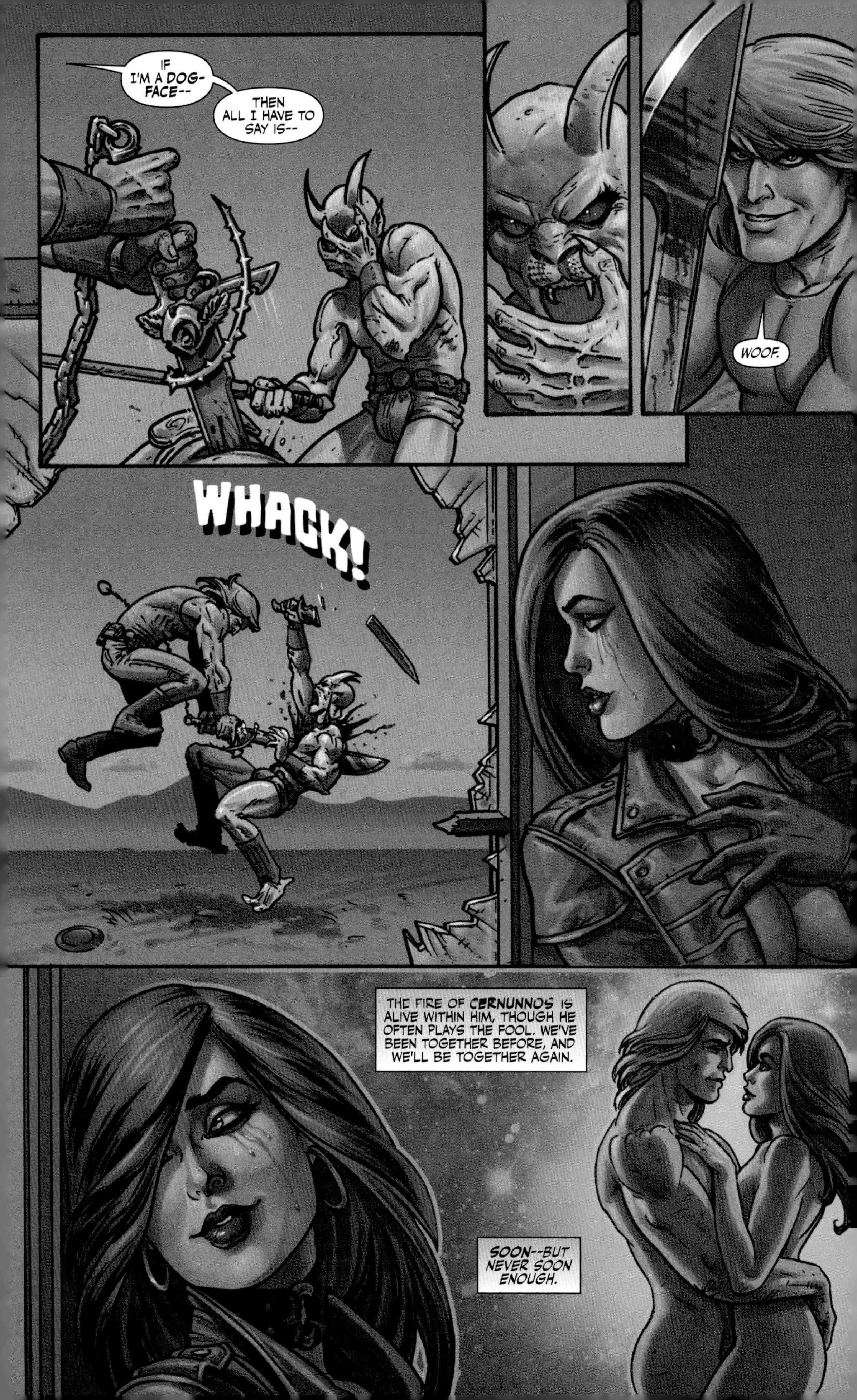
IF I'M A DOG-FACE--
THEN ALL I HAVE TO SAY IS--
WOOF.
WHACK!
THE FIRE OF CERNUNNOS IS ALIVE WITHIN HIM, THOUGH HE OFTEN PLAYS THE FOOL. WE'VE BEEN TOGETHER BEFORE, AND WE'LL BE TOGETHER AGAIN.
SOON--BUT NEVER SOON ENOUGH.

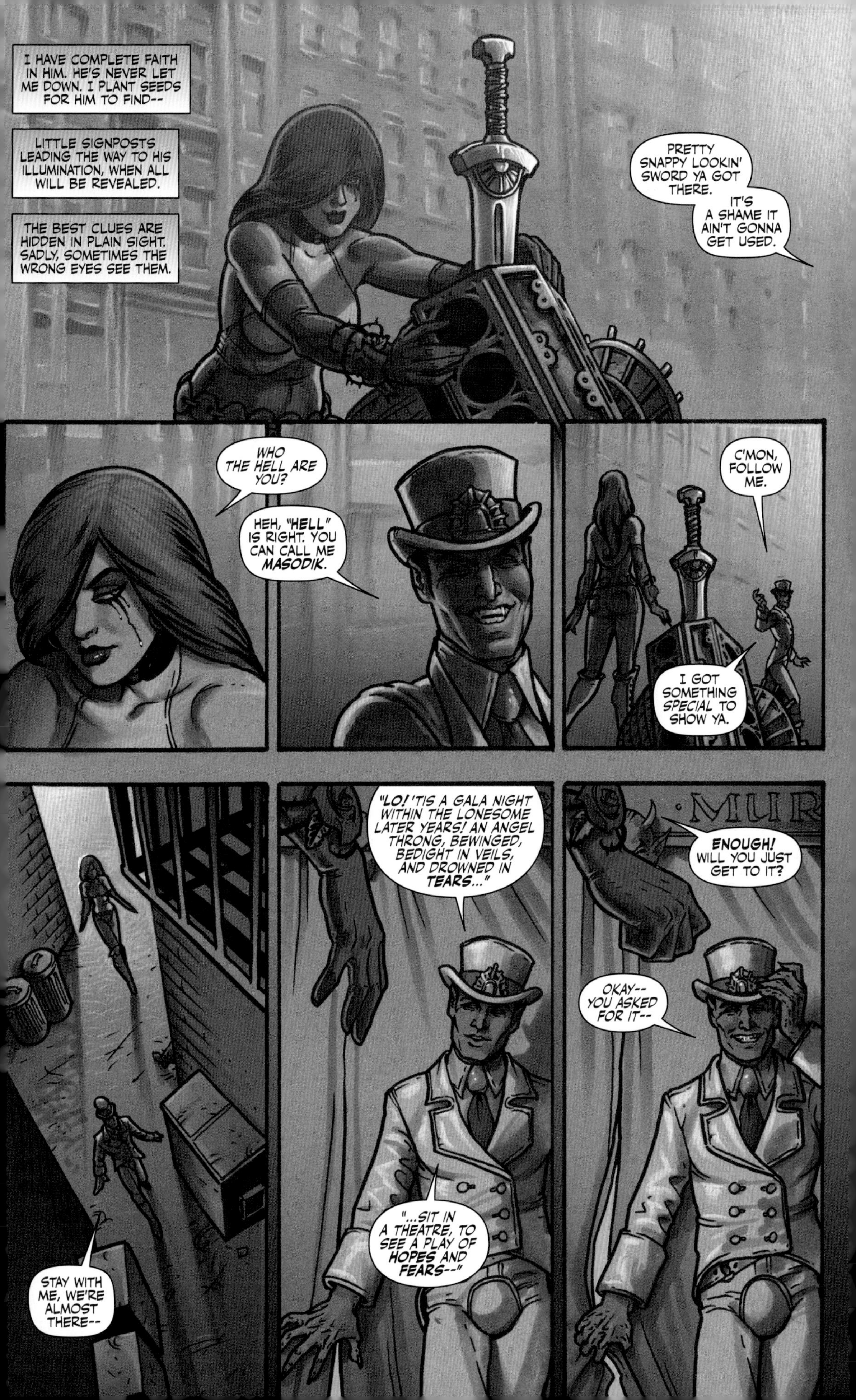
I HAVE COMPLETE FAITH IN HIM. HE'S NEVER LET ME DOWN. I PLANT SEEDS FOR HIM TO FIND--
LITTLE SIGNPOSTS LEADING THE WAY TO HIS ILLUMINATION, WHEN ALL WILL BE REVEALED.
THE BEST CLUES ARE HIDDEN IN PLAIN SIGHT. SADLY, SOMETIMES THE WRONG EYES SEE THEM.
PRETTY SNAPPY LOOKIN' SWORD YA GOT THERE.
IT'S A SHAME IT AIN'T GONNA GET USED.
WHO THE HELL ARE YOU?
HEH, "HELL" IS RIGHT. YOU CAN CALL ME MASODIK.
C'MON, FOLLOW ME.
I GOT SOMETHING SPECIAL TO SHOW YA.
STAY WITH ME, WE'RE ALMOST THERE--
"LO! 'TIS A GALA NIGHT WITHIN THE LONESOME LATER YEARS! AN ANGEL THRONG, BEWINGED, BEDIGHT IN VEILS, AND DROWNED IN TEARS..."
"...SIT IN A THEATRE, TO SEE A PLAY OF HOPES AND FEARS--"
MUR
ENOUGH! WILL YOU JUST GET TO IT?
OKAY-- YOU ASKED FOR IT--

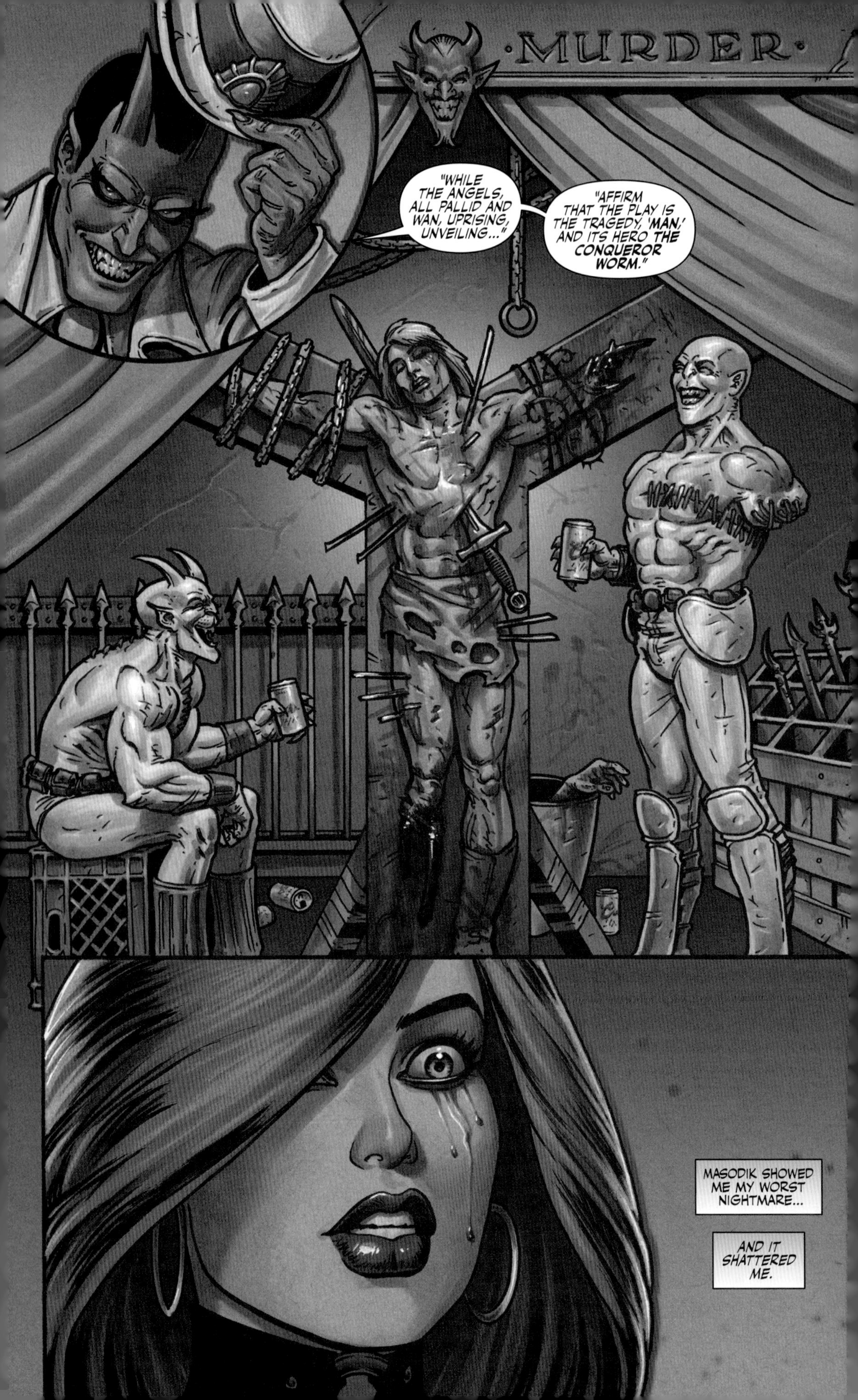
MURDER
"WHILE THE ANGELS, ALL PALLID AND WAN, UPRISING, UNVEILING..."
"AFFIRM THAT THE PLAY IS THE TRAGEDY, 'MAN,' AND ITS HERO THE CONQUEROR WORM."
MASODIK SHOWED ME MY WORST NIGHTMARE...
AND IT SHATTERED ME.

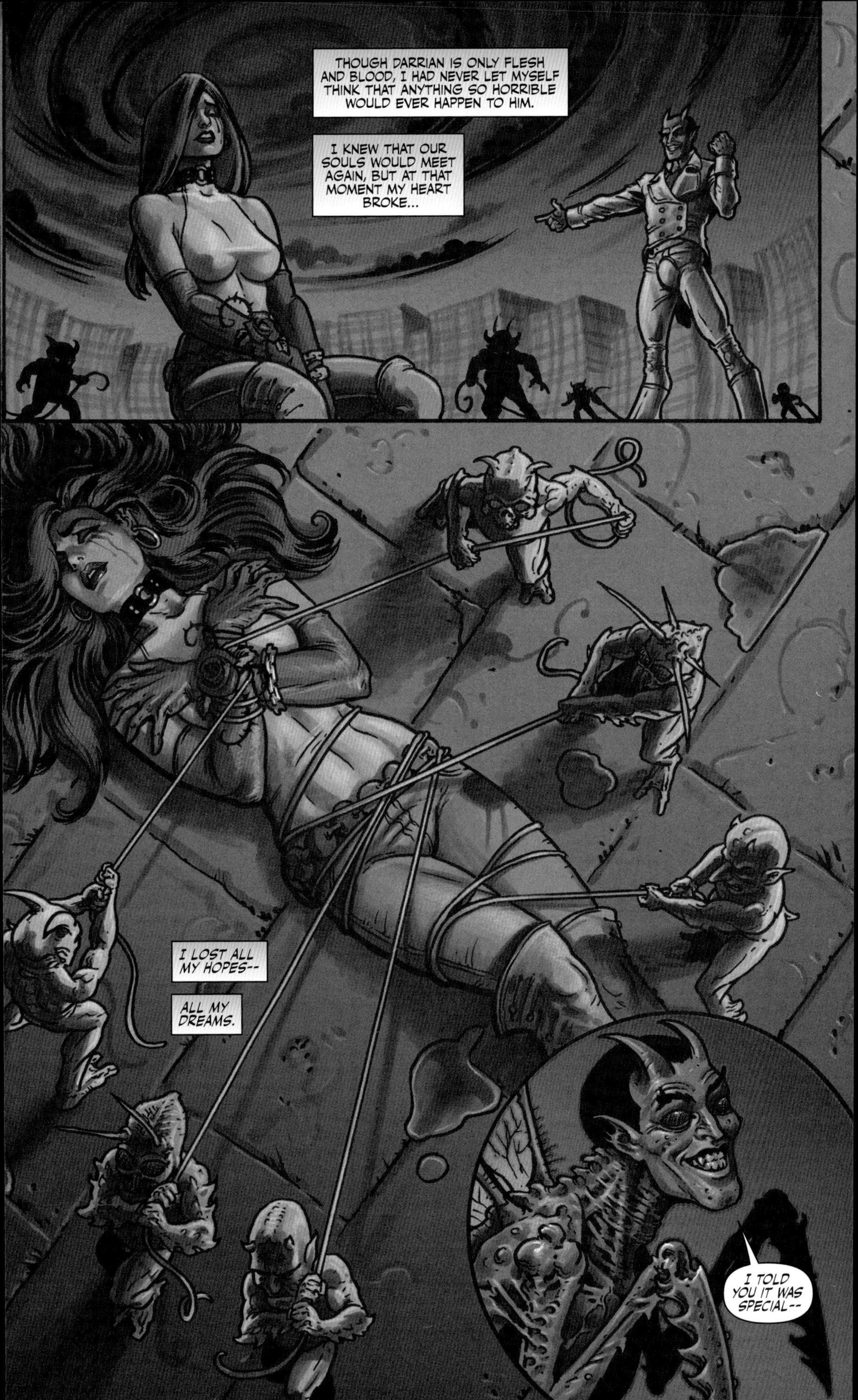
THOUGH DARRIAN IS ONLY FLESH AND BLOOD, I HAD NEVER LET MYSELF THINK THAT ANYTHING SO HORRIBLE WOULD EVER HAPPEN TO HIM.
I KNEW THAT OUR SOULS WOULD MEET AGAIN, BUT AT THAT MOMENT MY HEART BROKE...
I LOST ALL MY HOPES--
ALL MY DREAMS.
I TOLD YOU IT WAS SPECIAL--

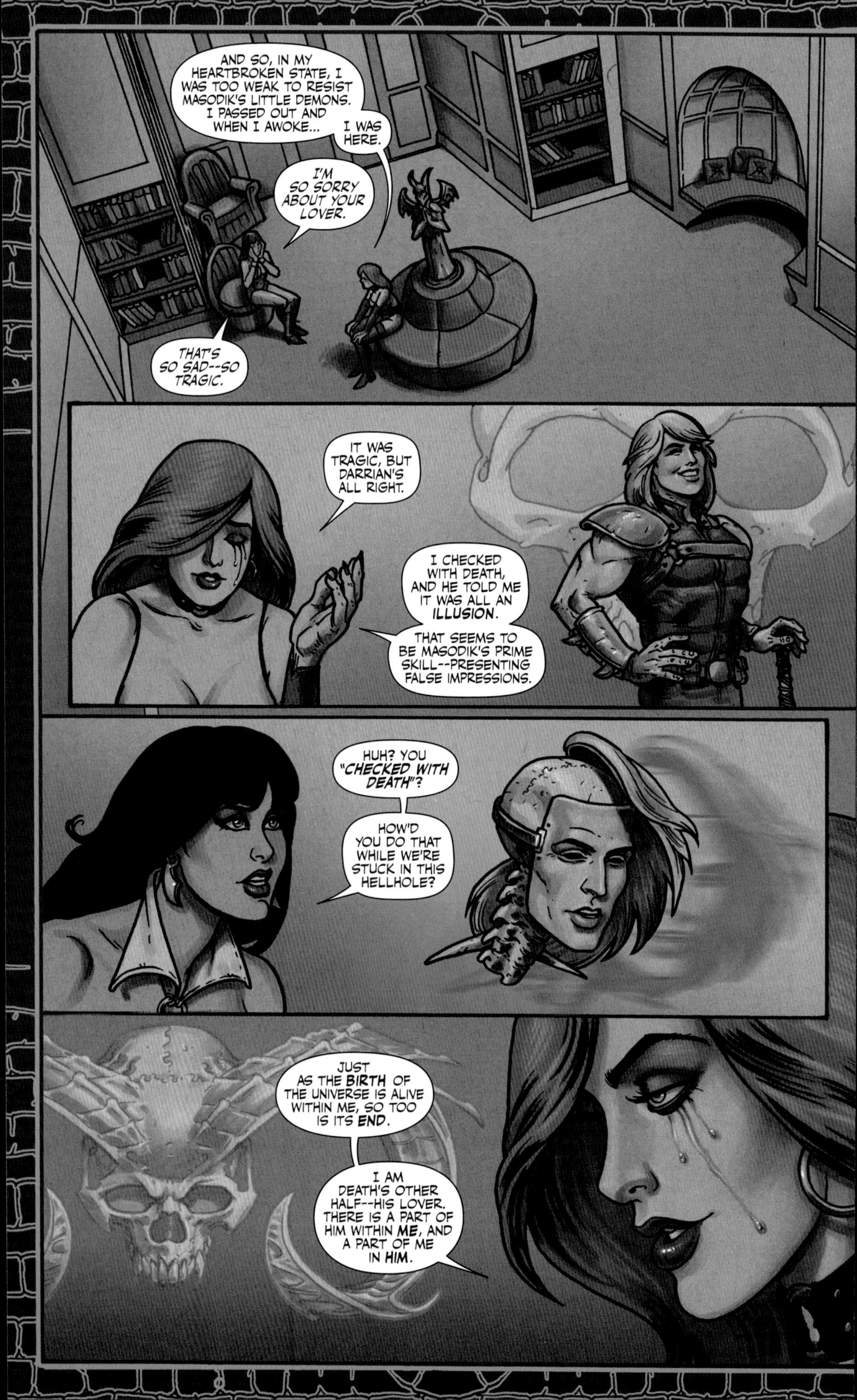

AND SO, IN MY HEARTBROKEN STATE, I WAS TOO WEAK TO RESIST MASODIK'S LITTLE DEMONS. I PASSED OUT AND WHEN I AWOKE...
I WAS HERE.
I'M SO SORRY ABOUT YOUR LOVER.
THAT'S SO SAD--SO TRAGIC.
IT WAS TRAGIC, BUT DARRIAN'S ALL RIGHT.
I CHECKED WITH DEATH, AND HE TOLD ME IT WAS ALL AN **ILLUSION**.
THAT SEEMS TO BE MASODIK'S PRIME SKILL--PRESENTING FALSE IMPRESSIONS.
HUH? YOU "***CHECKED WITH DEATH***"?
HOW'D YOU DO THAT WHILE WE'RE STUCK IN THIS HELLHOLE?
JUST AS THE **BIRTH** OF THE UNIVERSE IS ALIVE WITHIN ME, SO TOO IS ITS **END**.
I AM DEATH'S OTHER HALF--HIS LOVER. THERE IS A PART OF HIM WITHIN **ME**, AND A PART OF ME IN **HIM**.

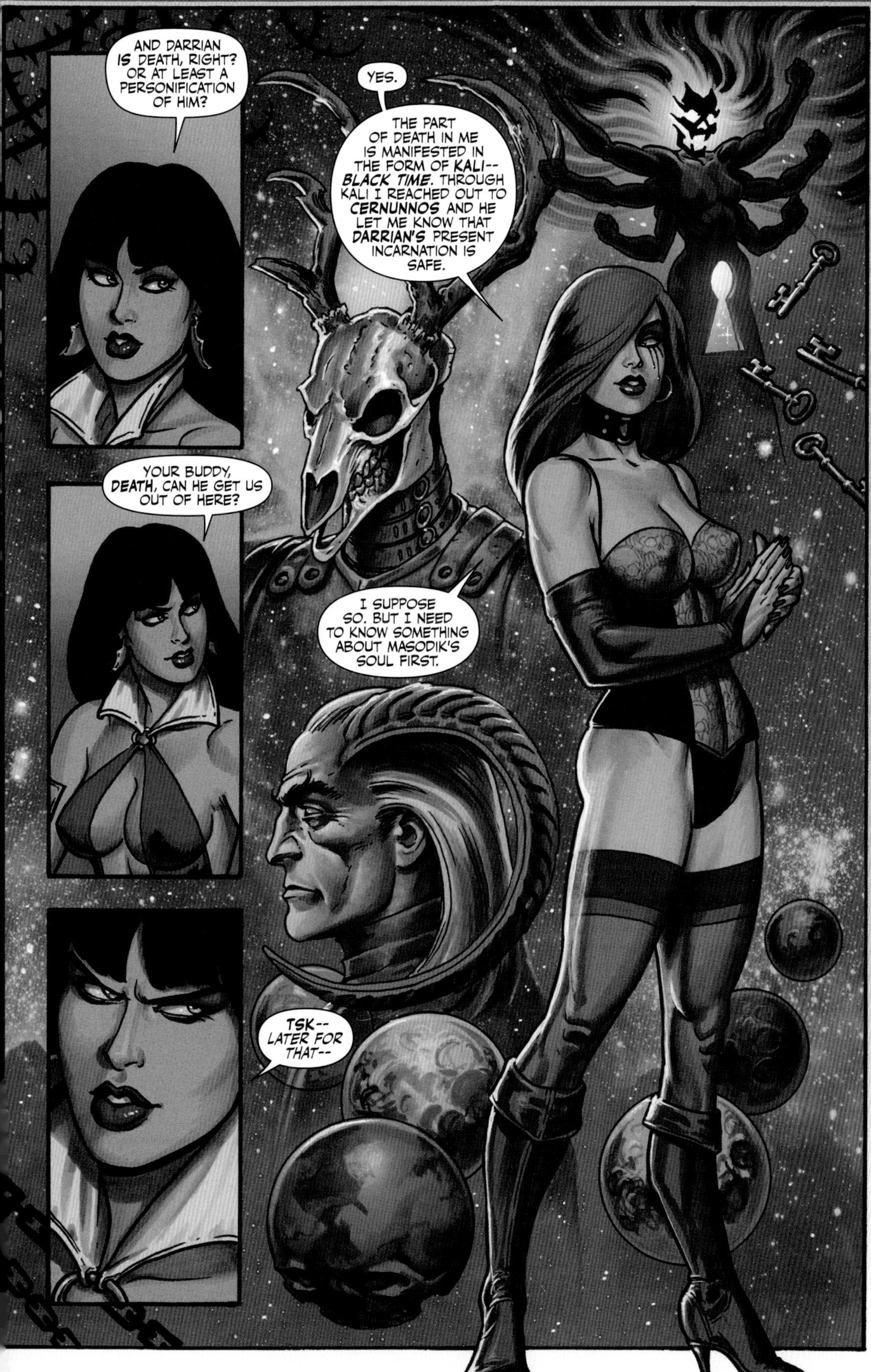
AND DARRIAN IS DEATH, RIGHT? OR AT LEAST A PERSONIFICATION OF HIM?
YES.
THE PART OF DEATH IN ME IS MANIFESTED IN THE FORM OF KALI-- BLACK TIME. THROUGH KALI I REACHED OUT TO CERNUNNOS AND HE LET ME KNOW THAT DARRIAN'S PRESENT INCARNATION IS SAFE.
YOUR BUDDY, DEATH, CAN HE GET US OUT OF HERE?
I SUPPOSE SO. BUT I NEED TO KNOW SOMETHING ABOUT MASODIK'S SOUL FIRST.
TSK-- LATER FOR THAT--

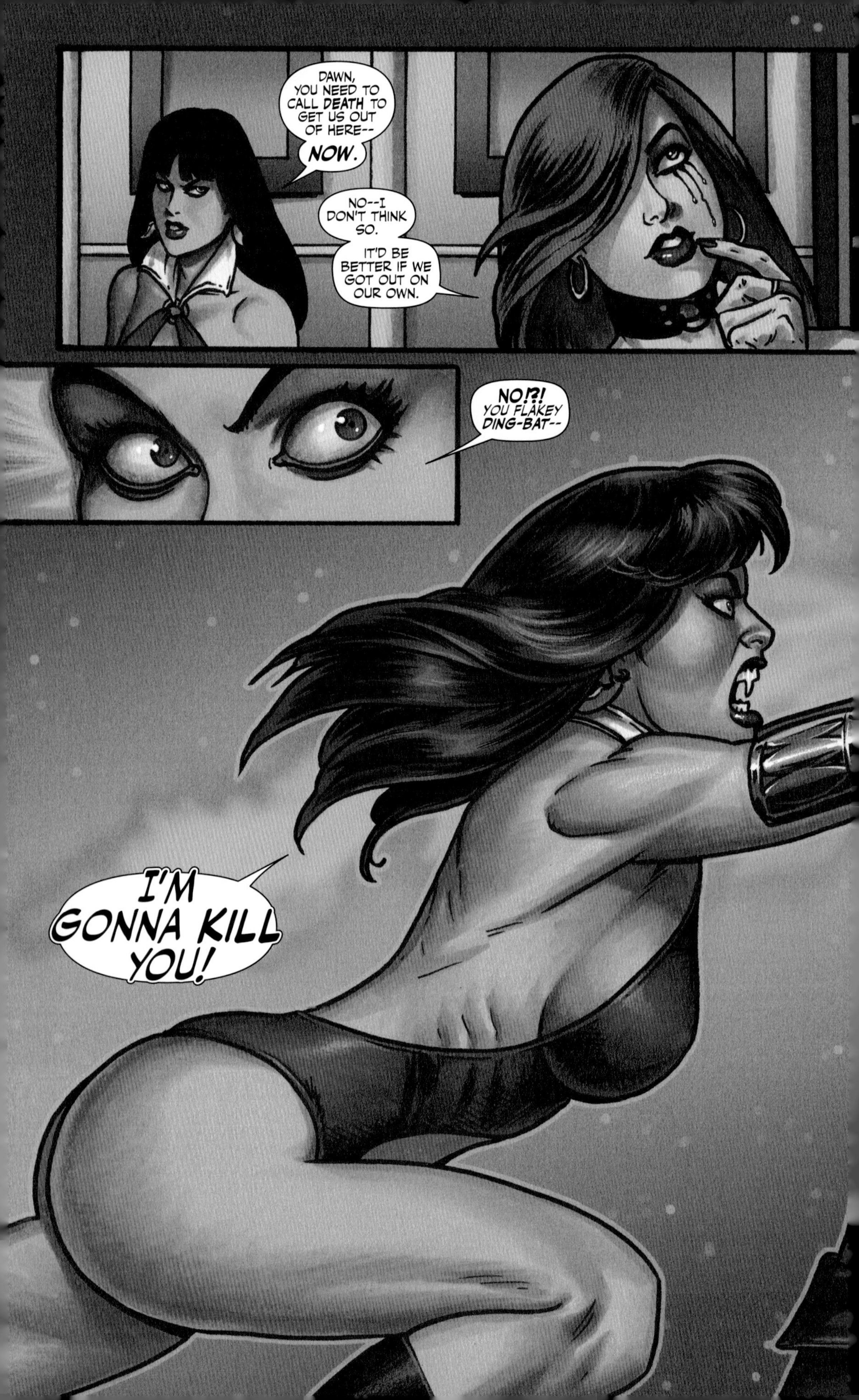

DAWN, YOU NEED TO CALL DEATH TO GET US OUT OF HERE-- NOW.
NO--I DON'T THINK SO.
IT'D BE BETTER IF WE GOT OUT ON OUR OWN.
NO!?! YOU FLAKEY DING-BAT--
I'M GONNA KILL YOU!

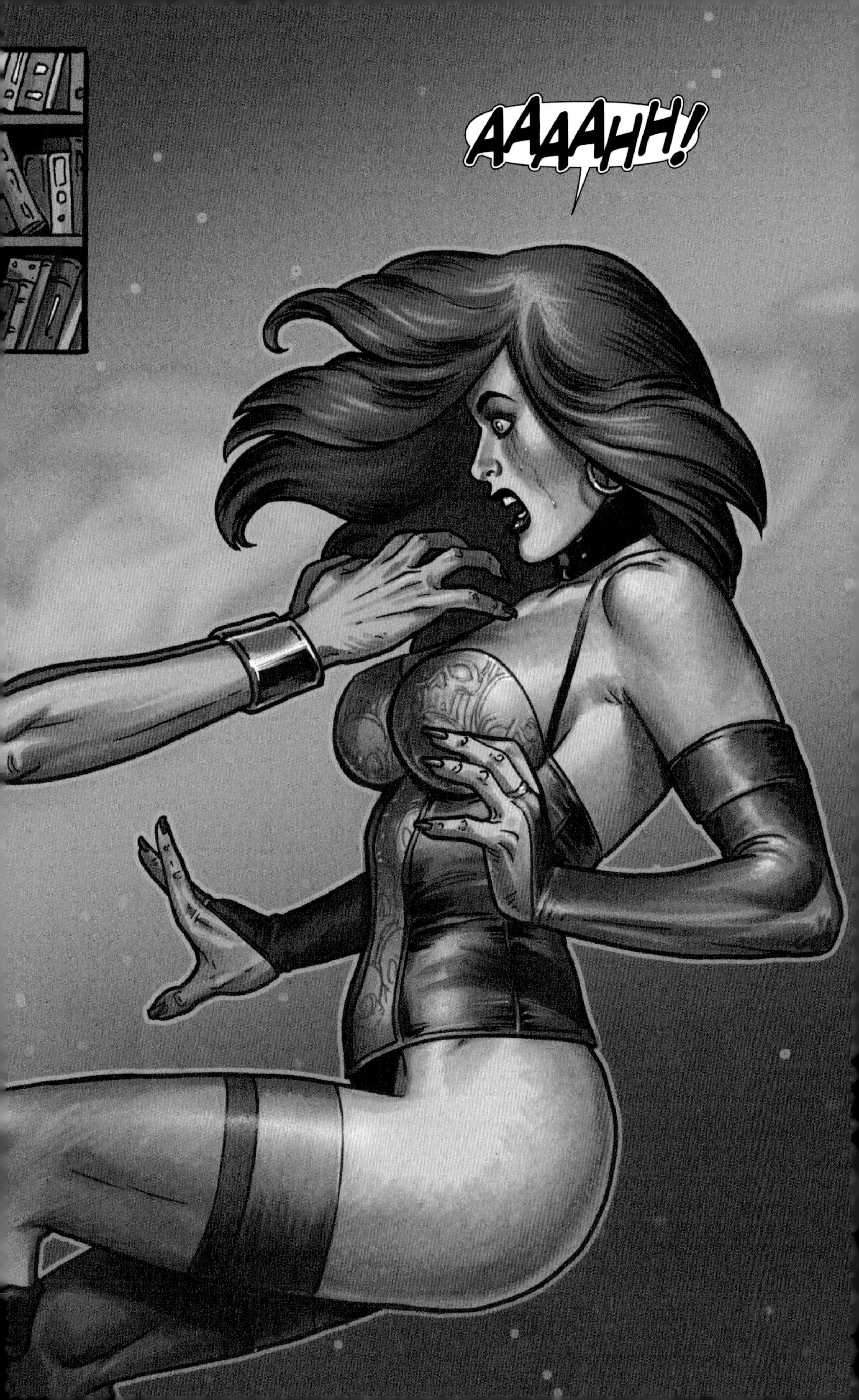
AAAAHH!

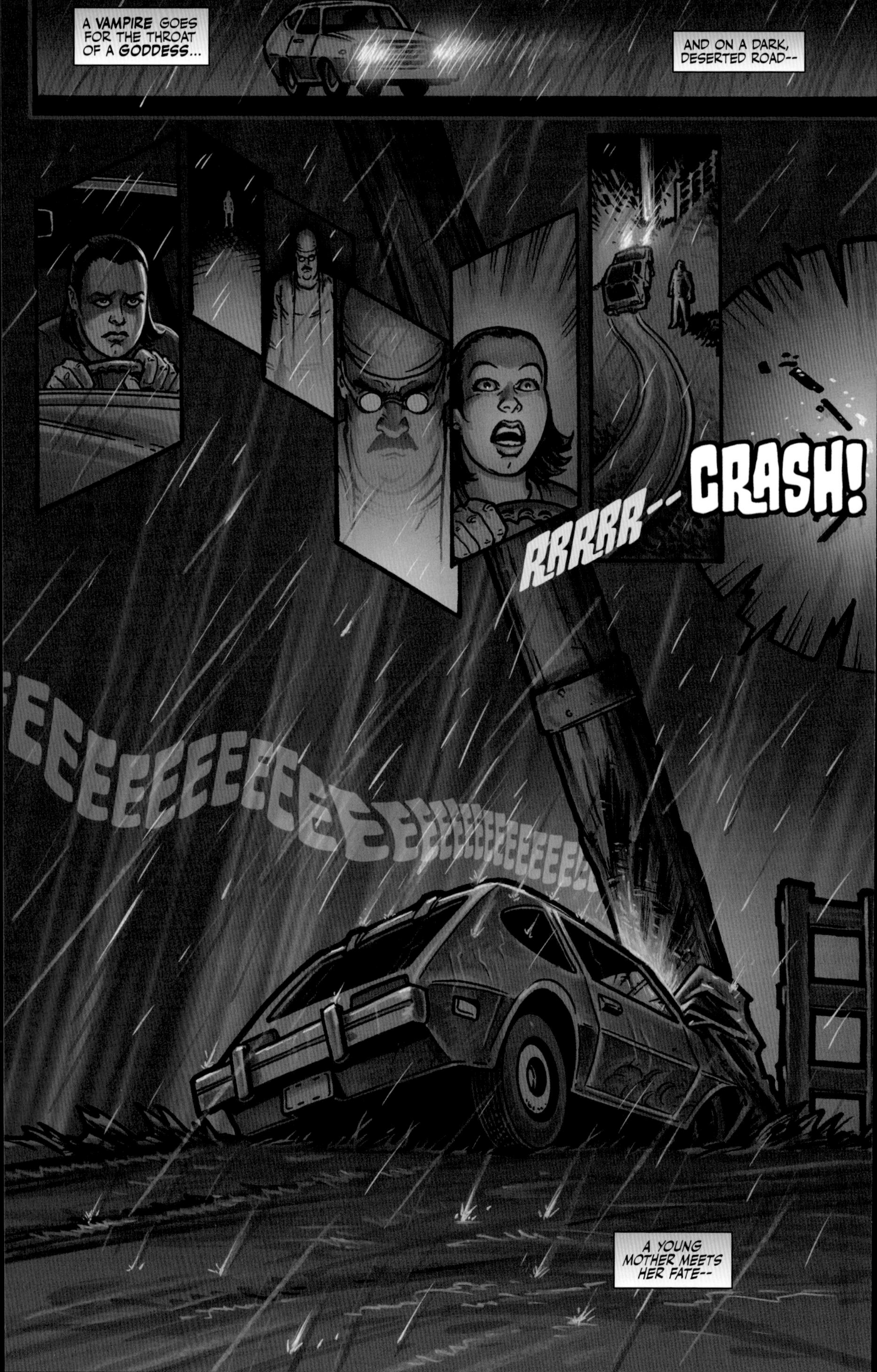

A VAMPIRE GOES FOR THE THROAT OF A GODDESS...
AND ON A DARK, DESERTED ROAD--
RRRRR-- CRASH!
EEEEEEEEEEEEEEEEEEEEEEEEEEEEEE
A YOUNG MOTHER MEETS HER FATE--

CHAPTER • FIVE

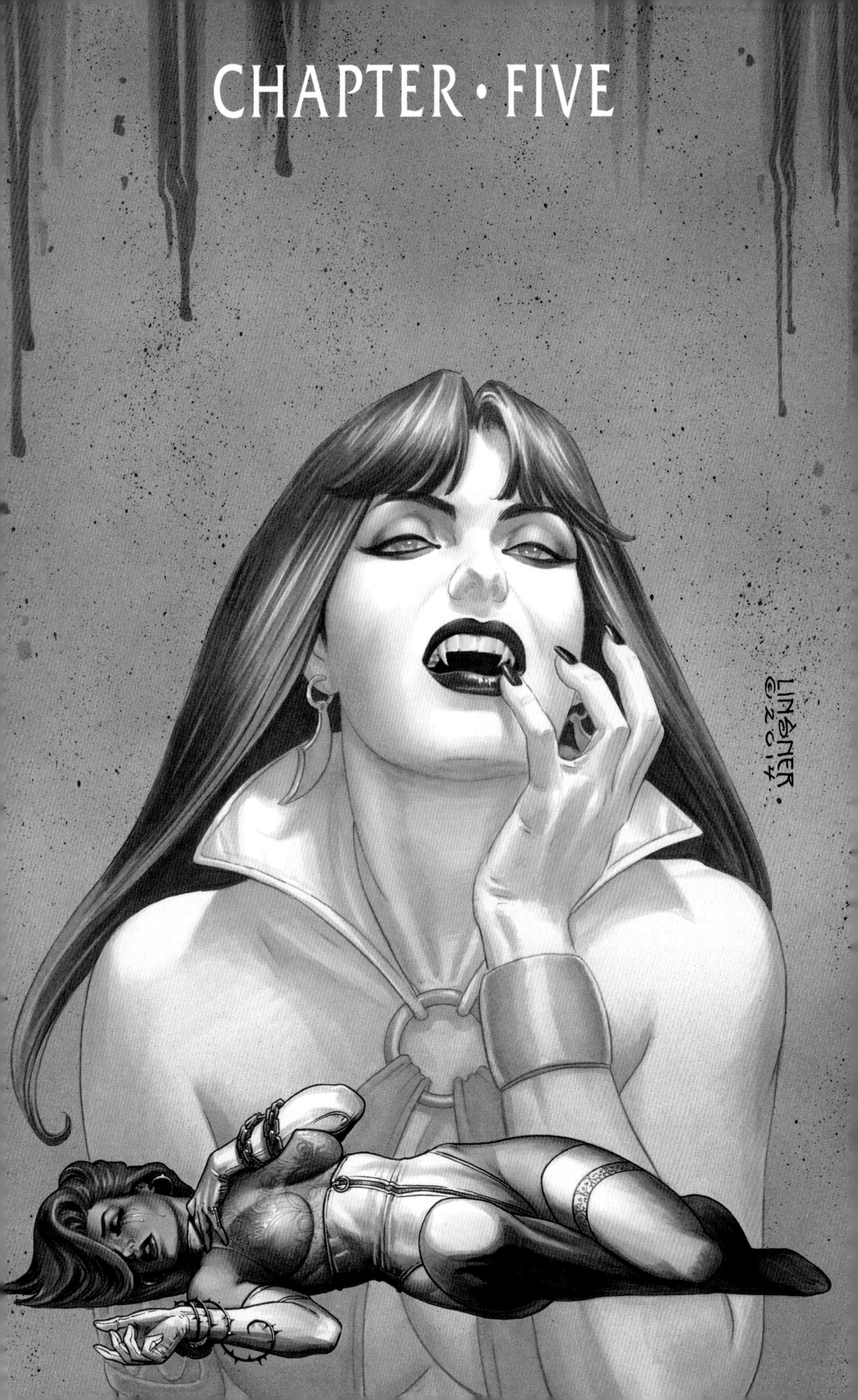
LINDNER
©2017

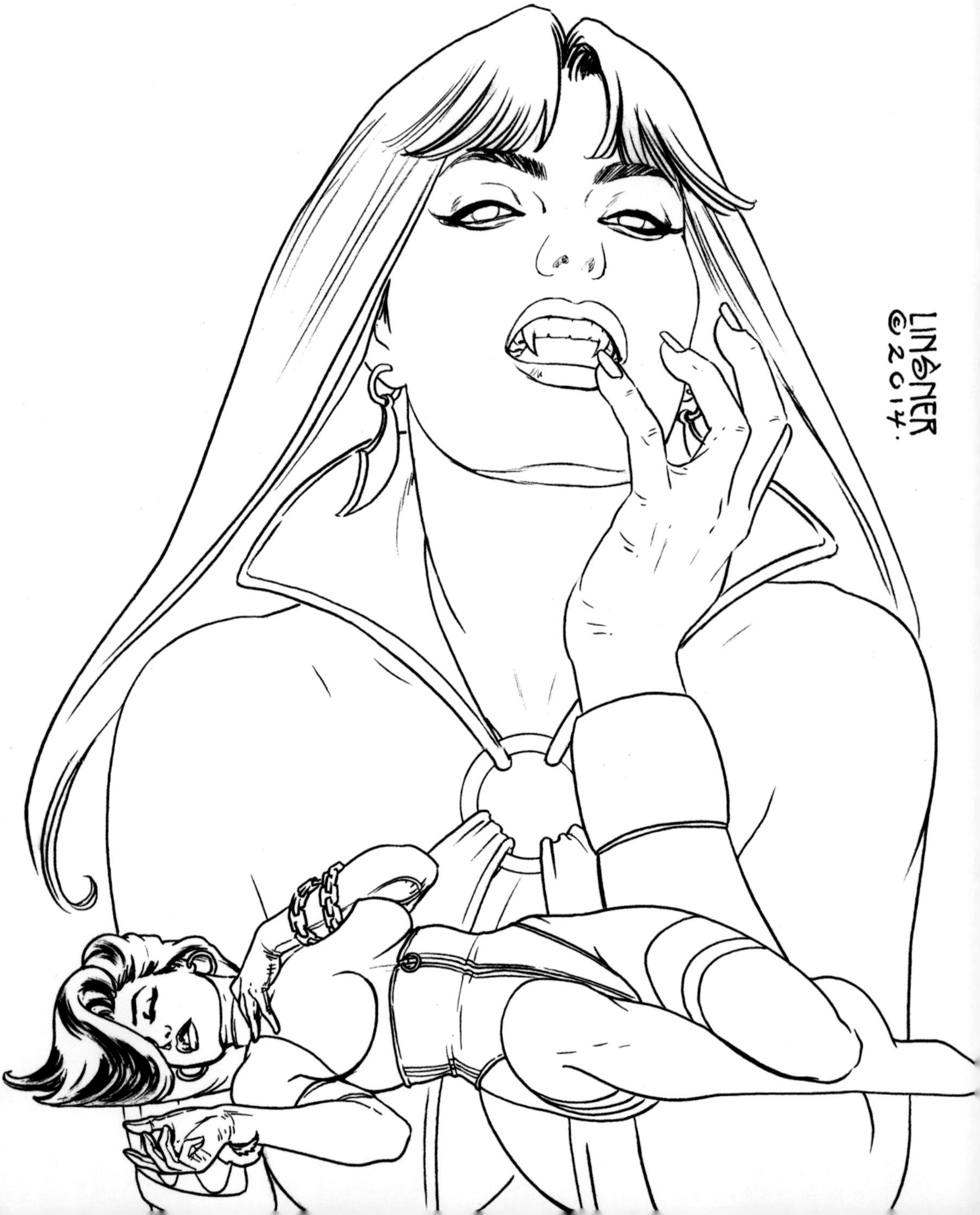
LINSNER
©2017.

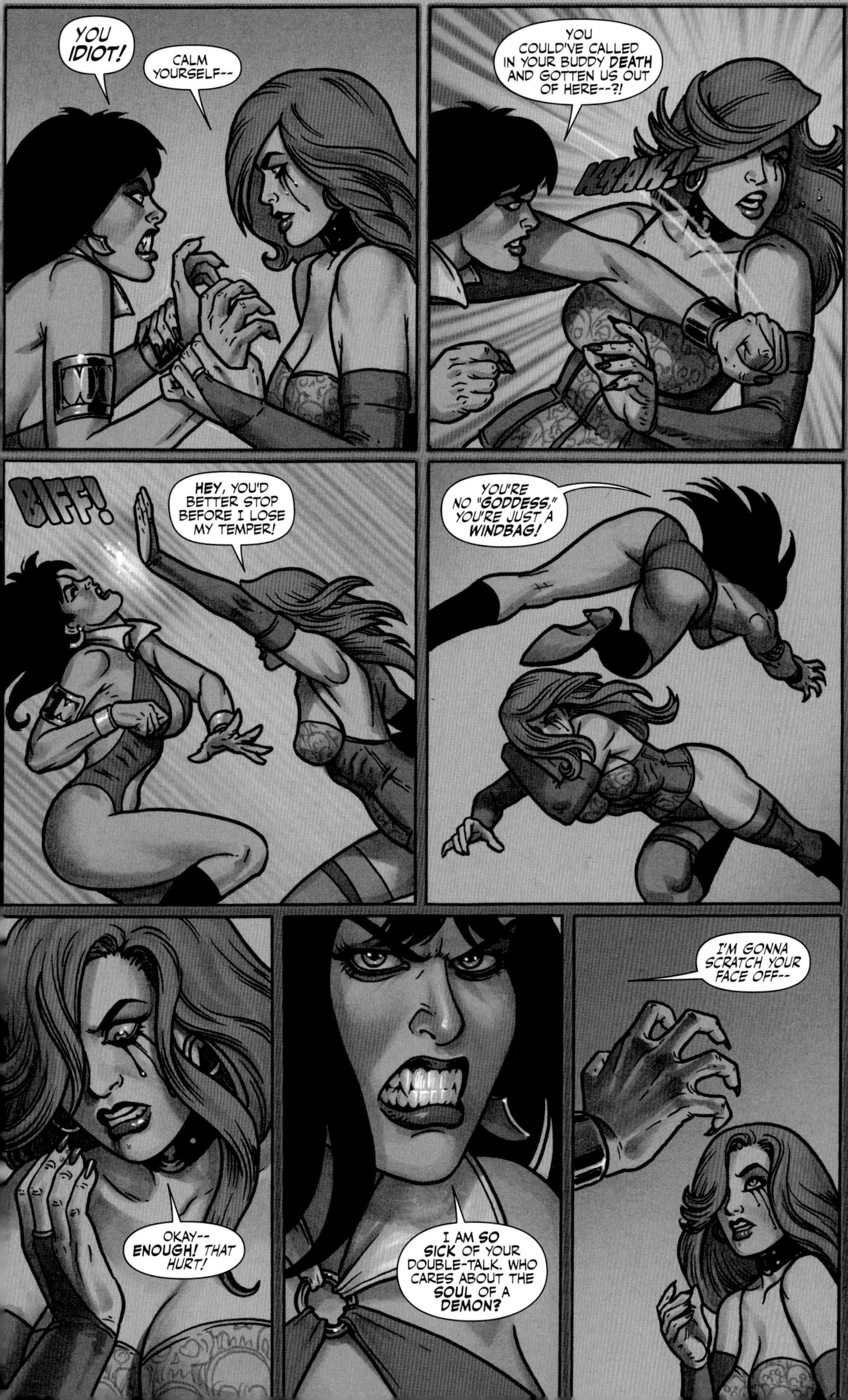
YOU IDIOT!
CALM YOURSELF--
YOU COULD'VE CALLED IN YOUR BUDDY DEATH AND GOTTEN US OUT OF HERE--?!
KRAK!
BIFF!
HEY, YOU'D BETTER STOP BEFORE I LOSE MY TEMPER!
YOU'RE NO "GODDESS," YOU'RE JUST A WINDBAG!
OKAY-- ENOUGH! THAT HURT!
I AM SO SICK OF YOUR DOUBLE-TALK. WHO CARES ABOUT THE SOUL OF A DEMON?
I'M GONNA SCRATCH YOUR FACE OFF--

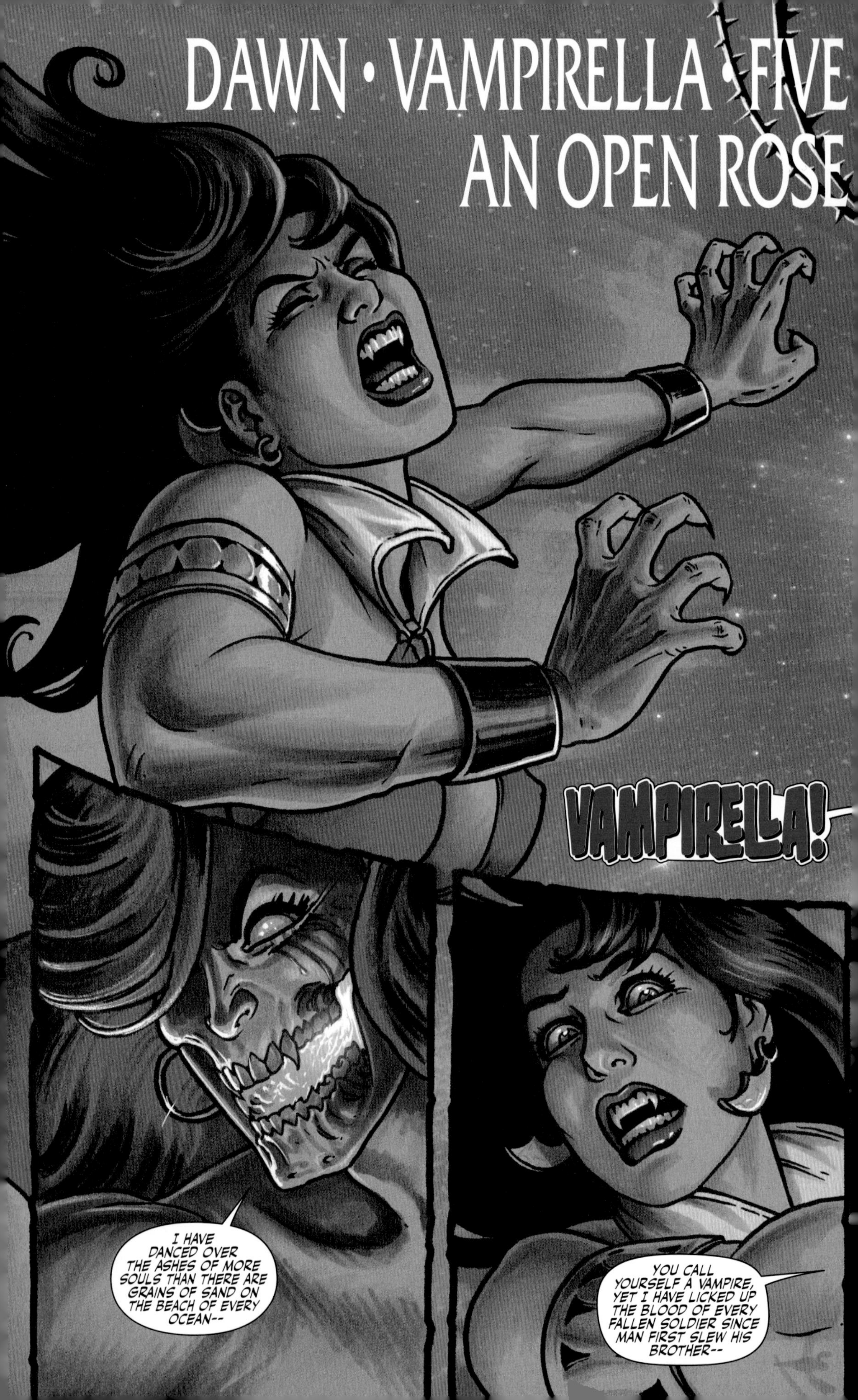
DAWN • VAMPIRELLA • FIVE
AN OPEN ROSE
VAMPIRELLA!
I HAVE DANCED OVER THE ASHES OF MORE SOULS THAN THERE ARE GRAINS OF SAND ON THE BEACH OF EVERY OCEAN--
YOU CALL YOURSELF A VAMPIRE, YET I HAVE LICKED UP THE BLOOD OF EVERY FALLEN SOLDIER SINCE MAN FIRST SLEW HIS BROTHER--

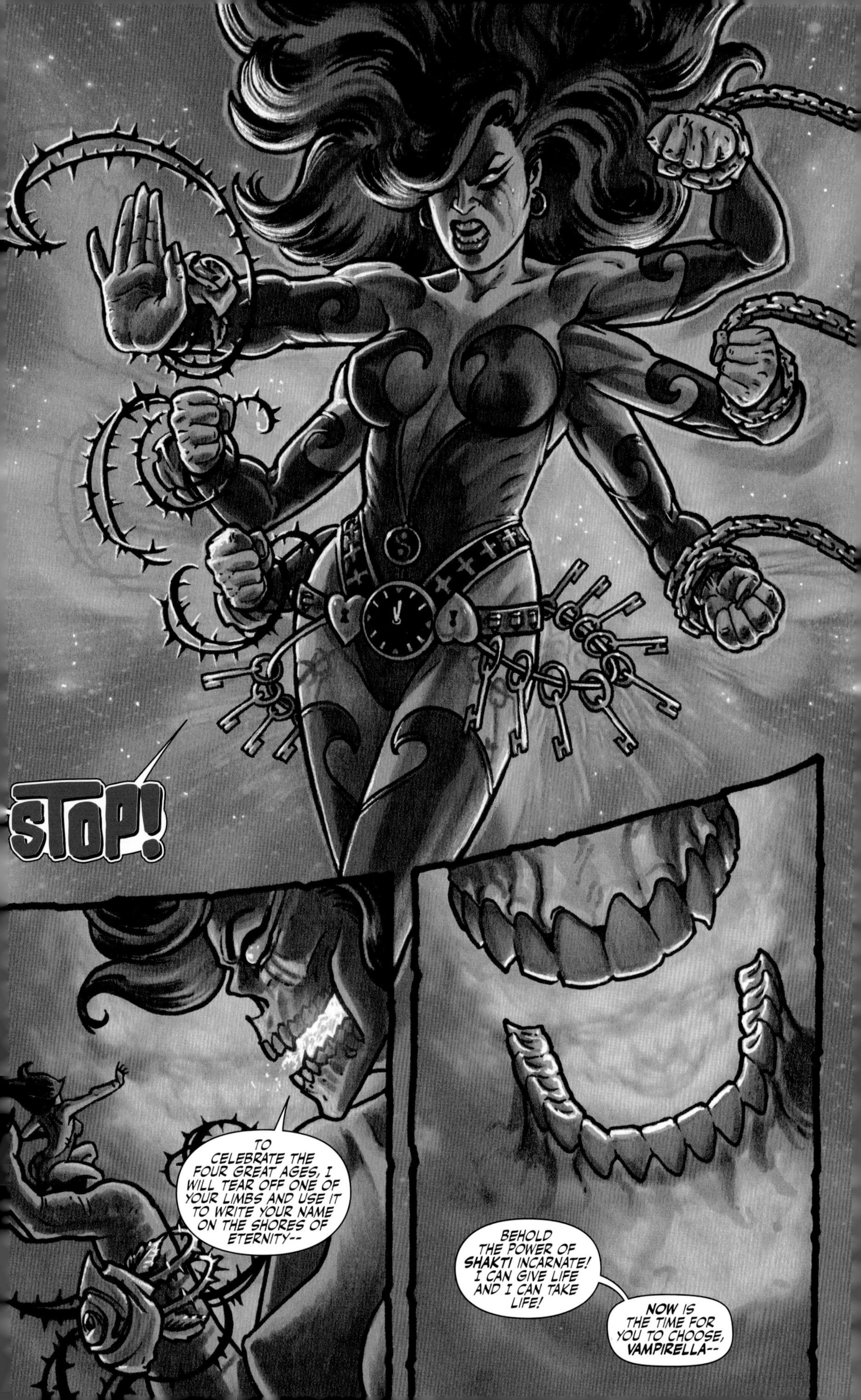
STOP!
TO CELEBRATE THE FOUR GREAT AGES, I WILL TEAR OFF ONE OF YOUR LIMBS AND USE IT TO WRITE YOUR NAME ON THE SHORES OF ETERNITY--
BEHOLD THE POWER OF SHAKTI INCARNATE! I CAN GIVE LIFE AND I CAN TAKE LIFE!
NOW IS THE TIME FOR YOU TO CHOOSE, VAMPIRELLA--

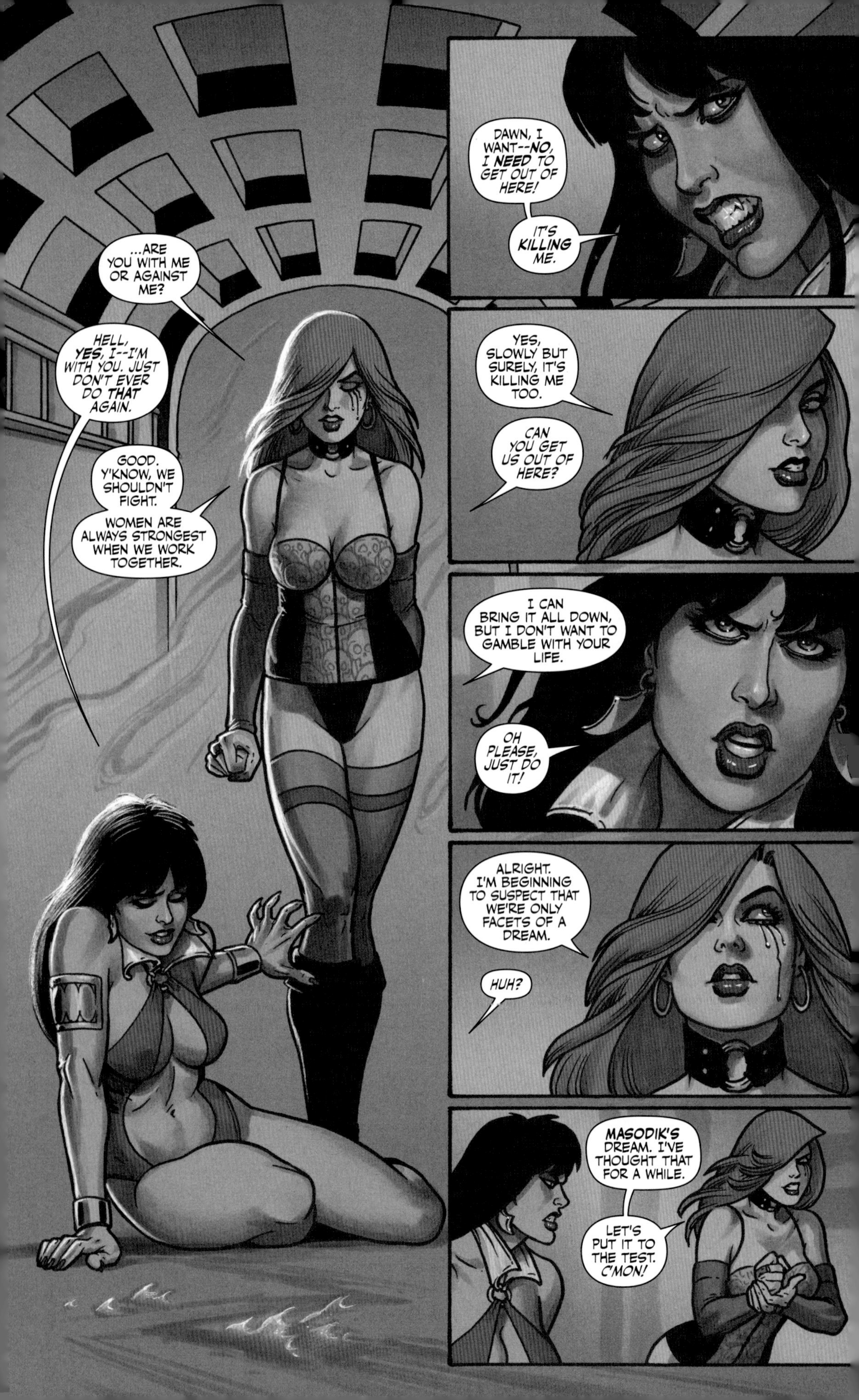

...ARE YOU WITH ME OR AGAINST ME?
HELL, YES, I--I'M WITH YOU. JUST DON'T EVER DO THAT AGAIN.
GOOD. Y'KNOW, WE SHOULDN'T FIGHT.
WOMEN ARE ALWAYS STRONGEST WHEN WE WORK TOGETHER.
DAWN, I WANT--NO, I NEED TO GET OUT OF HERE!
IT'S KILLING ME.
YES, SLOWLY BUT SURELY, IT'S KILLING ME TOO.
CAN YOU GET US OUT OF HERE?
I CAN BRING IT ALL DOWN, BUT I DON'T WANT TO GAMBLE WITH YOUR LIFE.
OH PLEASE, JUST DO IT!
ALRIGHT. I'M BEGINNING TO SUSPECT THAT WE'RE ONLY FACETS OF A DREAM.
HUH?
MASODIK'S DREAM. I'VE THOUGHT THAT FOR A WHILE.
LET'S PUT IT TO THE TEST. C'MON!

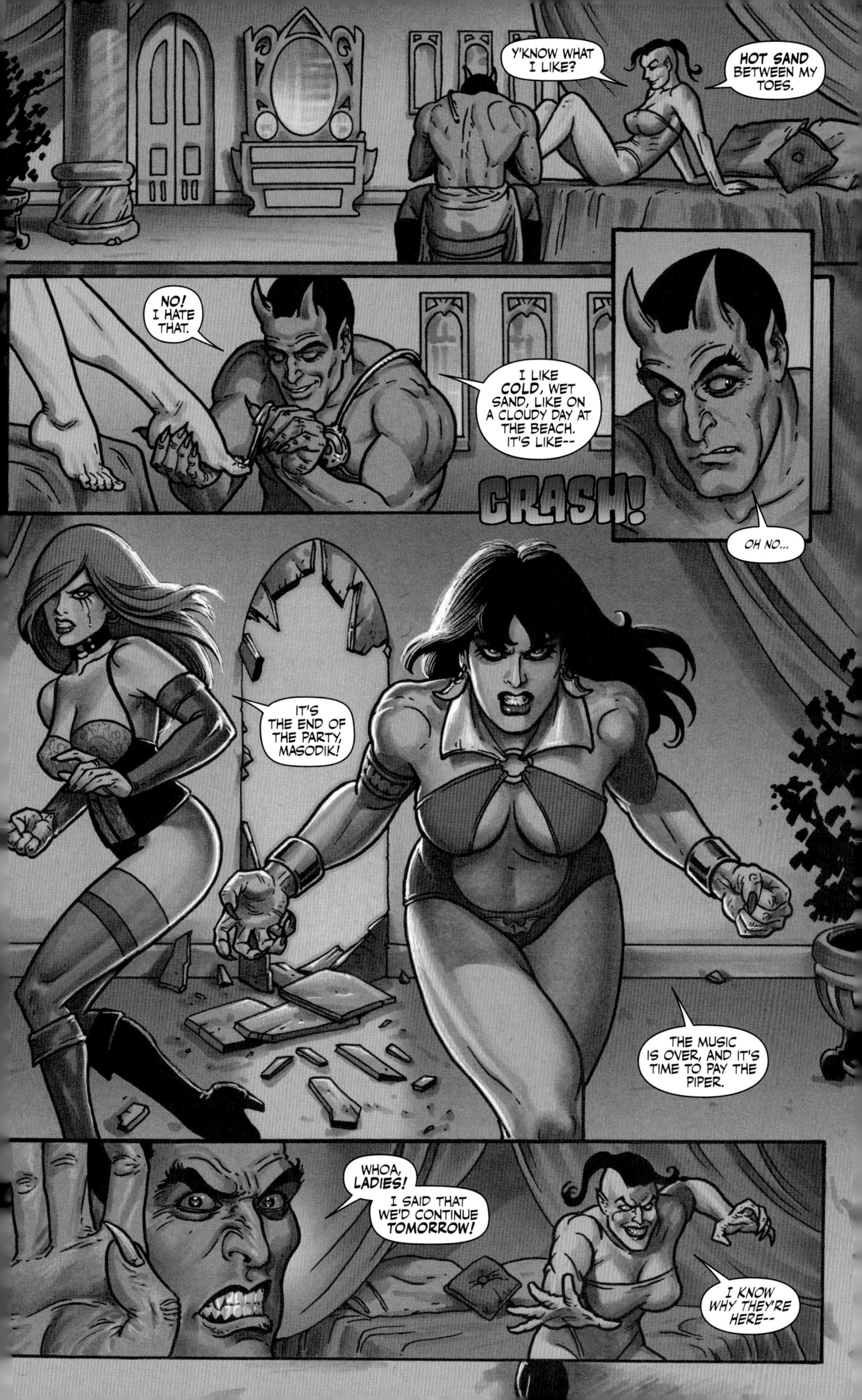
Y'KNOW WHAT I LIKE?
HOT SAND BETWEEN MY TOES.
NO! I HATE THAT.
I LIKE COLD, WET SAND, LIKE ON A CLOUDY DAY AT THE BEACH. IT'S LIKE--
CRASH!
OH NO...
IT'S THE END OF THE PARTY, MASODIK!
THE MUSIC IS OVER, AND IT'S TIME TO PAY THE PIPER.
WHOA, LADIES! I SAID THAT WE'D CONTINUE TOMORROW!
I KNOW WHY THEY'RE HERE--

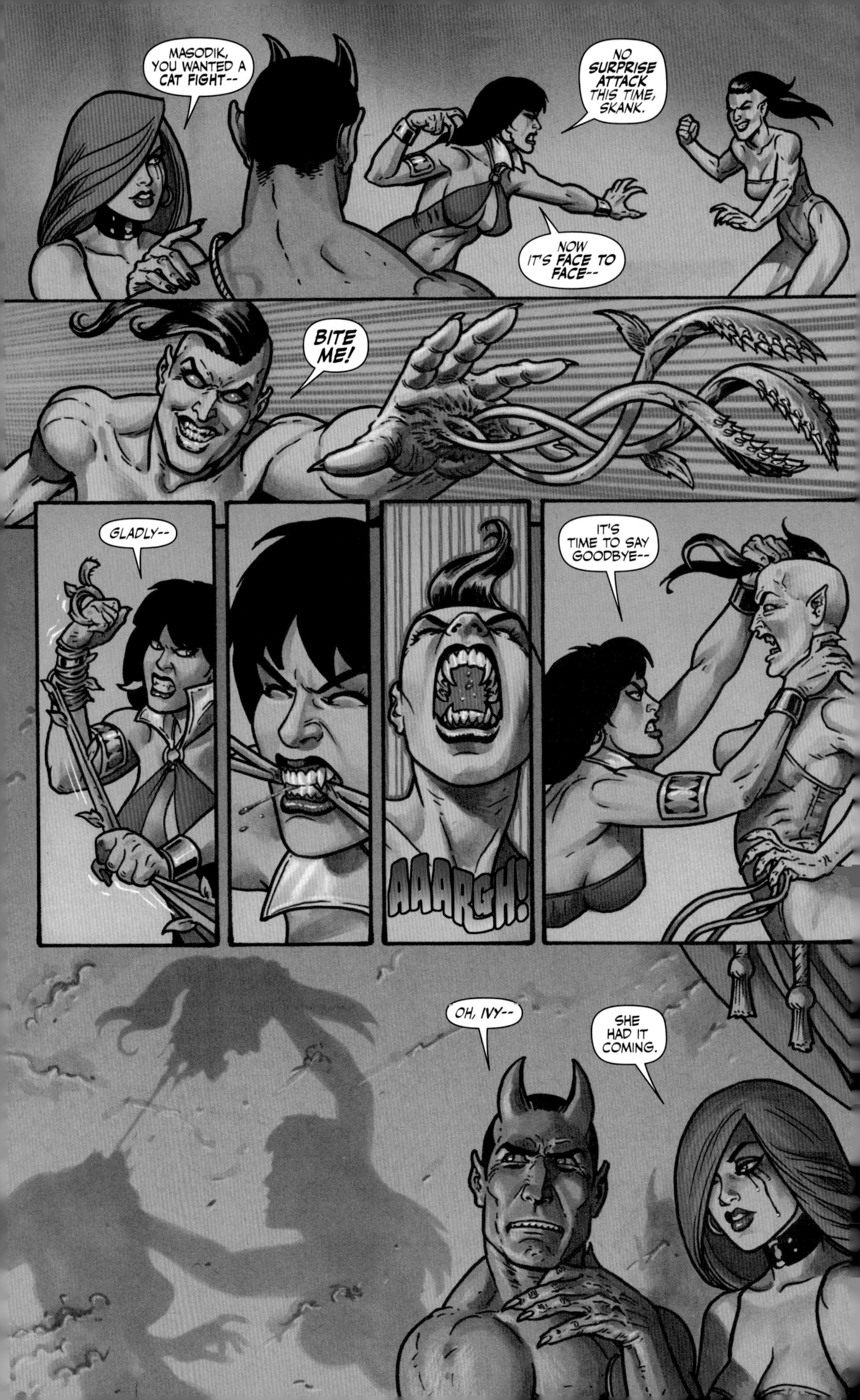
MASODIK, YOU WANTED A CAT FIGHT--
NO SURPRISE ATTACK THIS TIME, SKANK.
NOW IT'S FACE TO FACE--
BITE ME!
GLADLY--
AAARGH!
IT'S TIME TO SAY GOODBYE--
OH, IVY--
SHE HAD IT COMING.

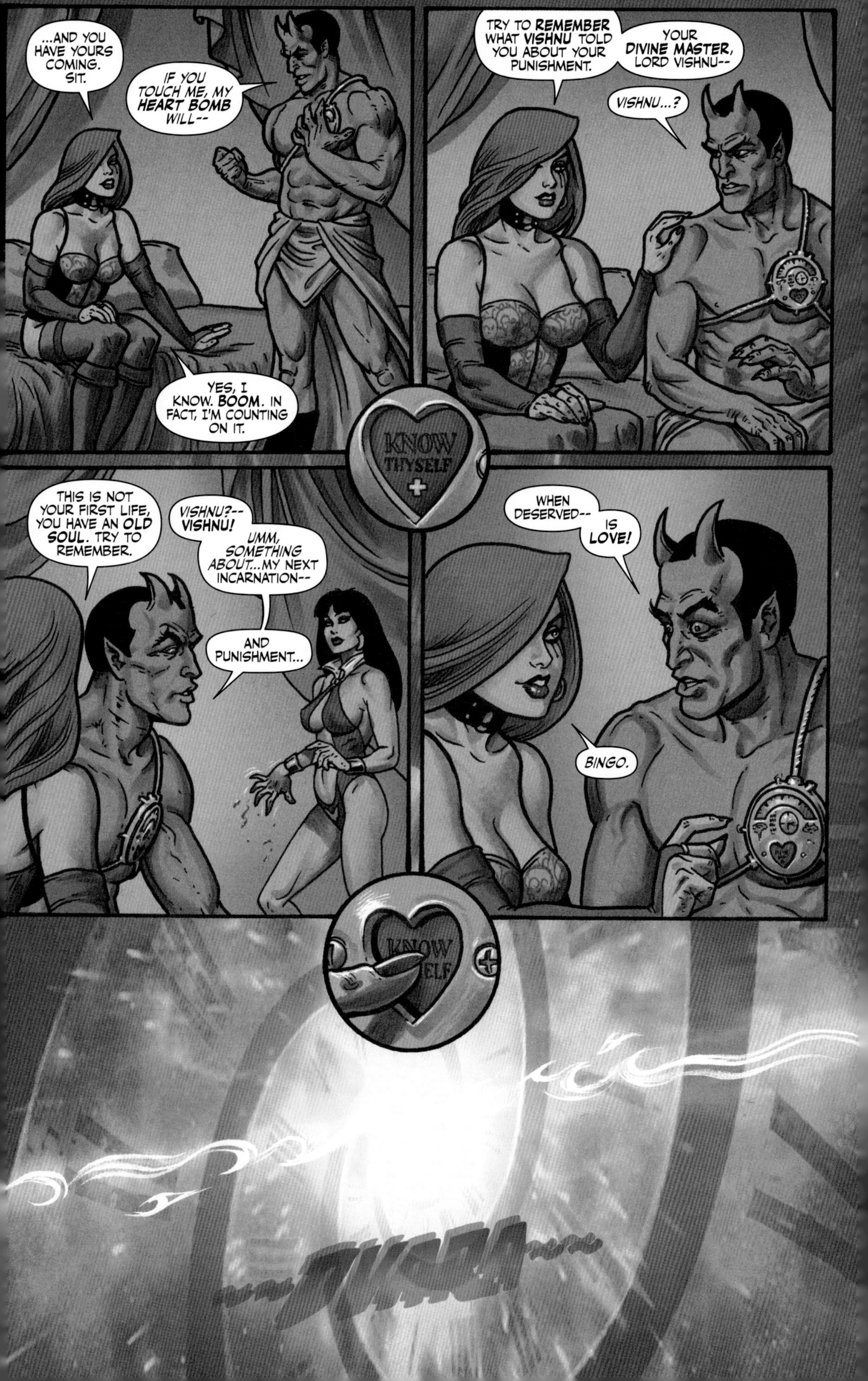
...AND YOU HAVE YOURS COMING. SIT.
IF YOU TOUCH ME, MY HEART BOMB WILL--
YES, I KNOW. BOOM. IN FACT, I'M COUNTING ON IT.
TRY TO REMEMBER WHAT VISHNU TOLD YOU ABOUT YOUR PUNISHMENT.
YOUR DIVINE MASTER, LORD VISHNU--
VISHNU...?
KNOW THYSELF
THIS IS NOT YOUR FIRST LIFE, YOU HAVE AN OLD SOUL. TRY TO REMEMBER.
VISHNU?-- VISHNU!
UMM, SOMETHING ABOUT...MY NEXT INCARNATION--
AND PUNISHMENT...
WHEN DESERVED--
IS LOVE!
BINGO.

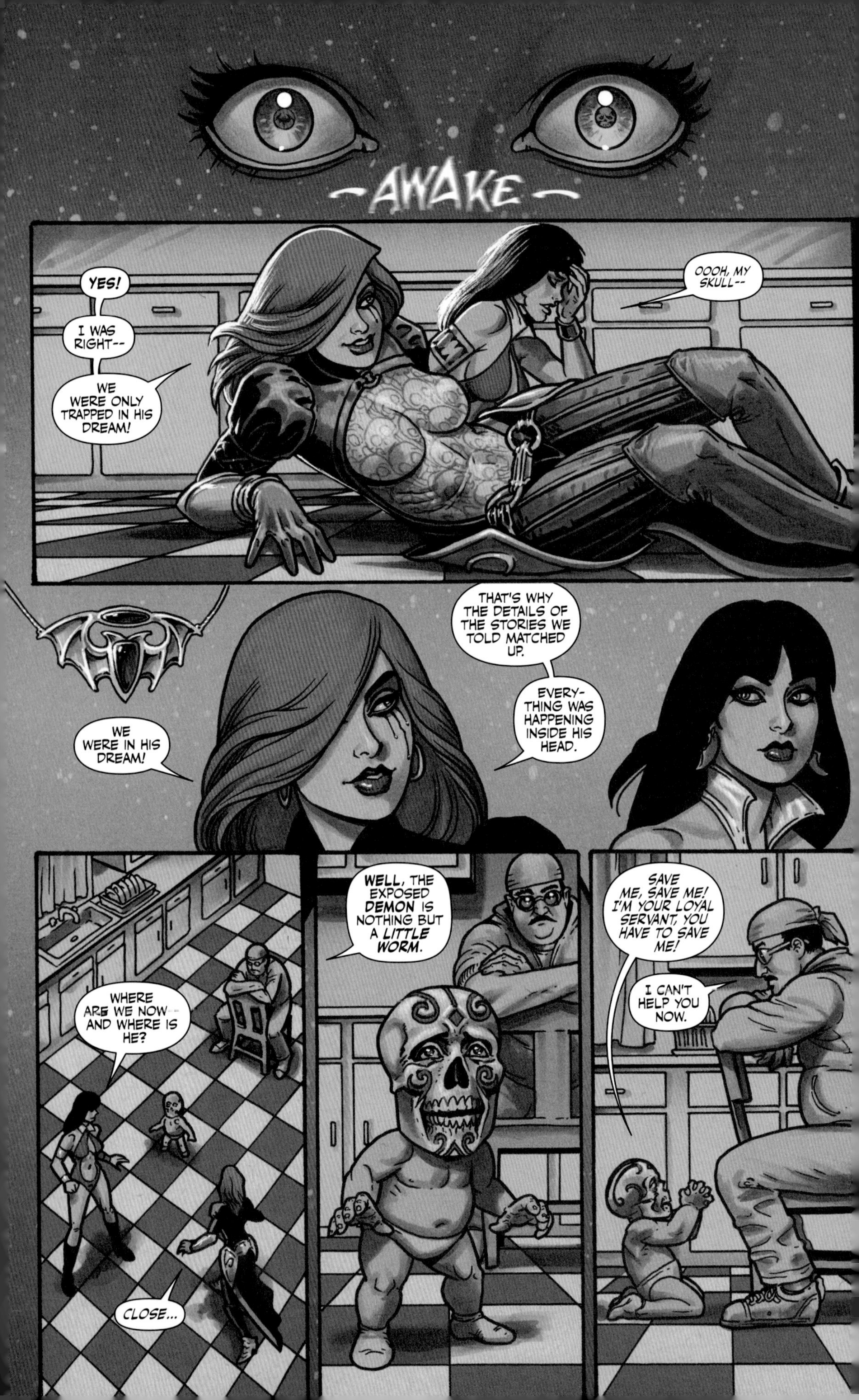
-AWAKE-
YES!
I WAS RIGHT--
WE WERE ONLY TRAPPED IN HIS DREAM!
OOOH, MY SKULL--
WE WERE IN HIS DREAM!
THAT'S WHY THE DETAILS OF THE STORIES WE TOLD MATCHED UP.
EVERY-THING WAS HAPPENING INSIDE HIS HEAD.
WHERE ARE WE NOW AND WHERE IS HE?
CLOSE...
WELL, THE EXPOSED DEMON IS NOTHING BUT A LITTLE WORM.
SAVE ME, SAVE ME! I'M YOUR LOYAL SERVANT, YOU HAVE TO SAVE ME!
I CAN'T HELP YOU NOW.

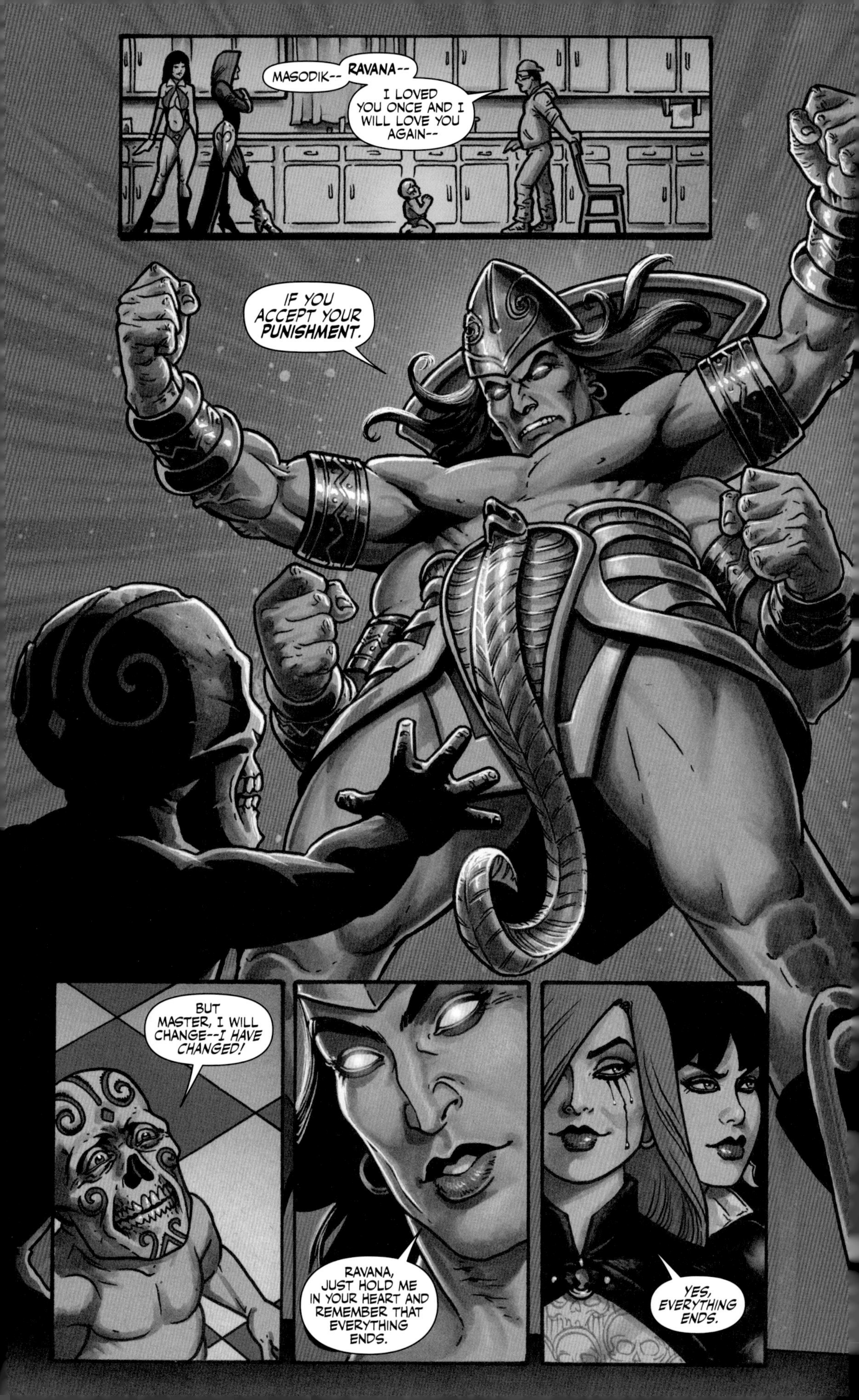
MASODIK--
RAVANA--
I LOVED YOU ONCE AND I WILL LOVE YOU AGAIN--
IF YOU ACCEPT YOUR PUNISHMENT.
BUT MASTER, I WILL CHANGE--I HAVE CHANGED!
RAVANA, JUST HOLD ME IN YOUR HEART AND REMEMBER THAT EVERYTHING ENDS.
YES, EVERYTHING ENDS.

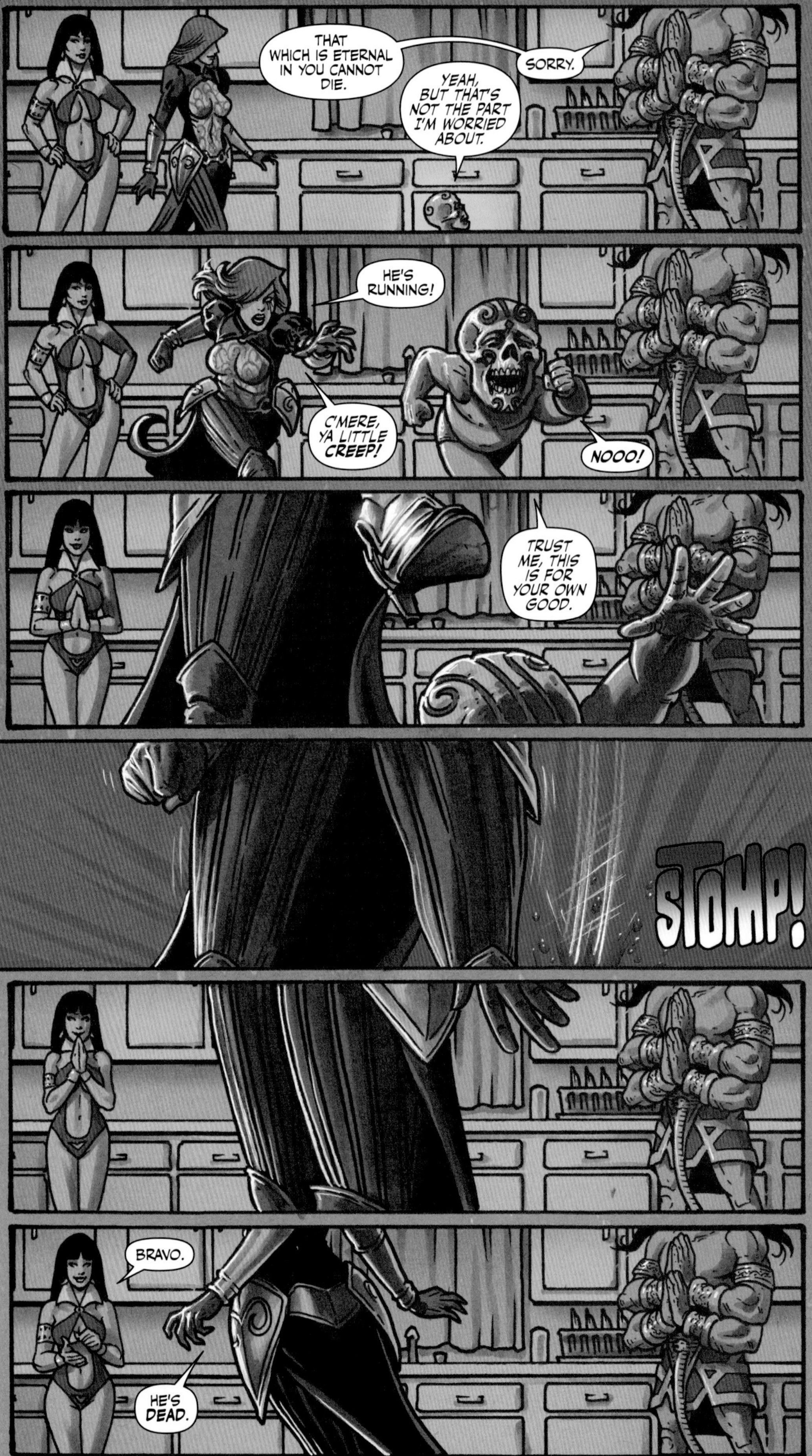
THAT WHICH IS ETERNAL IN YOU CANNOT DIE.
SORRY.
YEAH, BUT THAT'S NOT THE PART I'M WORRIED ABOUT.
HE'S RUNNING!
C'MERE, YA LITTLE CREEP!
NOOO!
TRUST ME, THIS IS FOR YOUR OWN GOOD.
STOMP!
BRAVO.
HE'S DEAD.

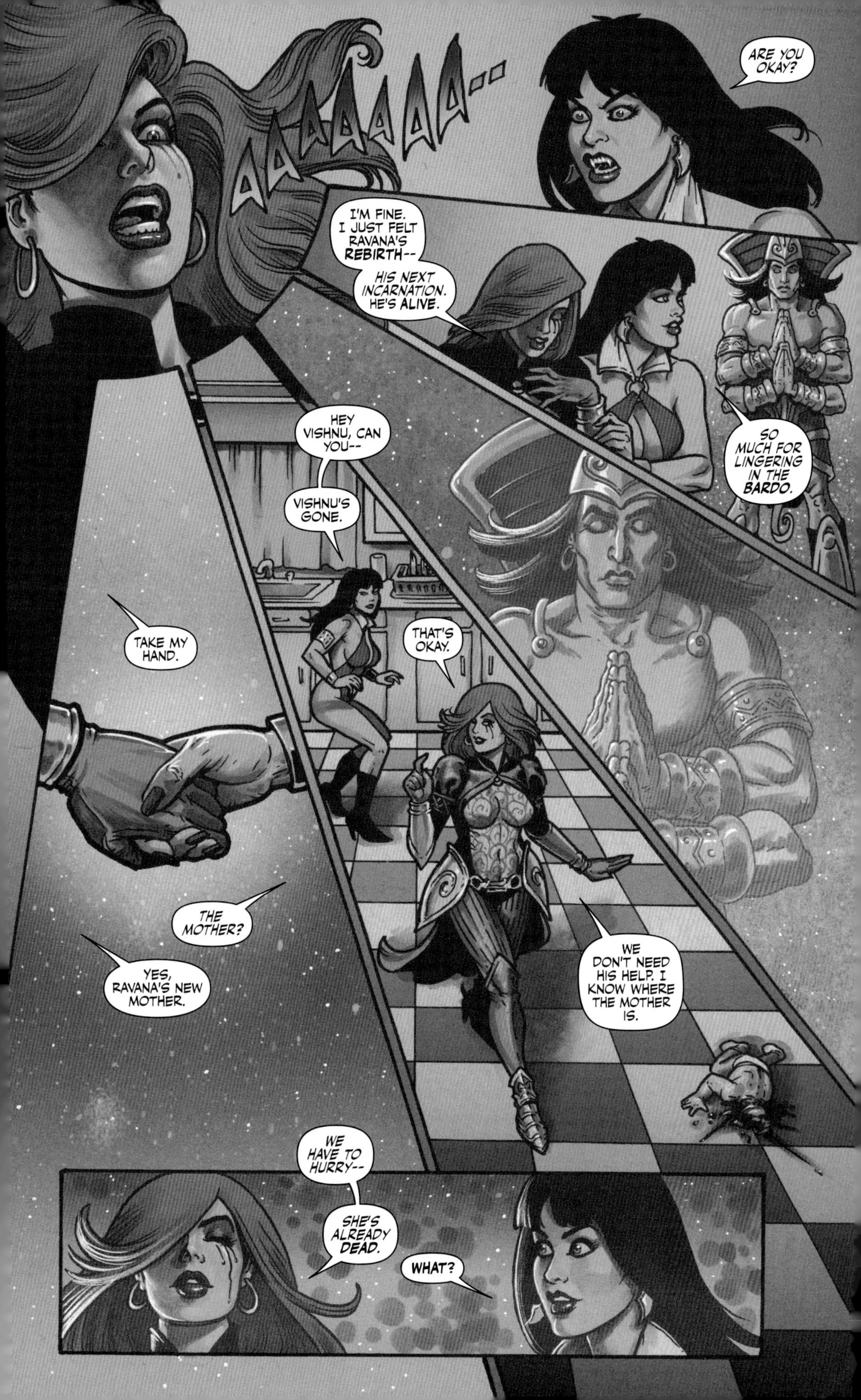
AAAAAAA--
ARE YOU OKAY?
I'M FINE. I JUST FELT RAVANA'S REBIRTH--
HIS NEXT INCARNATION. HE'S ALIVE.
SO MUCH FOR LINGERING IN THE BARDO.
HEY VISHNU, CAN YOU--
VISHNU'S GONE.
THAT'S OKAY.
WE DON'T NEED HIS HELP. I KNOW WHERE THE MOTHER IS.
TAKE MY HAND.
THE MOTHER?
YES, RAVANA'S NEW MOTHER.
WE HAVE TO HURRY--
SHE'S ALREADY DEAD.
WHAT?

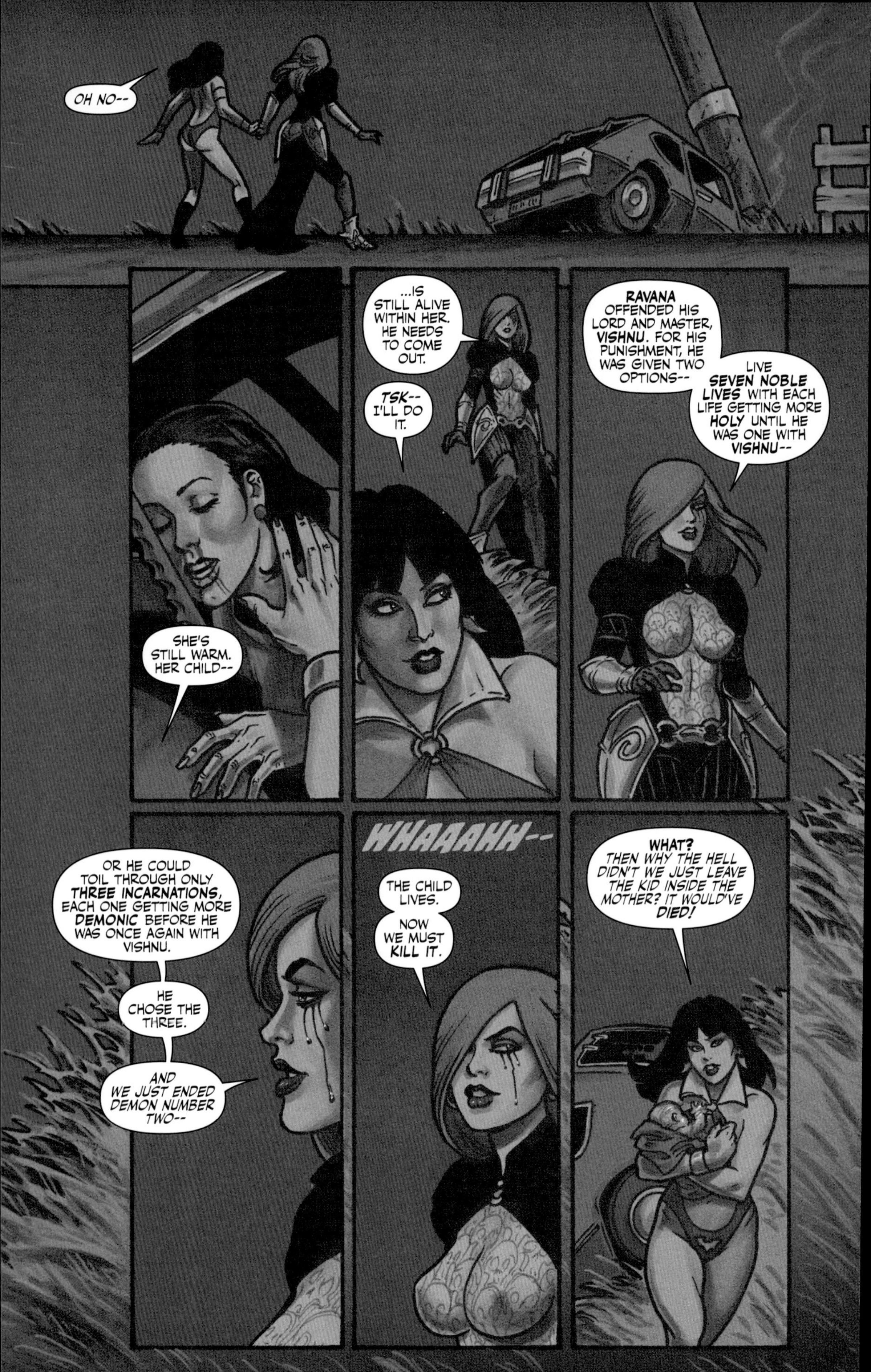
OH NO--
SHE'S STILL WARM. HER CHILD--
...IS STILL ALIVE WITHIN HER. HE NEEDS TO COME OUT.
TSK-- I'LL DO IT.
RAVANA OFFENDED HIS LORD AND MASTER, VISHNU. FOR HIS PUNISHMENT, HE WAS GIVEN TWO OPTIONS--
LIVE SEVEN NOBLE LIVES WITH EACH LIFE GETTING MORE HOLY UNTIL HE WAS ONE WITH VISHNU--
OR HE COULD TOIL THROUGH ONLY THREE INCARNATIONS, EACH ONE GETTING MORE DEMONIC BEFORE HE WAS ONCE AGAIN WITH VISHNU.
HE CHOSE THE THREE.
AND WE JUST ENDED DEMON NUMBER TWO--
WHAAAHH--
THE CHILD LIVES.
NOW WE MUST KILL IT.
WHAT? THEN WHY THE HELL DIDN'T WE JUST LEAVE THE KID INSIDE THE MOTHER? IT WOULD'VE DIED!

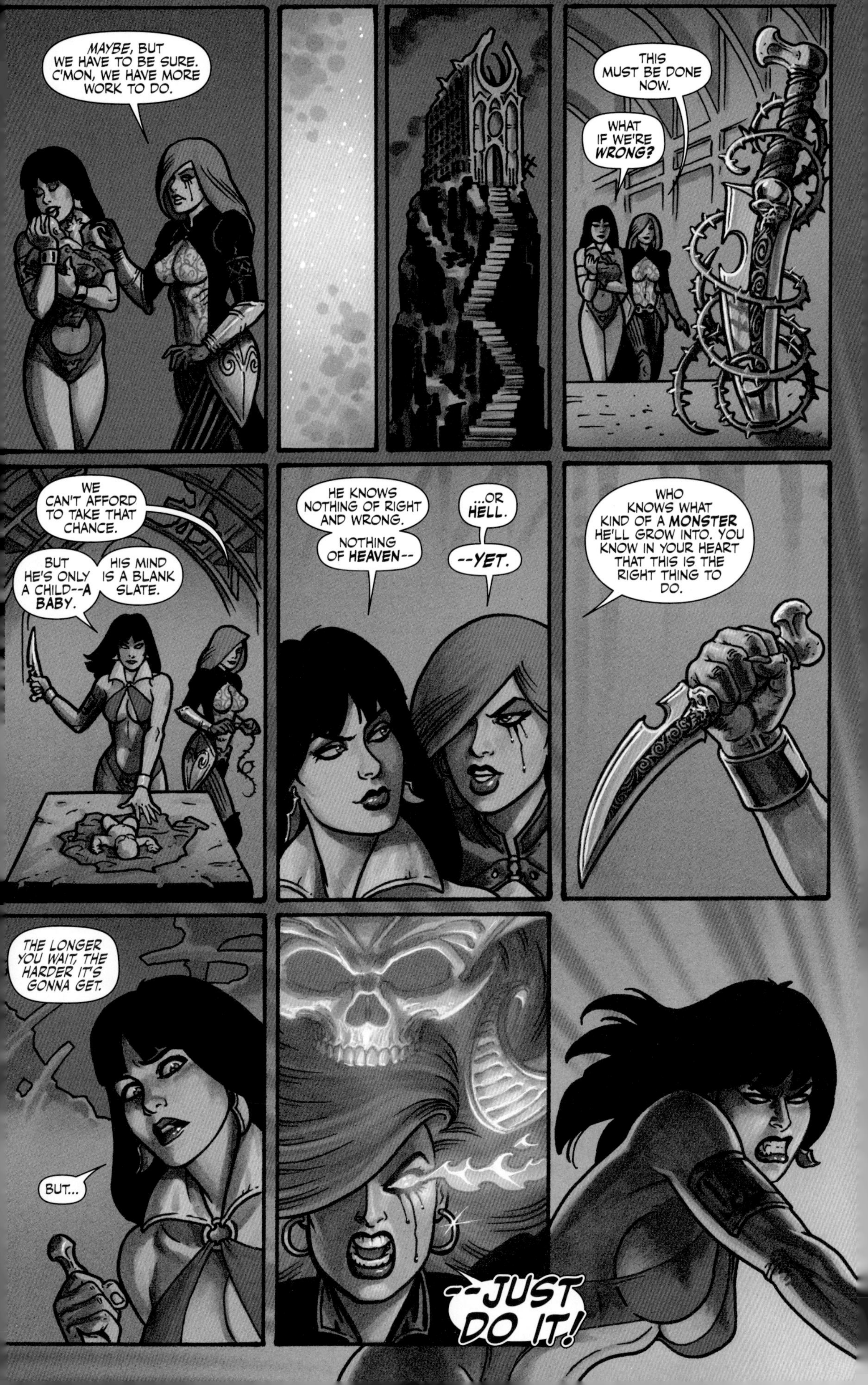
MAYBE, BUT WE HAVE TO BE SURE. C'MON, WE HAVE MORE WORK TO DO.
THIS MUST BE DONE NOW.
WHAT IF WE'RE WRONG?
WE CAN'T AFFORD TO TAKE THAT CHANCE.
BUT HE'S ONLY A CHILD--A BABY.
HIS MIND IS A BLANK SLATE.
HE KNOWS NOTHING OF RIGHT AND WRONG.
NOTHING OF HEAVEN--
...OR HELL.
--YET.
WHO KNOWS WHAT KIND OF A MONSTER HE'LL GROW INTO. YOU KNOW IN YOUR HEART THAT THIS IS THE RIGHT THING TO DO.
THE LONGER YOU WAIT, THE HARDER IT'S GONNA GET.
BUT...
--JUST DO IT!

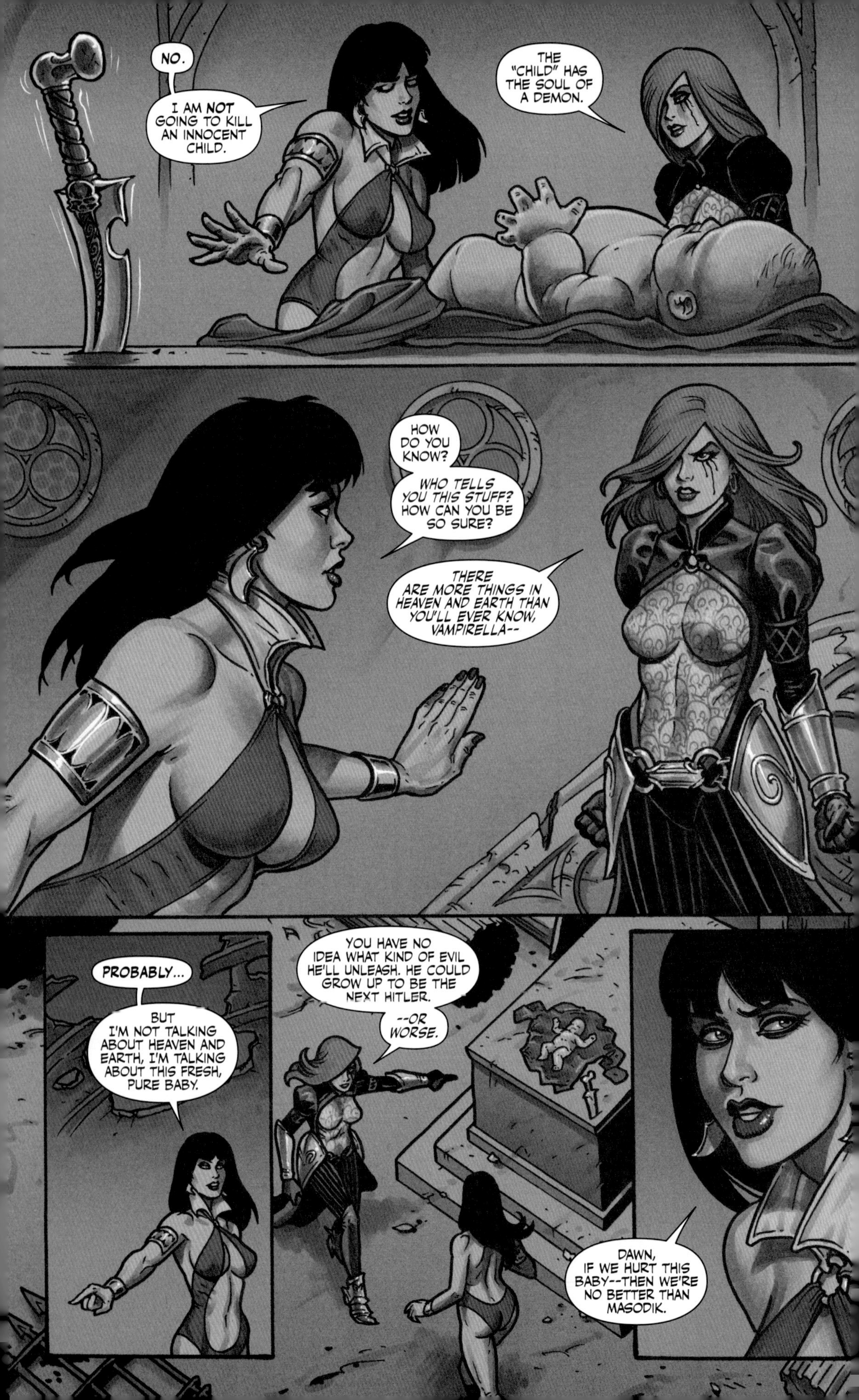
NO.
I AM NOT GOING TO KILL AN INNOCENT CHILD.
THE "CHILD" HAS THE SOUL OF A DEMON.
HOW DO YOU KNOW?
WHO TELLS YOU THIS STUFF? HOW CAN YOU BE SO SURE?
THERE ARE MORE THINGS IN HEAVEN AND EARTH THAN YOU'LL EVER KNOW, VAMPIRELLA--
PROBABLY...
BUT I'M NOT TALKING ABOUT HEAVEN AND EARTH, I'M TALKING ABOUT THIS FRESH, PURE BABY.
YOU HAVE NO IDEA WHAT KIND OF EVIL HE'LL UNLEASH. HE COULD GROW UP TO BE THE NEXT HITLER.
--OR WORSE.
DAWN, IF WE HURT THIS BABY--THEN WE'RE NO BETTER THAN MASODIK.

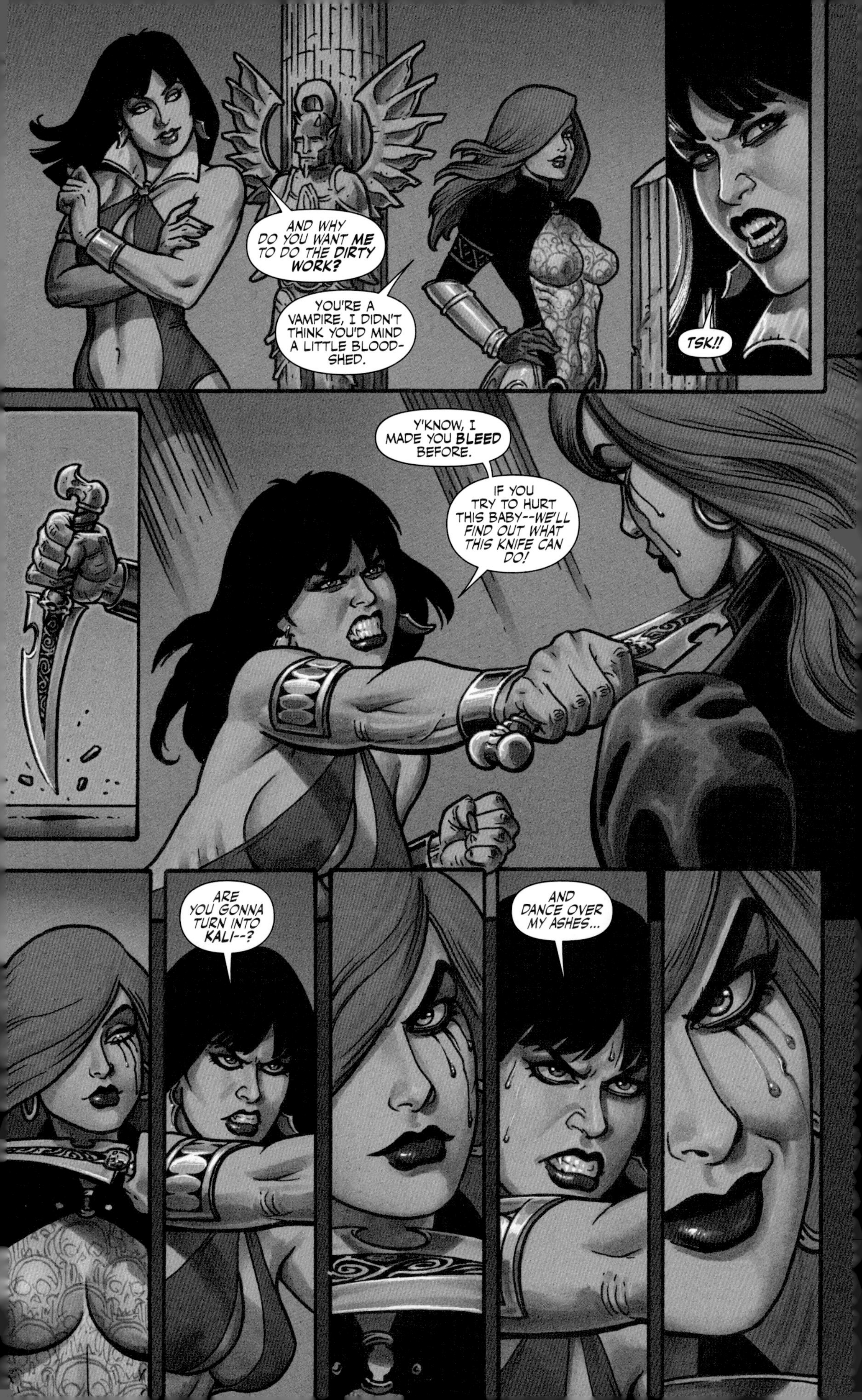
AND WHY DO YOU WANT ME TO DO THE DIRTY WORK?
YOU'RE A VAMPIRE, I DIDN'T THINK YOU'D MIND A LITTLE BLOOD-SHED.
TSK!!
Y'KNOW, I MADE YOU BLEED BEFORE.
IF YOU TRY TO HURT THIS BABY--WE'LL FIND OUT WHAT THIS KNIFE CAN DO!
ARE YOU GONNA TURN INTO KALI--?
AND DANCE OVER MY ASHES...

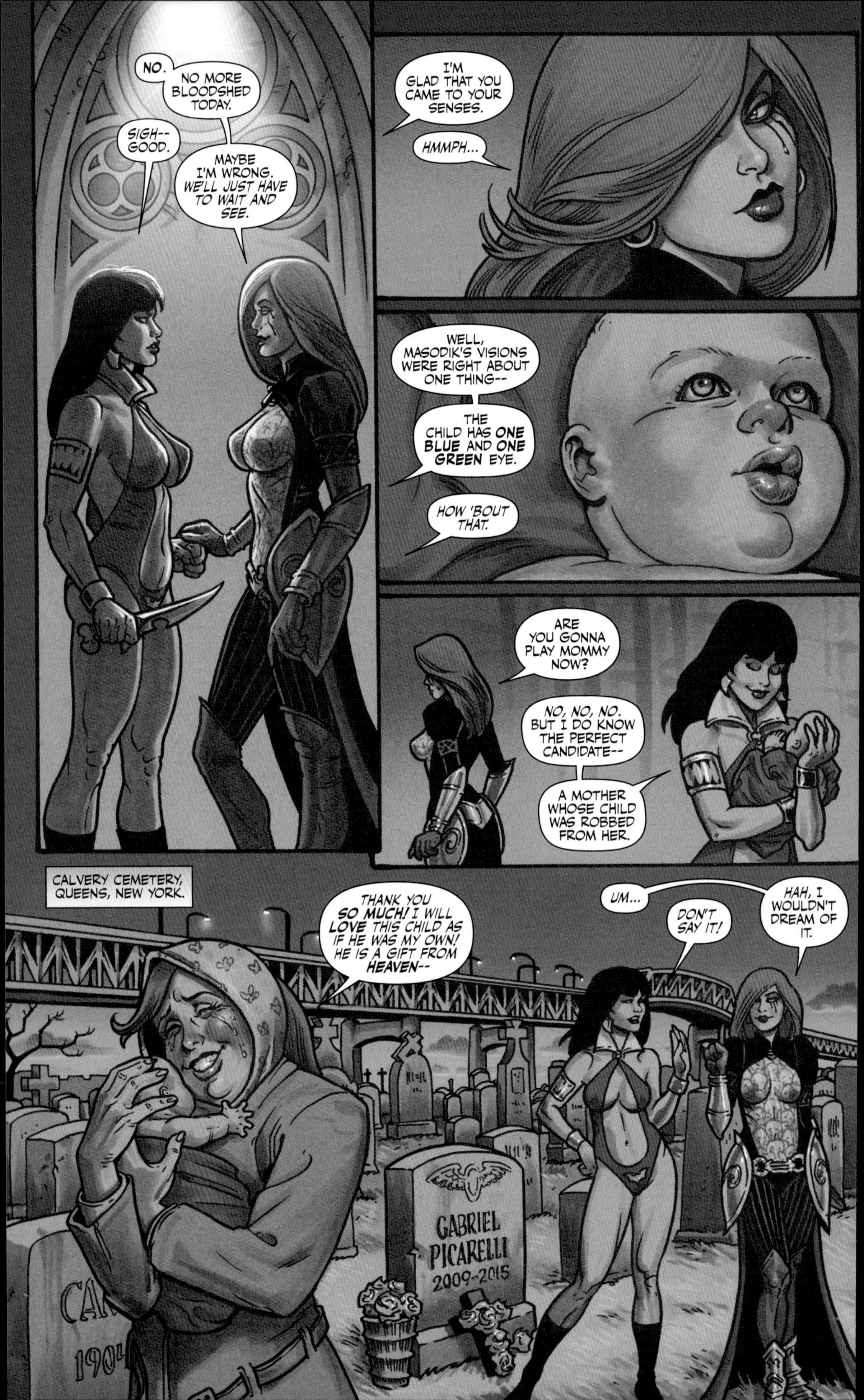
NO.
NO MORE BLOODSHED TODAY.
SIGH-- GOOD.
MAYBE I'M WRONG. WE'LL JUST HAVE TO WAIT AND SEE.
I'M GLAD THAT YOU CAME TO YOUR SENSES.
HMMPH...
WELL, MASODIK'S VISIONS WERE RIGHT ABOUT ONE THING--
THE CHILD HAS ONE BLUE AND ONE GREEN EYE.
HOW 'BOUT THAT.
ARE YOU GONNA PLAY MOMMY NOW?
NO, NO, NO. BUT I DO KNOW THE PERFECT CANDIDATE--
A MOTHER WHOSE CHILD WAS ROBBED FROM HER.
CALVERY CEMETERY, QUEENS, NEW YORK.
THANK YOU SO MUCH! I WILL LOVE THIS CHILD AS IF HE WAS MY OWN! HE IS A GIFT FROM HEAVEN--
UM...
DON'T SAY IT!
HAH, I WOULDN'T DREAM OF IT.
GABRIEL PICARELLI 2009-2015

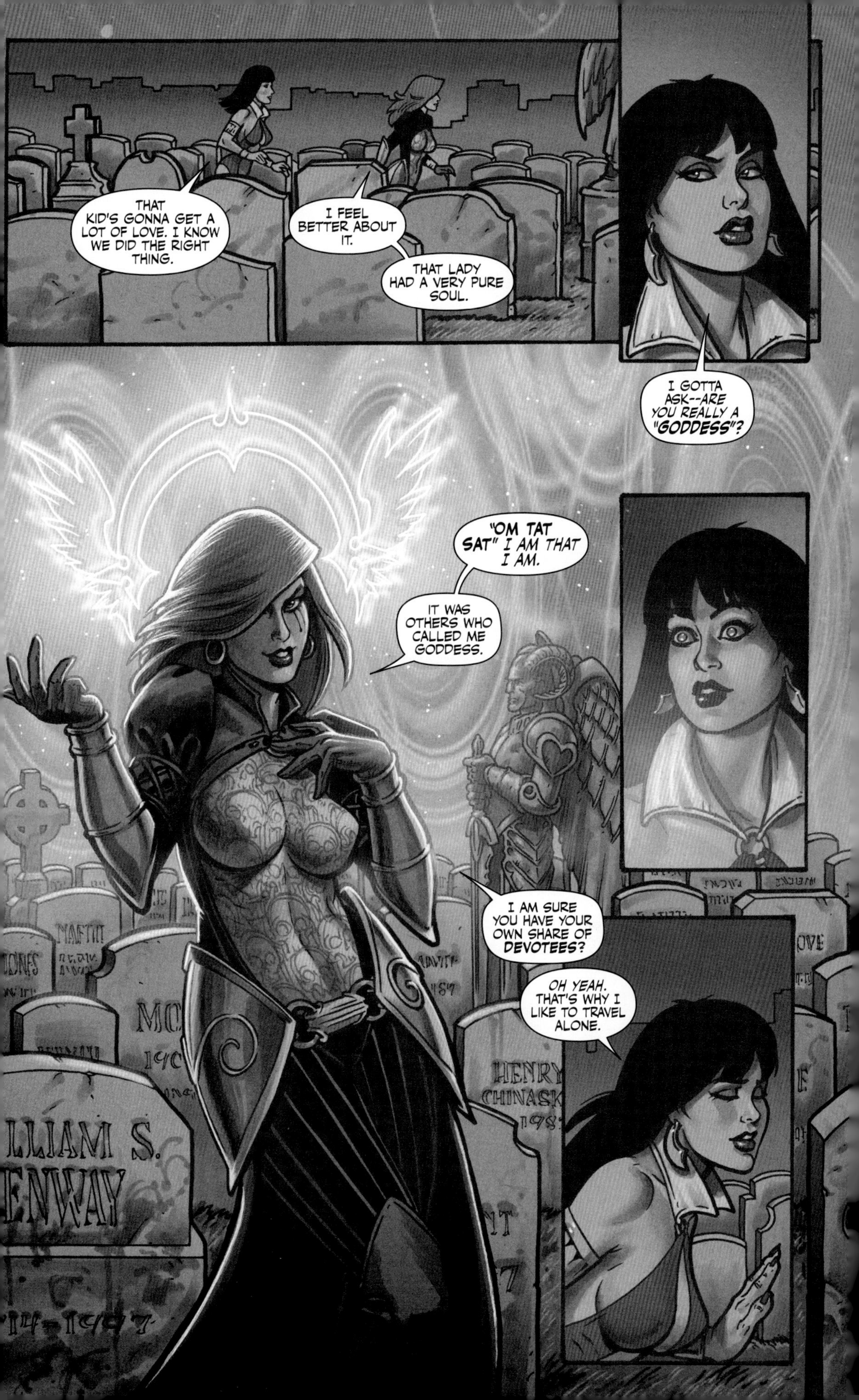
THAT KID'S GONNA GET A LOT OF LOVE. I KNOW WE DID THE RIGHT THING.
I FEEL BETTER ABOUT IT.
THAT LADY HAD A VERY PURE SOUL.
I GOTTA ASK--ARE YOU REALLY A "GODDESS"?
"OM TAT SAT" I AM THAT I AM.
IT WAS OTHERS WHO CALLED ME GODDESS.
I AM SURE YOU HAVE YOUR OWN SHARE OF DEVOTEES?
OH YEAH. THAT'S WHY I LIKE TO TRAVEL ALONE.
HENRY CHINASK
LLIAM S. ENWAY

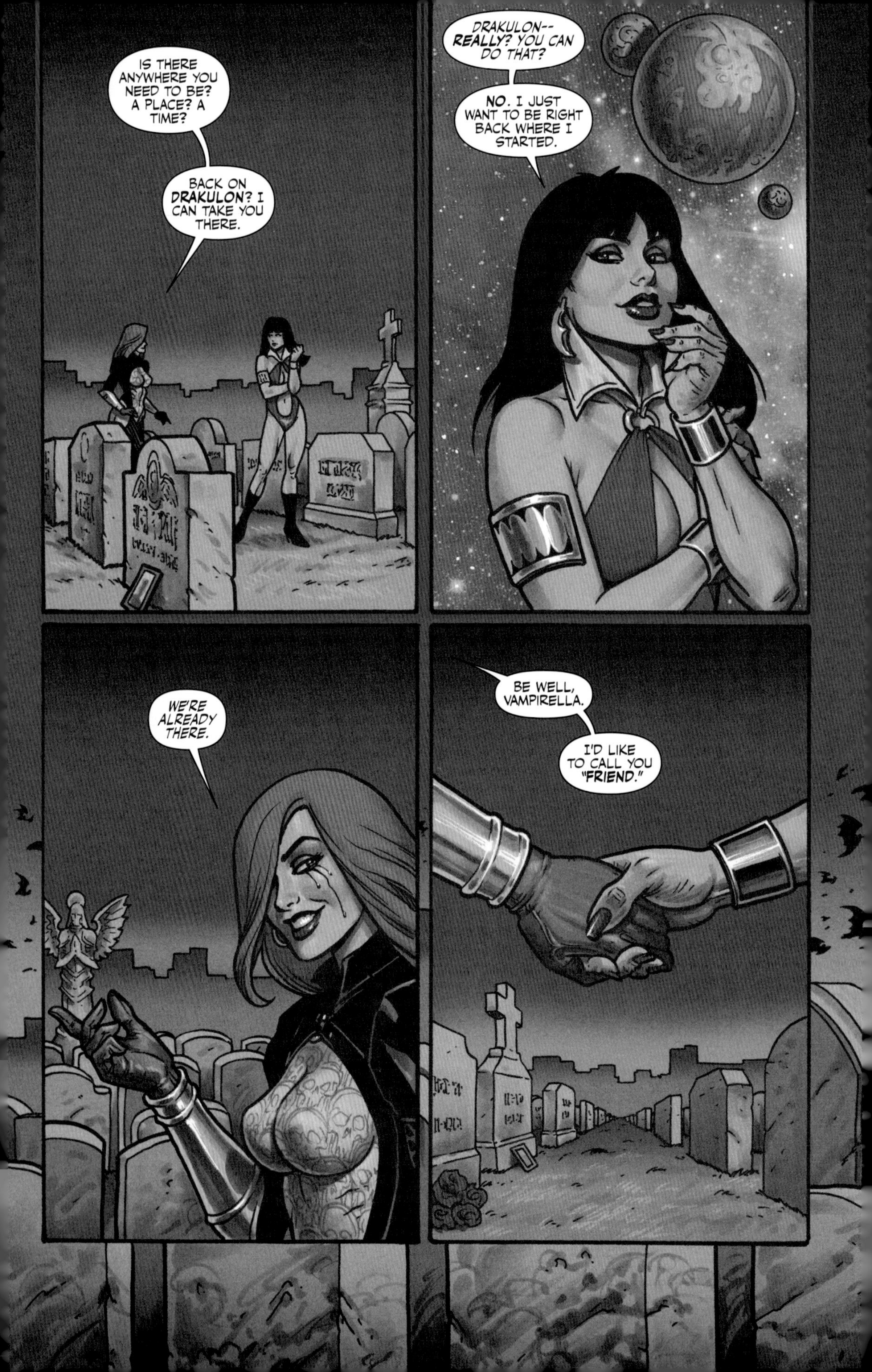
IS THERE ANYWHERE YOU NEED TO BE? A PLACE? A TIME?
BACK ON DRAKULON? I CAN TAKE YOU THERE.
DRAKULON-- REALLY? YOU CAN DO THAT?
NO. I JUST WANT TO BE RIGHT BACK WHERE I STARTED.
WE'RE ALREADY THERE.
BE WELL, VAMPIRELLA.
I'D LIKE TO CALL YOU "FRIEND."

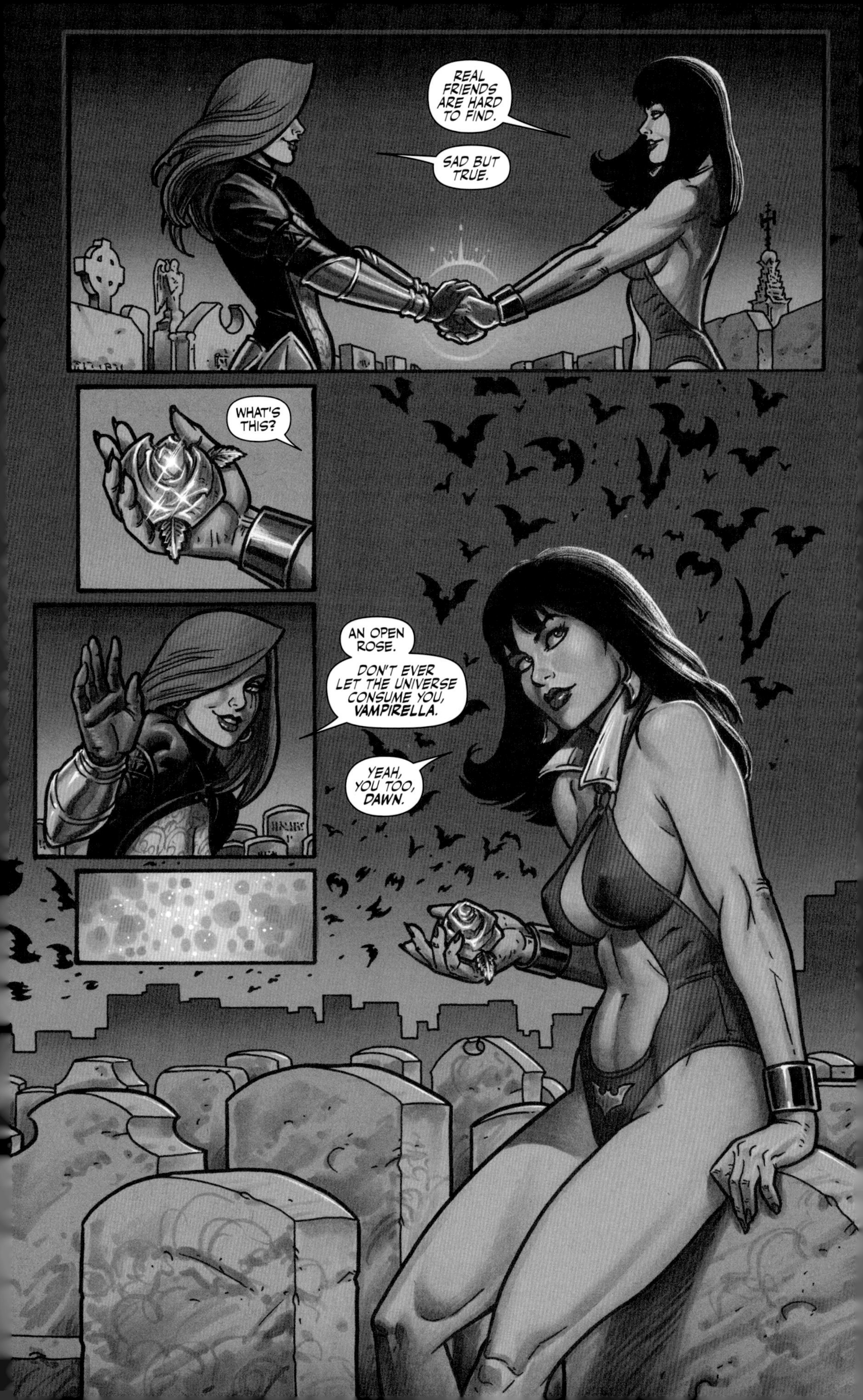
REAL FRIENDS ARE HARD TO FIND.
SAD BUT TRUE.
WHAT'S THIS?
AN OPEN ROSE.
DON'T EVER LET THE UNIVERSE CONSUME YOU, **VAMPIRELLA.**
YEAH, YOU TOO, **DAWN.**

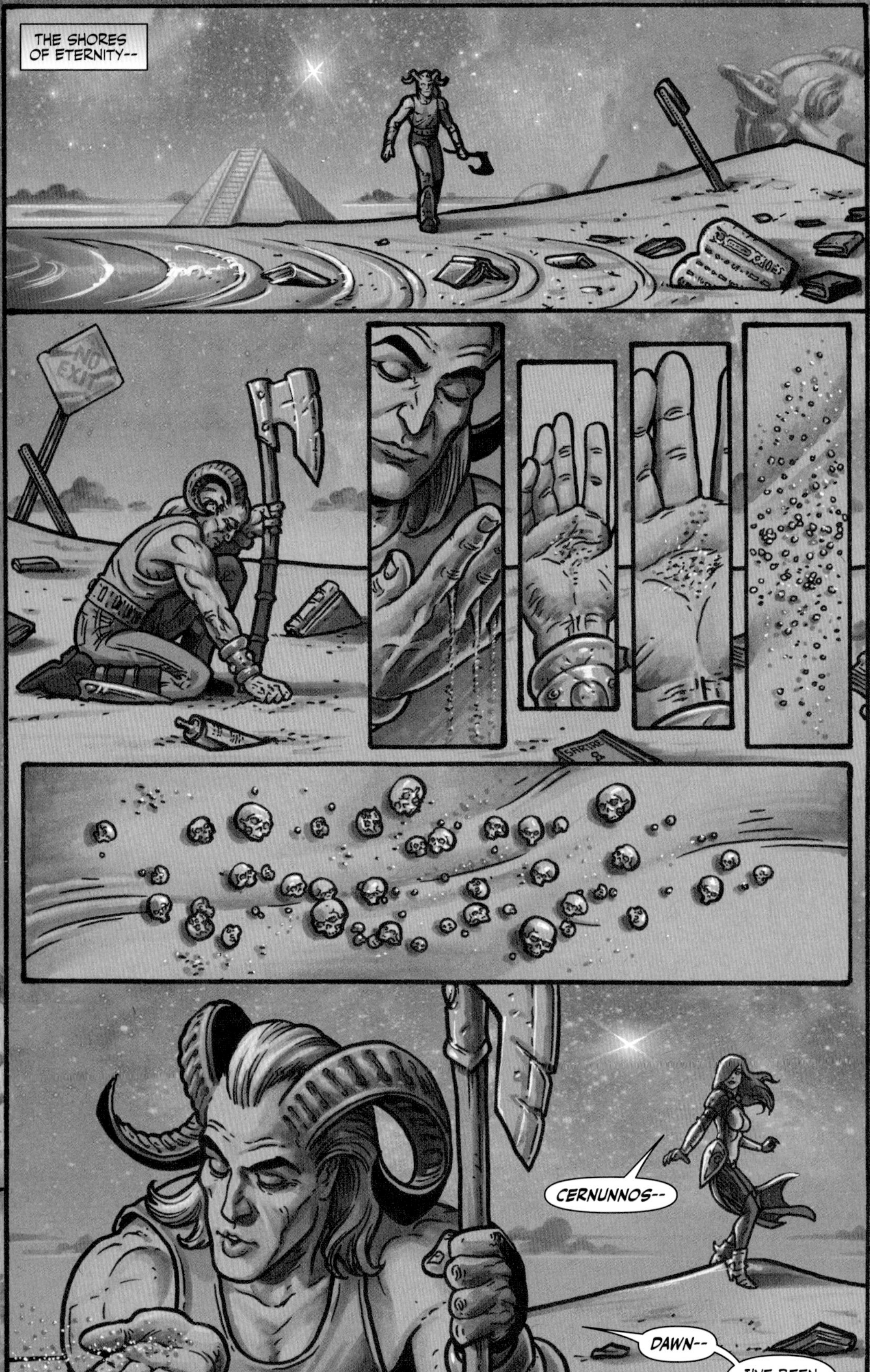
THE SHORES OF ETERNITY--
CERNUNNOS--
DAWN--
I'VE BEEN WAITING FOR YOU.

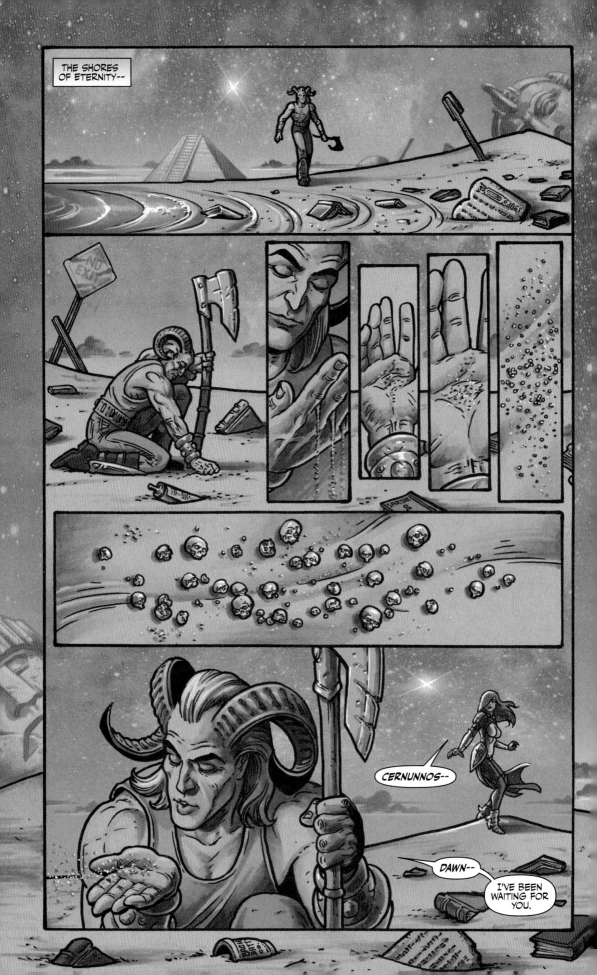

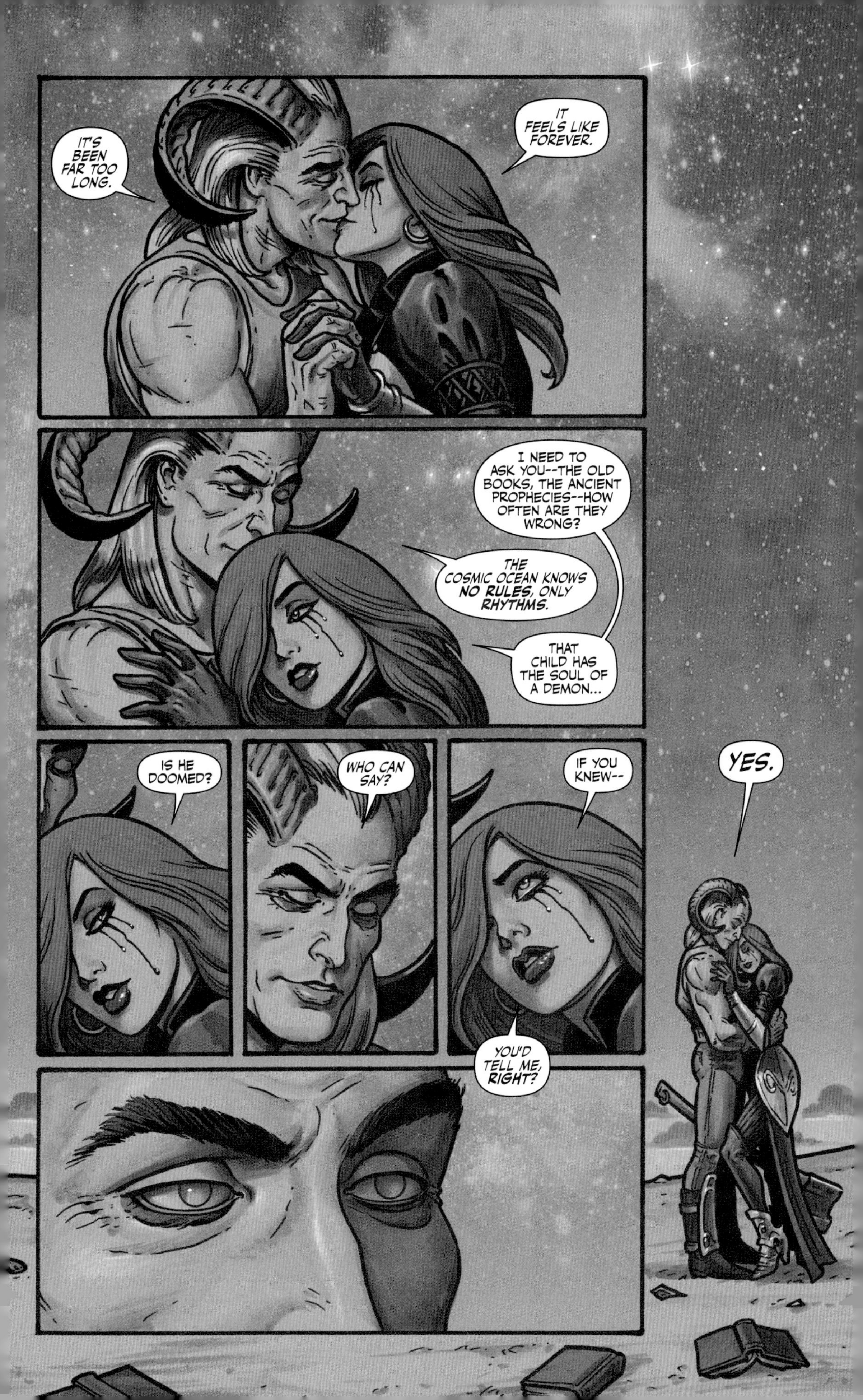
IT'S BEEN FAR TOO LONG.
IT FEELS LIKE FOREVER.
I NEED TO ASK YOU--THE OLD BOOKS, THE ANCIENT PROPHECIES--HOW OFTEN ARE THEY WRONG?
THE COSMIC OCEAN KNOWS NO RULES, ONLY RHYTHMS.
THAT CHILD HAS THE SOUL OF A DEMON...
IS HE DOOMED?
WHO CAN SAY?
IF YOU KNEW--
YOU'D TELL ME, RIGHT?
YES.

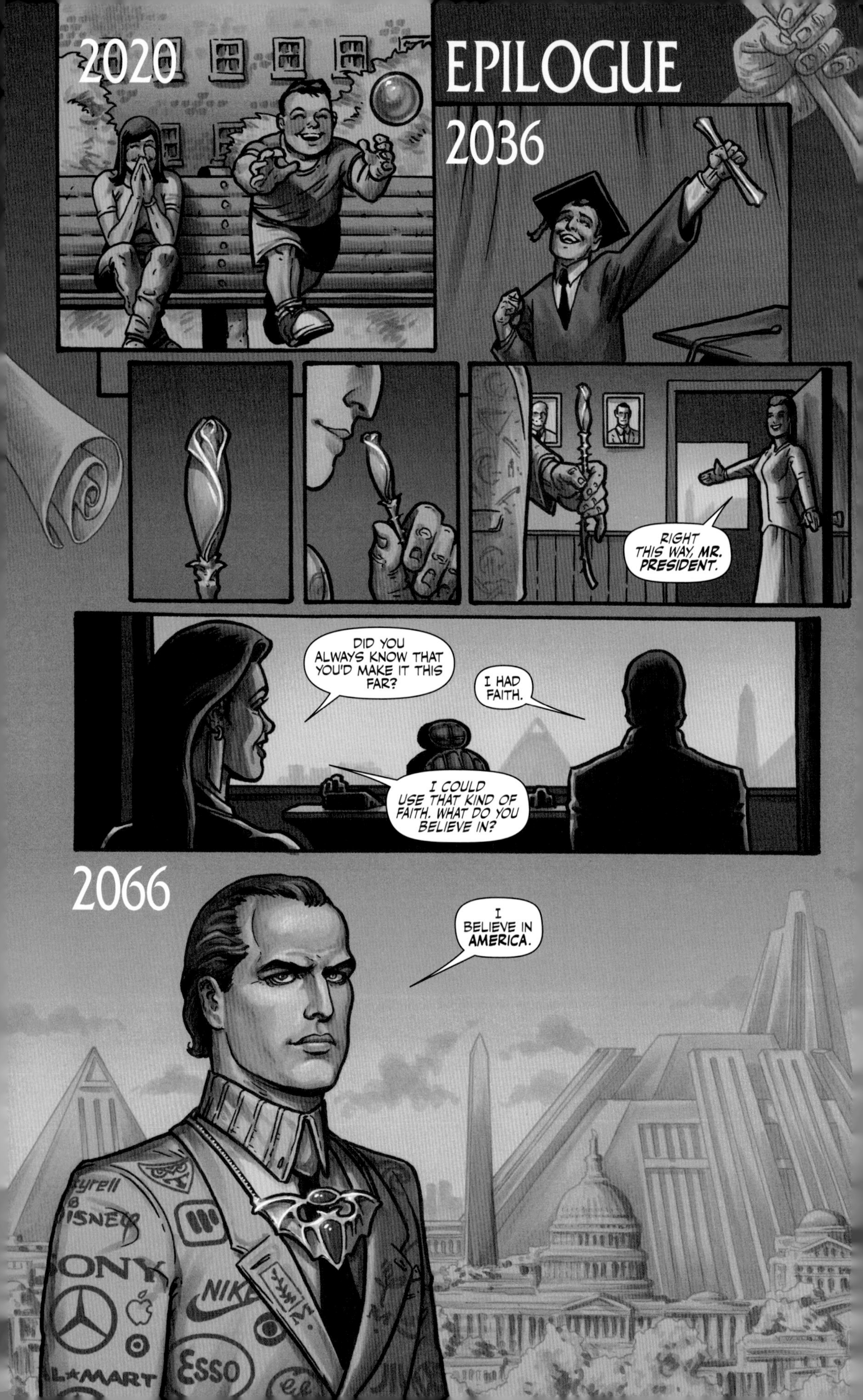
2020
EPILOGUE
2036
RIGHT THIS WAY, MR. PRESIDENT.
DID YOU ALWAYS KNOW THAT YOU'D MAKE IT THIS FAR?
I HAD FAITH.
I COULD USE THAT KIND OF FAITH. WHAT DO YOU BELIEVE IN?
2066
I BELIEVE IN AMERICA.
SONY
NIKE
ESSO

DAWN · VAMPIRELLA
SUPPLEMENTAL SECTION

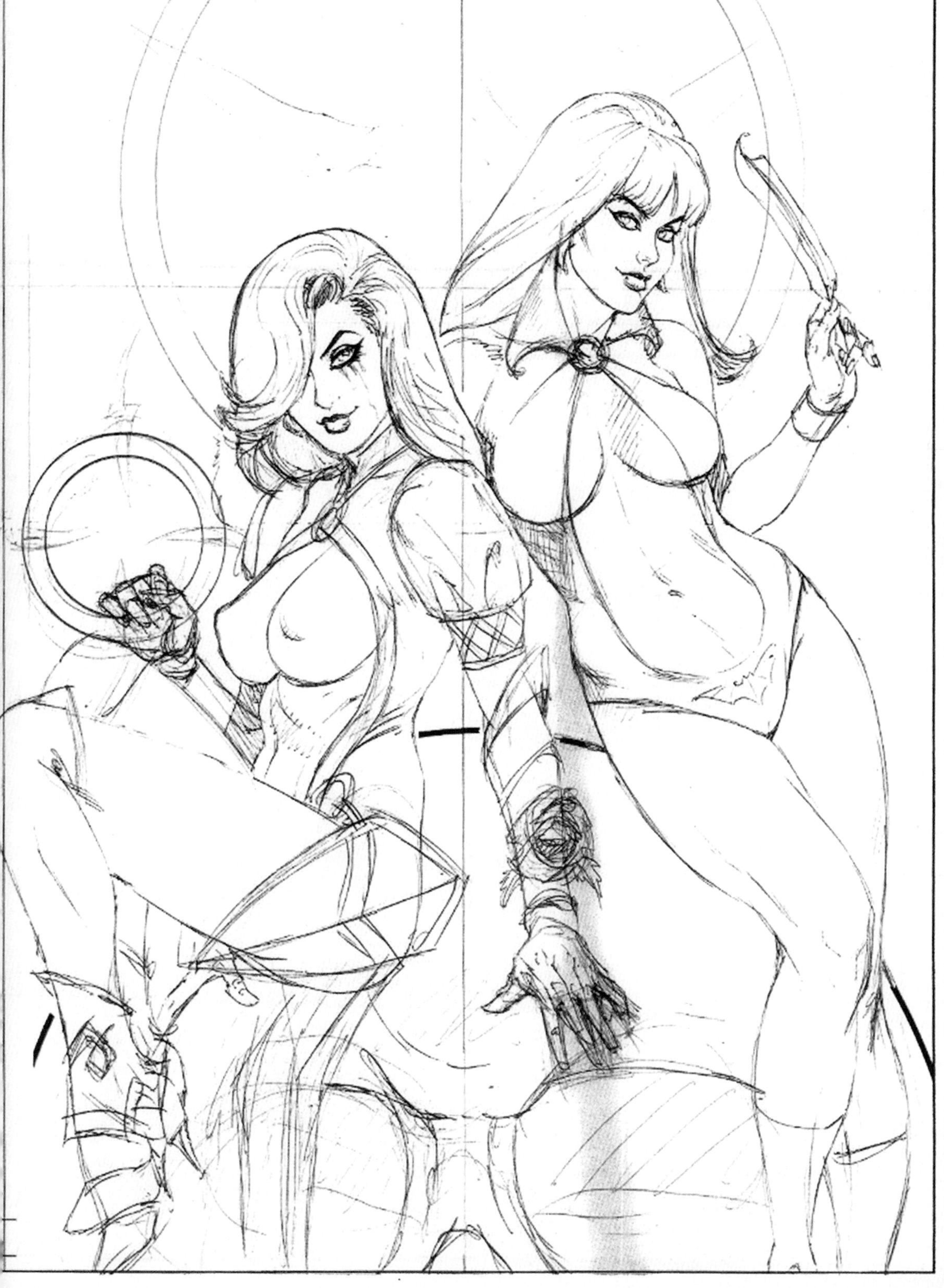

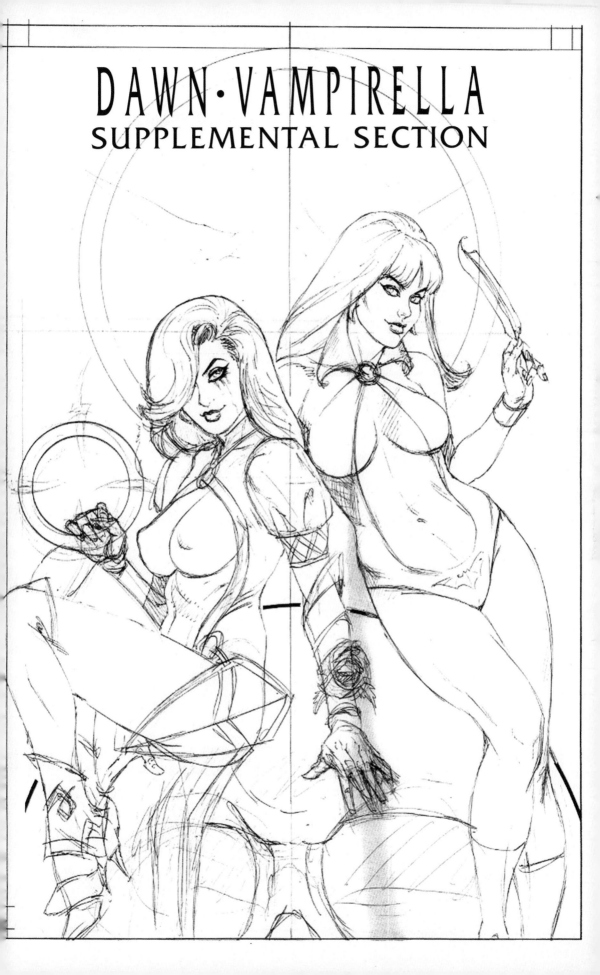

It's tough sharing a stage.

Dawn is usually the star of her own show, front row and center, but on these covers, I knew she'd have to move over.

It was a nice challenge.

Hands and arms were constantly being redrawn and shifted in an attempt to get both divas to look fabulous at all times.

A few of the best, most iconic poses from the story pages were reworked into variant covers.

Whenever possibly, I tried to 're-do' images from the ground up so that it would have some visual integrity of its own.

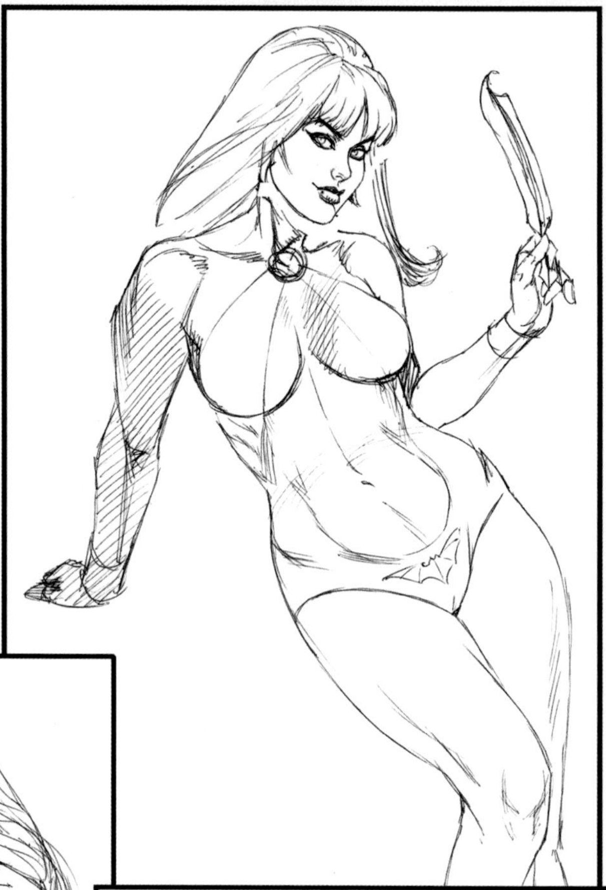

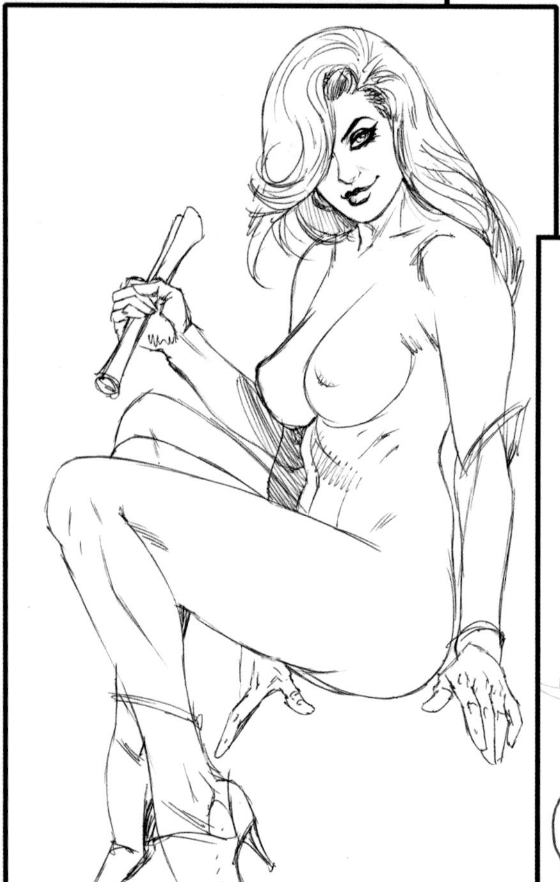

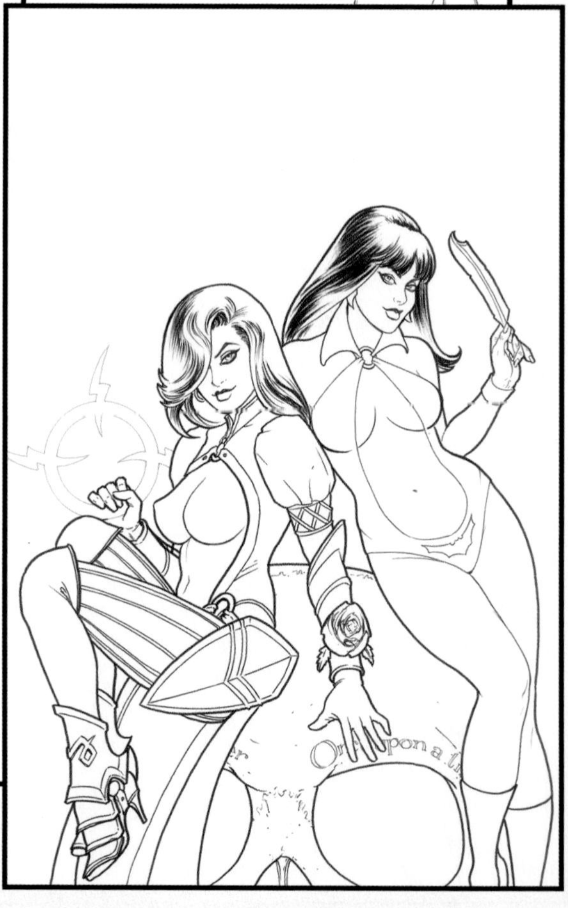

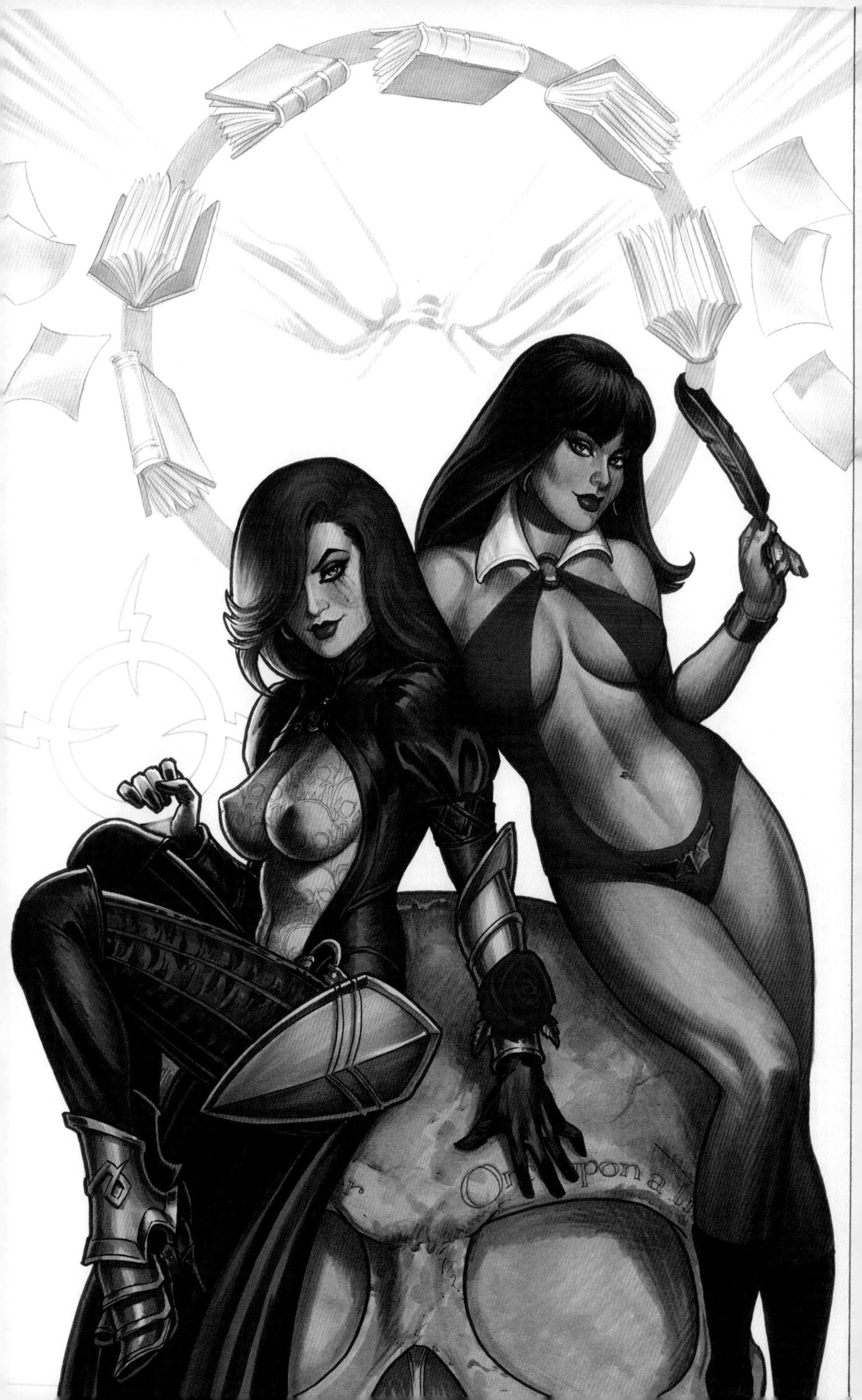

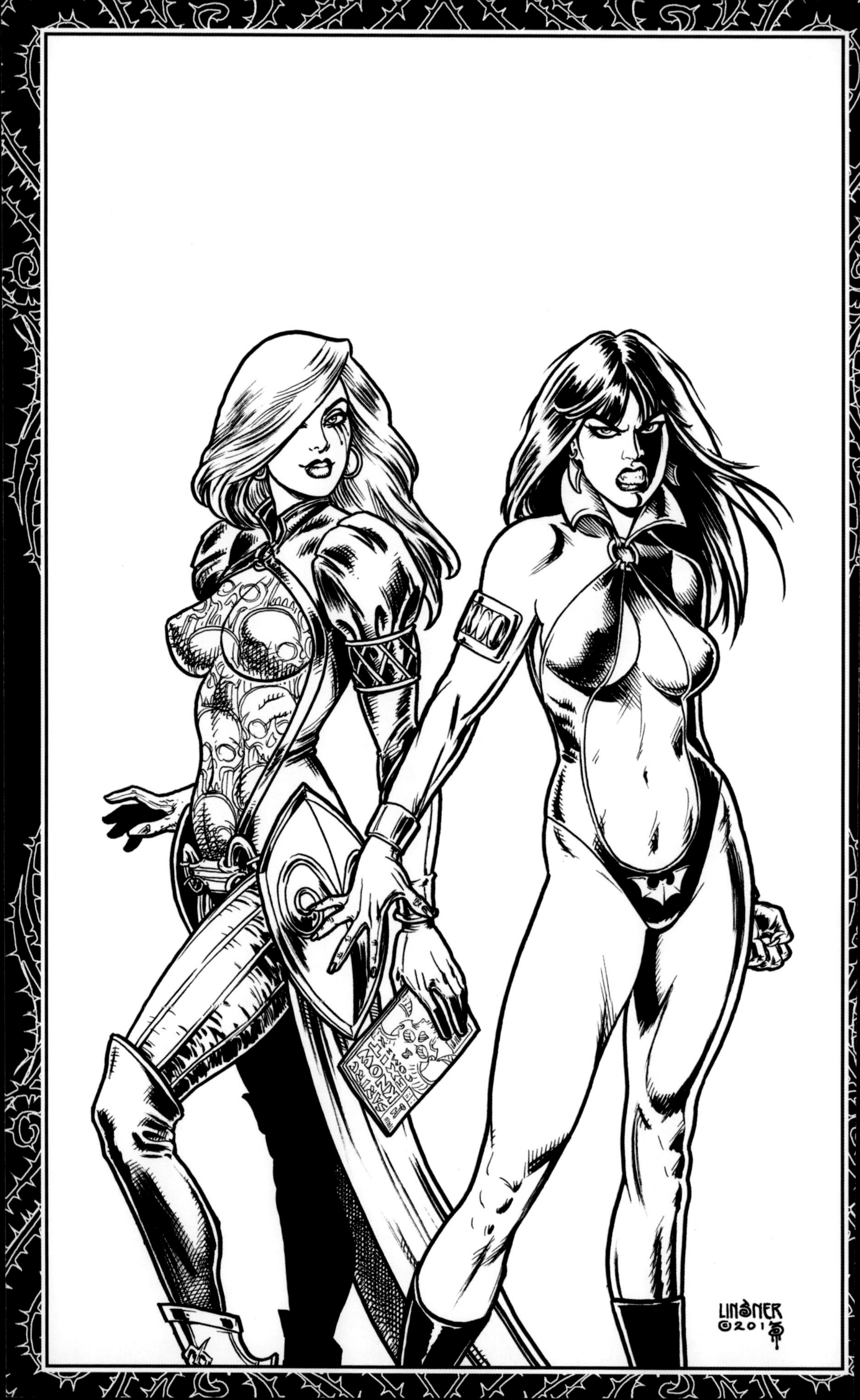
LINSNER
©201

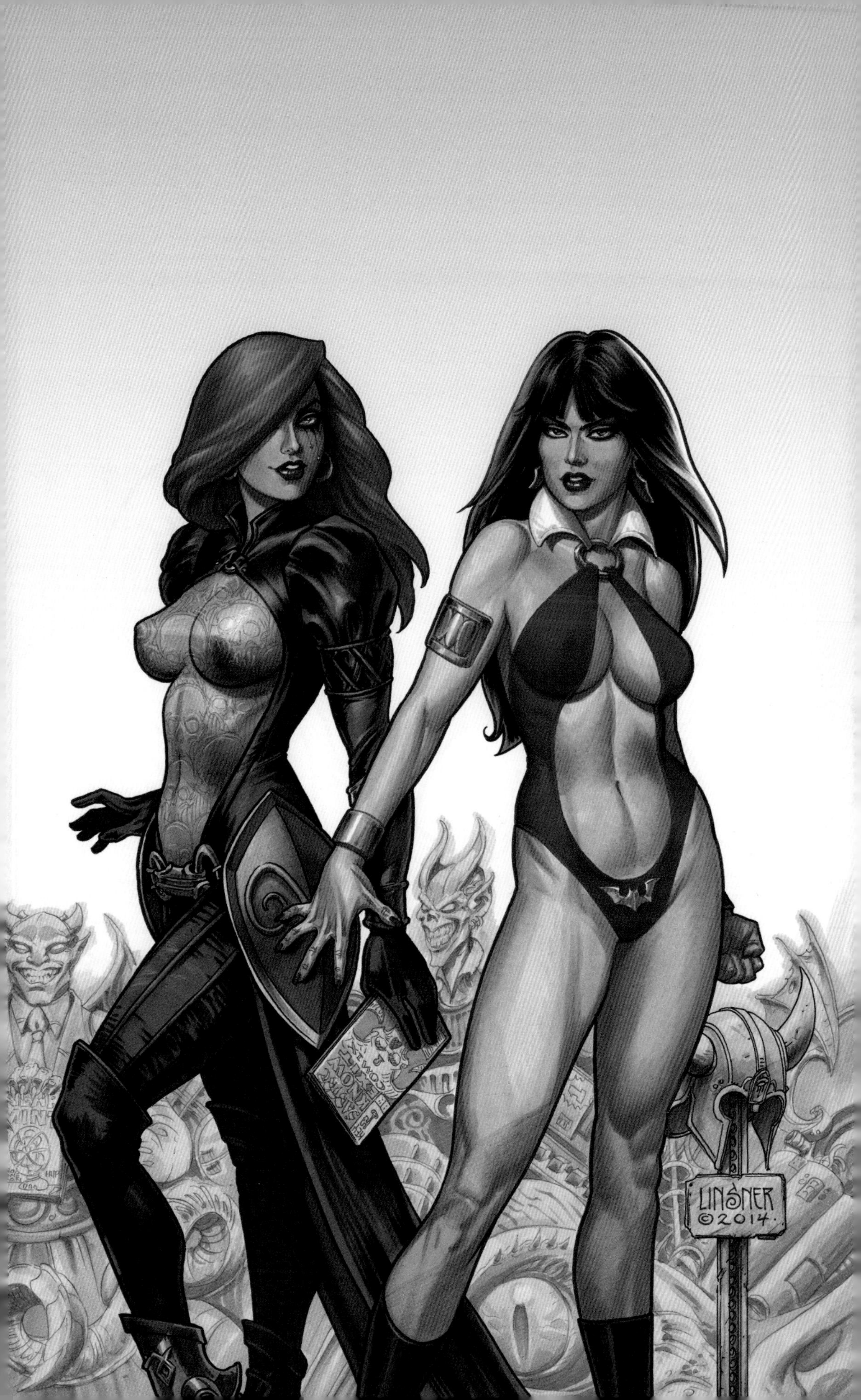
LINSNER
©2014.

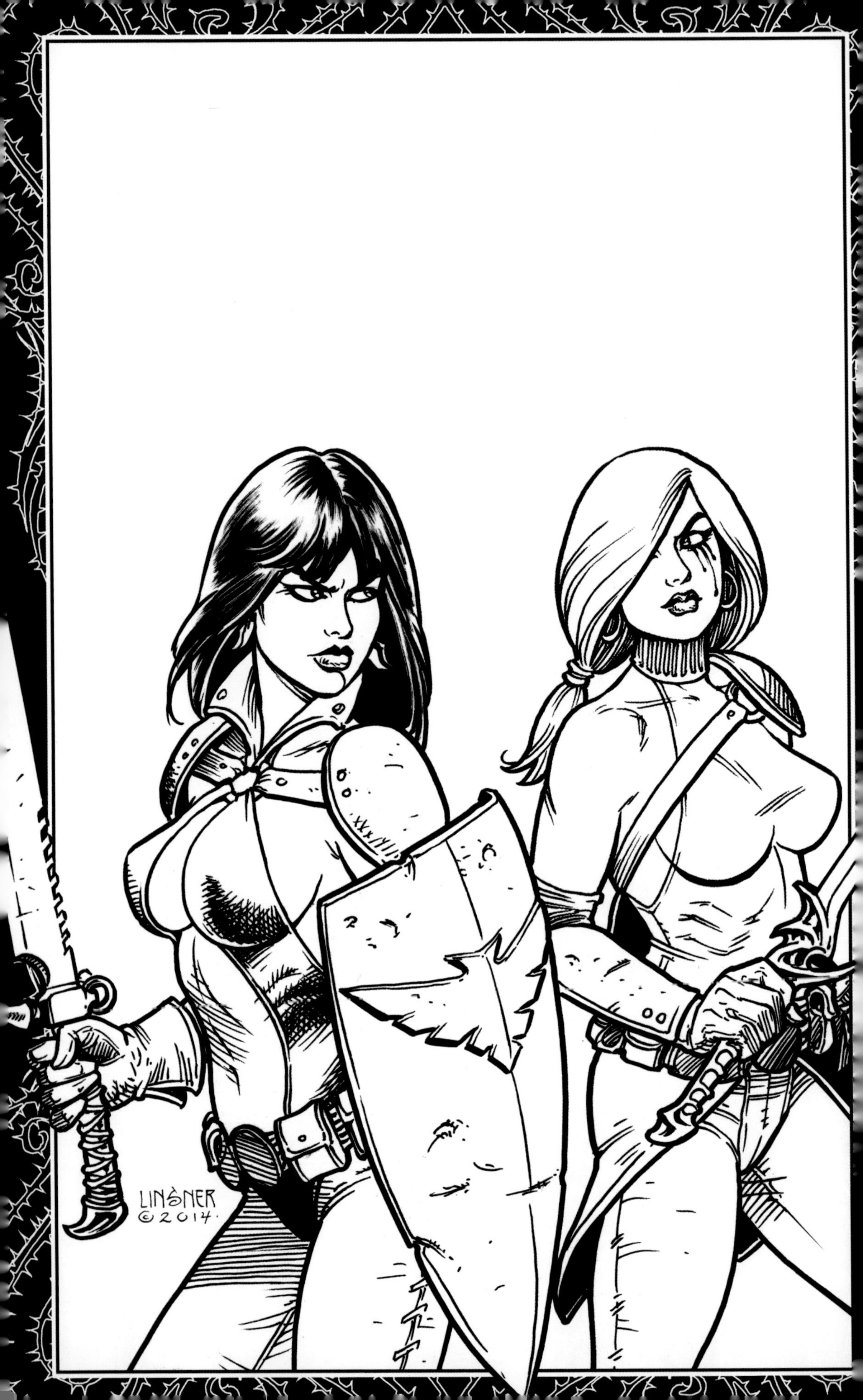
LINSNER
©2014.

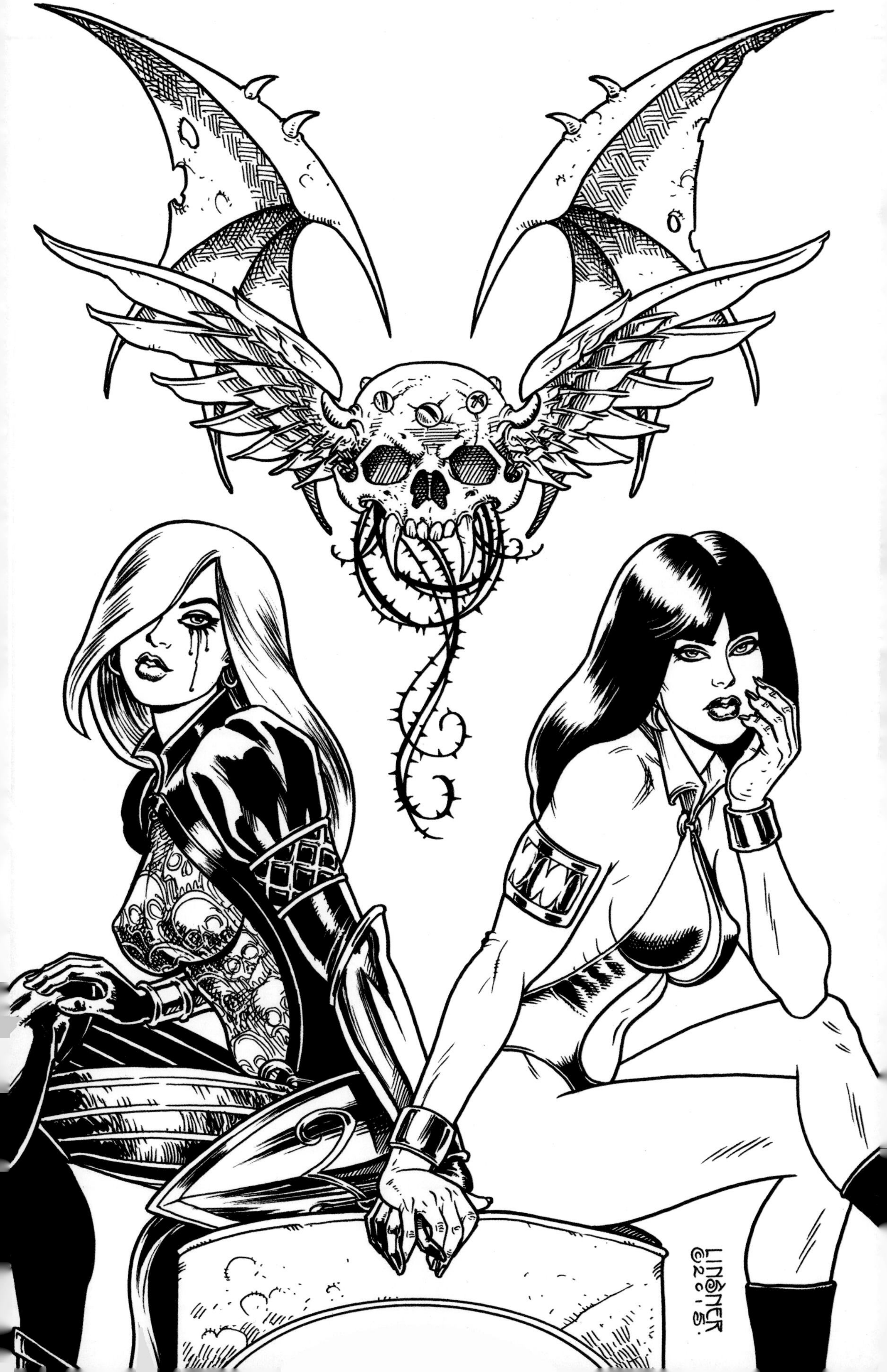
LINSNER ©2015.

I love clever demons.

Slobbering ghouls can be fun, but if a demon is really gonna stick it to you, he's going to try and outsmart you. I wanted my villain to be charming and somehow sympathetic.

Right from the beginning he had a backstory involving multiple incarnations.

in fact, 'MASODIK' means 'SECOND' in Hungarian.

He's on his second evil incarnation on his way to the bottom before he can be reborn and have his slate wiped clean.

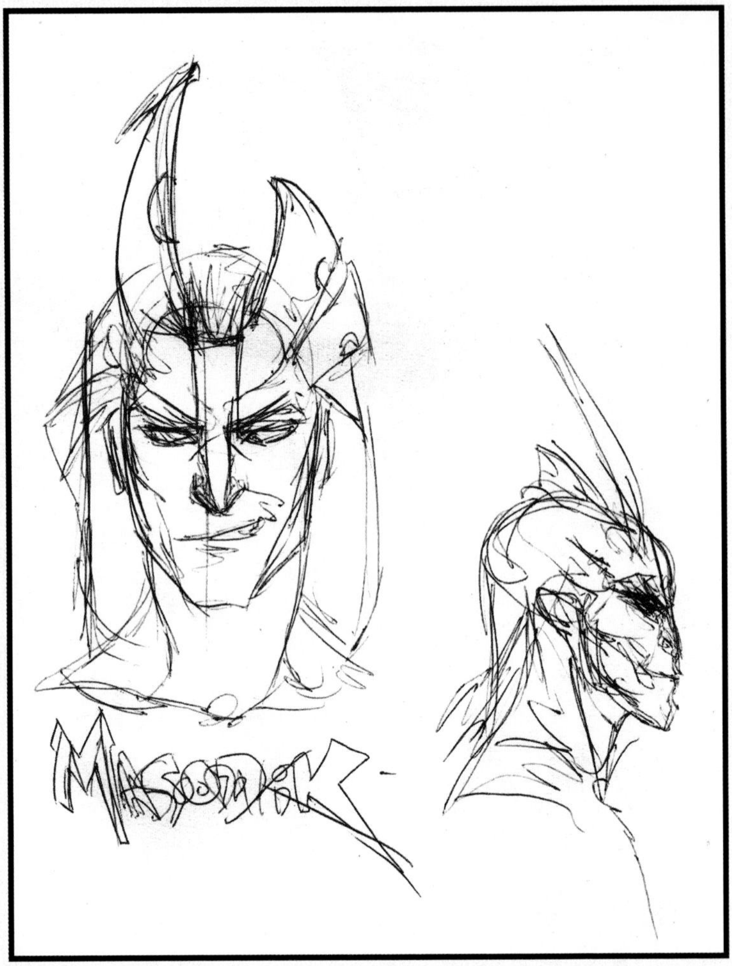
MASODIK

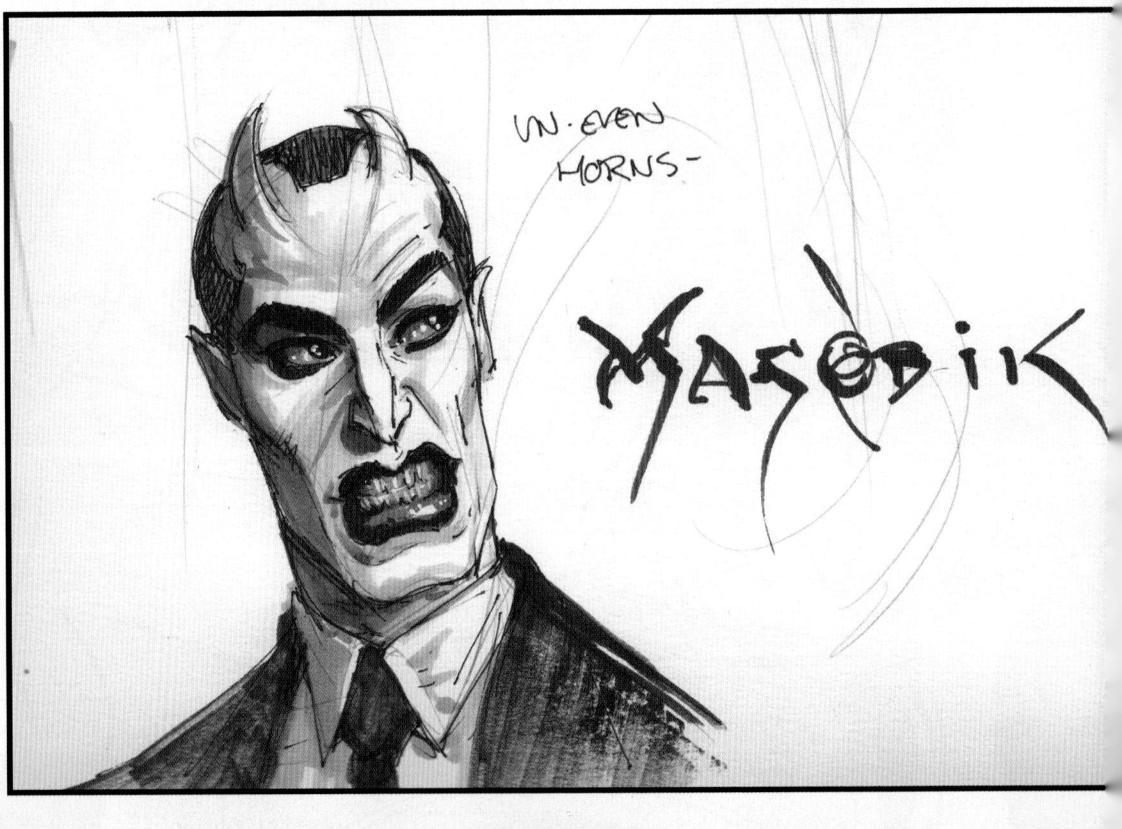
UN-EVEN HORNS-
MASODIK

Excerpt from a color guide by JML

DAMN VAMPIRELLA

NO EXIT

One of my favorite sequences to draw was th 'Girl from Drakulon' short story.

As a long time Vampirella lover, I have a deep fondness for her original appearances.

I drew great inspiration from her early days--even the Aurora model kit--which I actually owned as a tyke back in the 70's.

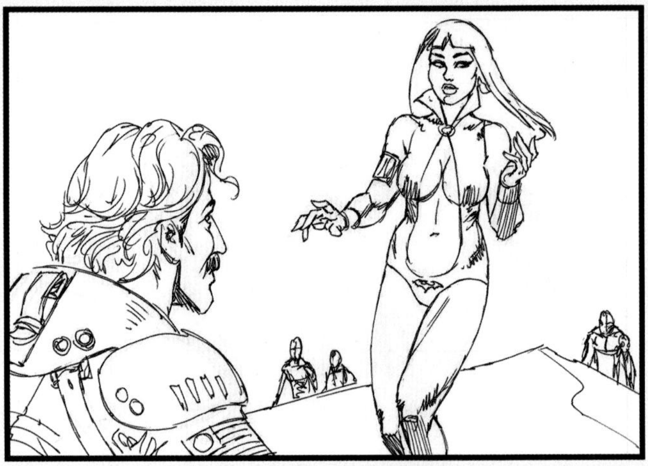

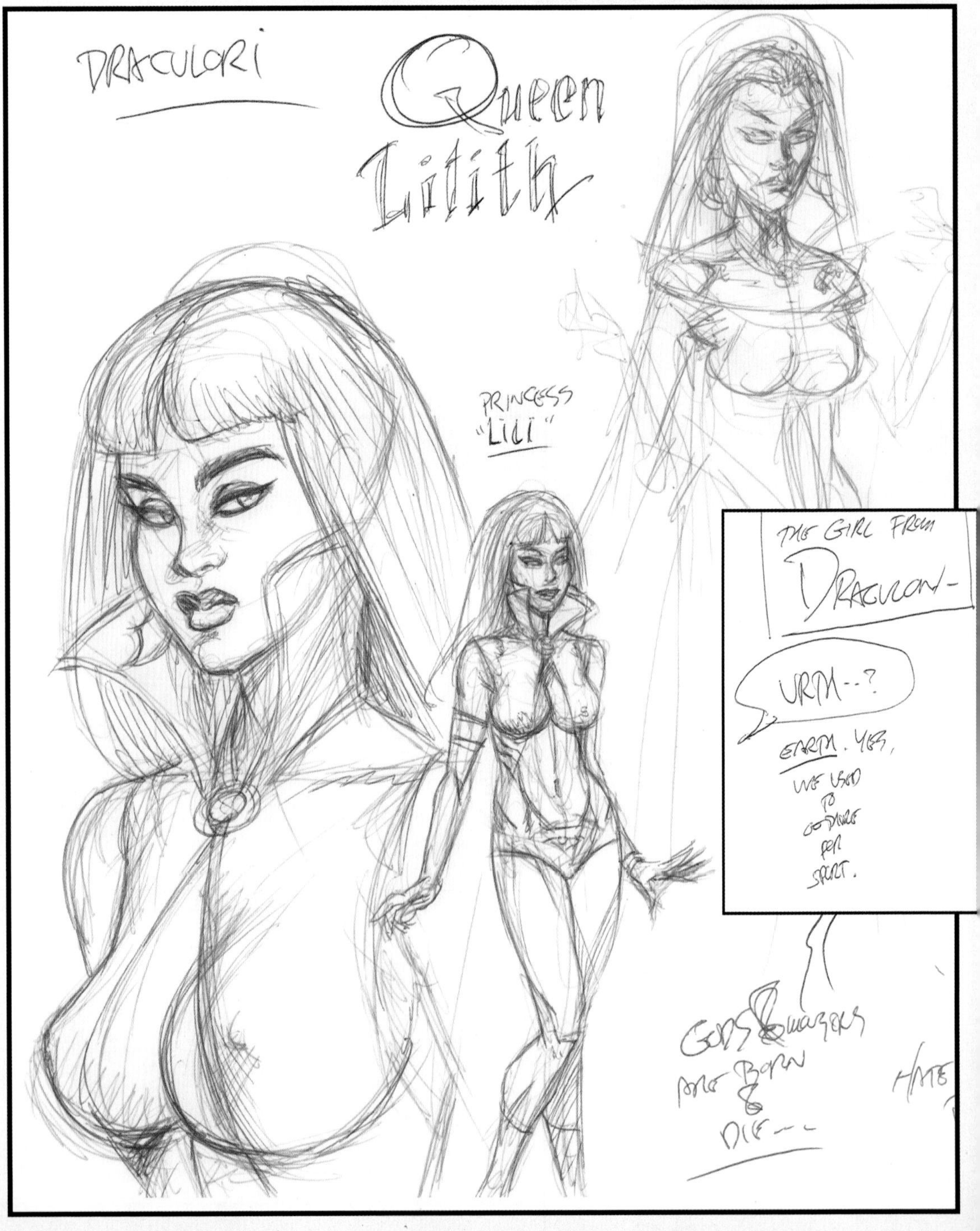
DRACULORI
Queen Lilith
PRINCESS "LILI"
THE GIRL FROM DRAKULON-
URM--?
EARTH. YES,
GODS & MORTALS ARE BORN & DIE--
HATE

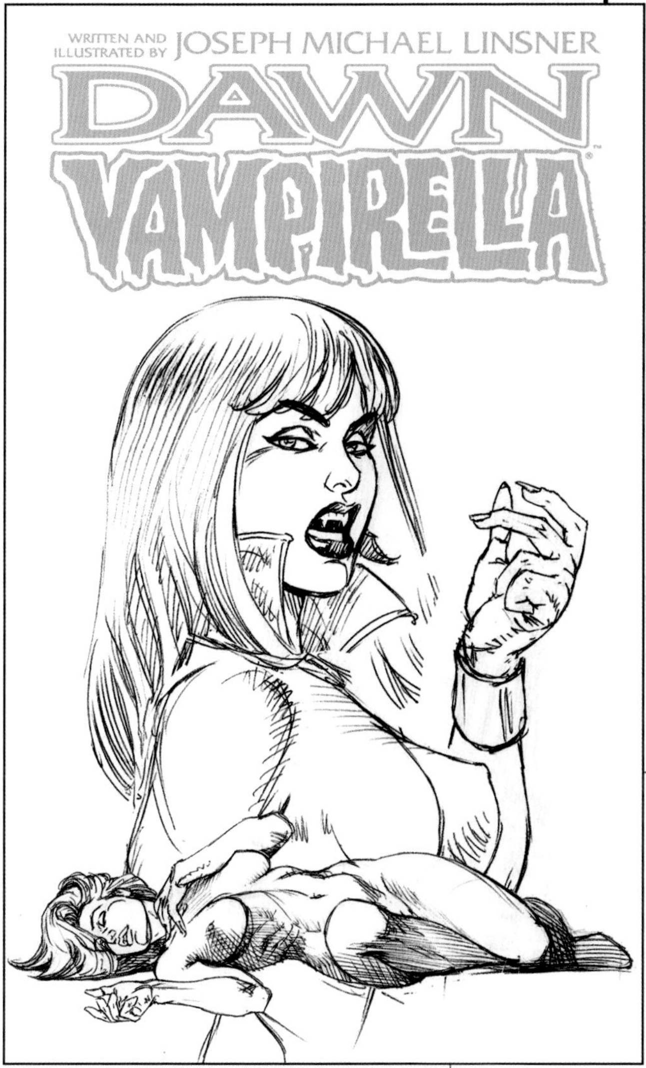
WRITTEN AND ILLUSTRATED BY JOSEPH MICHAEL LINSNER
DAWN
VAMPIRELLA

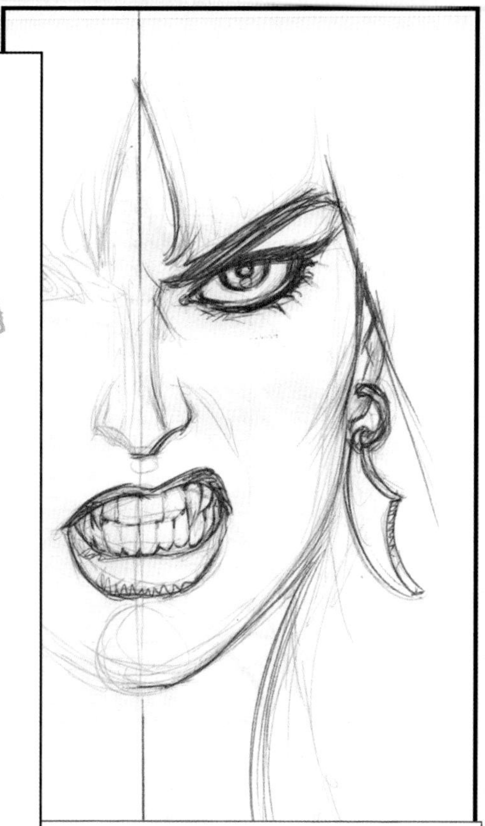

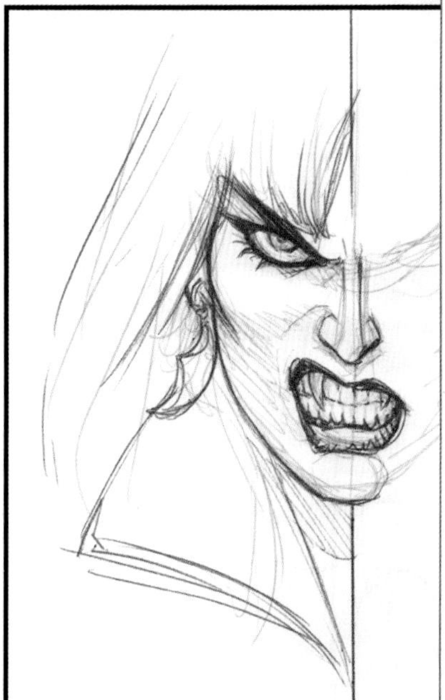

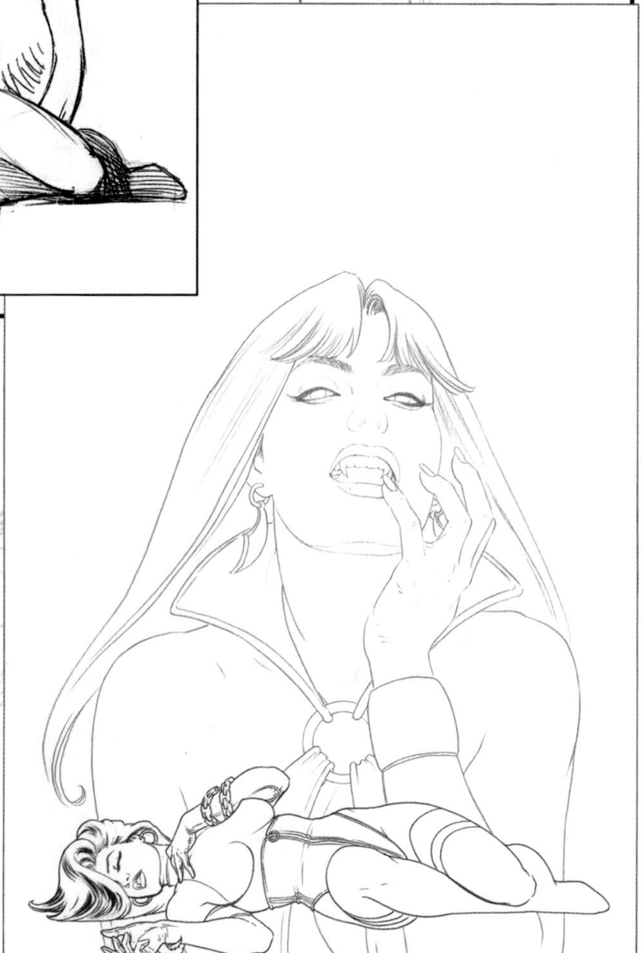

A F T E R W O R D

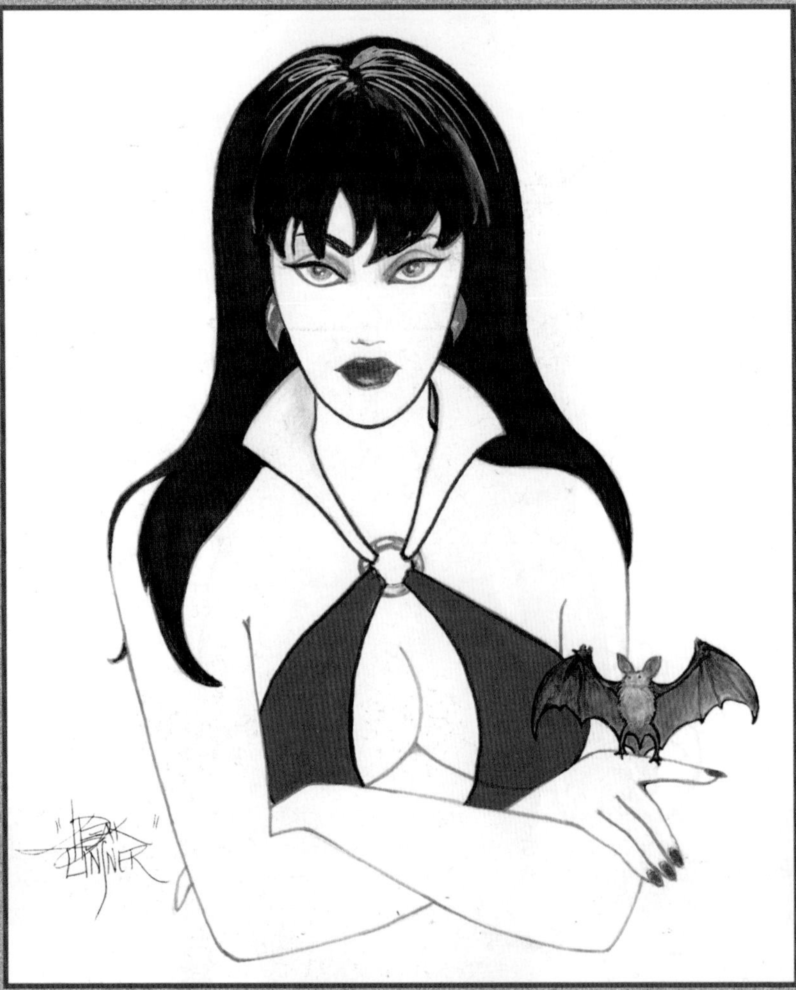

Art by Kristina Deak Linsner

My first introduction to VAMPIRELLA was in 1973 via the "life size" 6ft. Warren poster on my Uncle's closet door. I recall being totally entranced by it every time I entered the room. I wanted to know all about her. Who was she? What was her story? Where did she come from? As I later came to read in the pages of VAMPIRELLA, she was a vampire, a magician's assistant, a B-Grade movie star and so much more. I was hooked - a Vampi fan for life!

I came to know of DAWN in a quite different manner. At my local comic book shop one week, among my regula Wednesday pulls, I found a copy of Cry For Dawn #1. The store manager had put it in there because it "seemec right up my alley." It was. And then some. I would meet Joe about a month or so later, in January 1990 at a NYC convention. And thus would begin a very long and fulfilling friendship between the two of us, which led eventuall (all these years later) to our marriage.

Both ladies are strong characters that deserve to share the stage with one another. So when I heard the news o the crossover I was very excited for Joe that this team-up was coming to fruition.

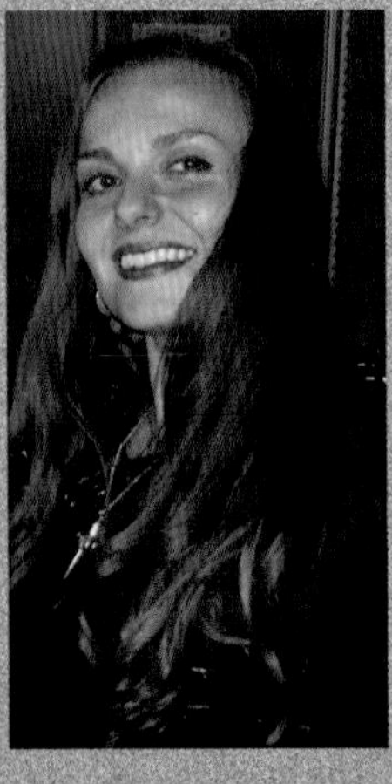

Additionally, it was an absolute honor and a true pleasure to oversee as Creative Edito on this series. Working alongside Joe, to steer him in the right direction when, and if, he faltered on a couple of things. For instance, the female voice and element in story-telling from a woman's perspective, and so on. Or sometimes, just being there in a pinch - like posing for the cover to #5.

Joe's dynamic visuals and snappy dialogue already provide a strong backbone to flesh out the story. I do hope that my contributions to DAWN·VAMPIRELLA help to elevate the series as a whole, and produce a pleasant experience for the reader. Something tha both devotees of the goddess DAWN and long-time fans of VAMPIRELLA can really sin their teeth into.

Kristina Deak - Linsner
Creative Editor
@KristinaDeak - twitter
facebook.com/lightisthenewdark

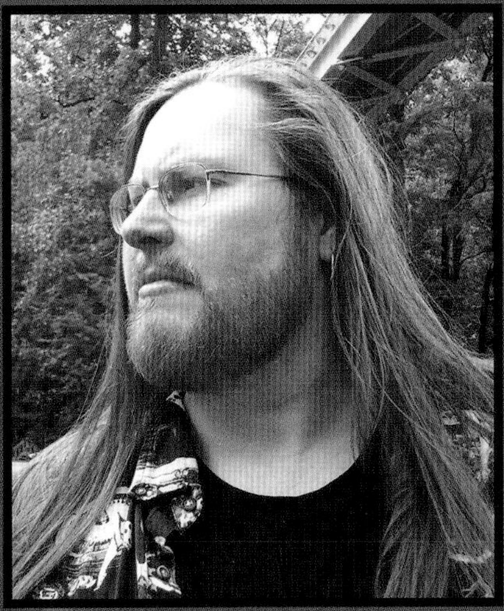

ABOUT THE AUTHOR

Joseph Michael Linsner is most well-known for writing, drawing and coloring the adventures of his creation DAWN, his personal Pin-Up Goddess. Since her debut appearance on the cover of the first CRY FOR DAWN in 1989, Dawn struck a chord with thousands of fans on an international level. She is currently published in six languages and has come to life in the form of statues, action figures, t-shirts, lithographs, lunch boxes and trading cards.

An award winning illustrator, Linsner has done covers for all of the major comics publishers, painting Wolverine, Black Cat, Killraven, Conan, Mystique, Vampirella, Harley Quinn and countless others. One of his proudest moments was getting to illustrate a short story written by Stan Lee for 'Actor Comics Presents.'

Dawn will next appear in late 2016.

'Like' JML's official FACEBOOK page:
facebook.com/josephmichaellinsner

& Follow JML on TWITTER
@JosephLinsner - Twitter

BOOKS BY JML:
- Dawn: Lucifer's Halo
- Dawn: Return Of The Goddess
- Dawn: Three Tiers
- Angry Christ Comix: The Cry For Dawn stories of JML
- The Vampire's Christmas
- The Art Of Joseph Michael Linsner Vol. One
- Girl & Goddesses: The Pin-Up Art of JML
- Claws; Wolverine & the Black Cat Vol. One & Two (written by Jimmy Palmiotti & Justin Gray)

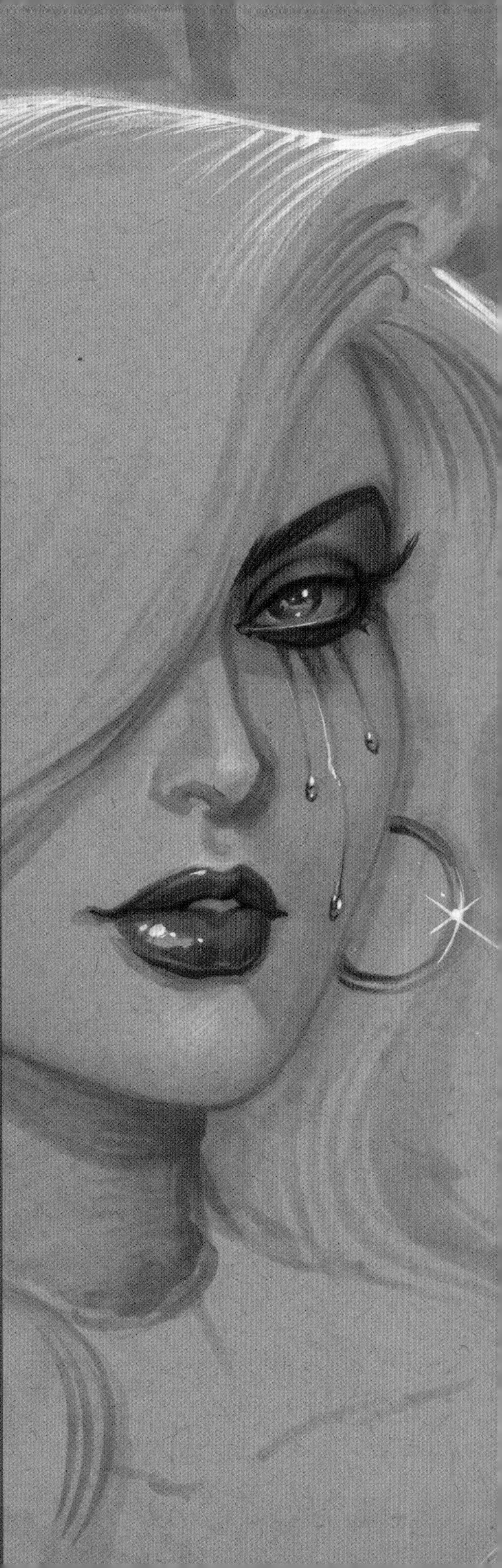

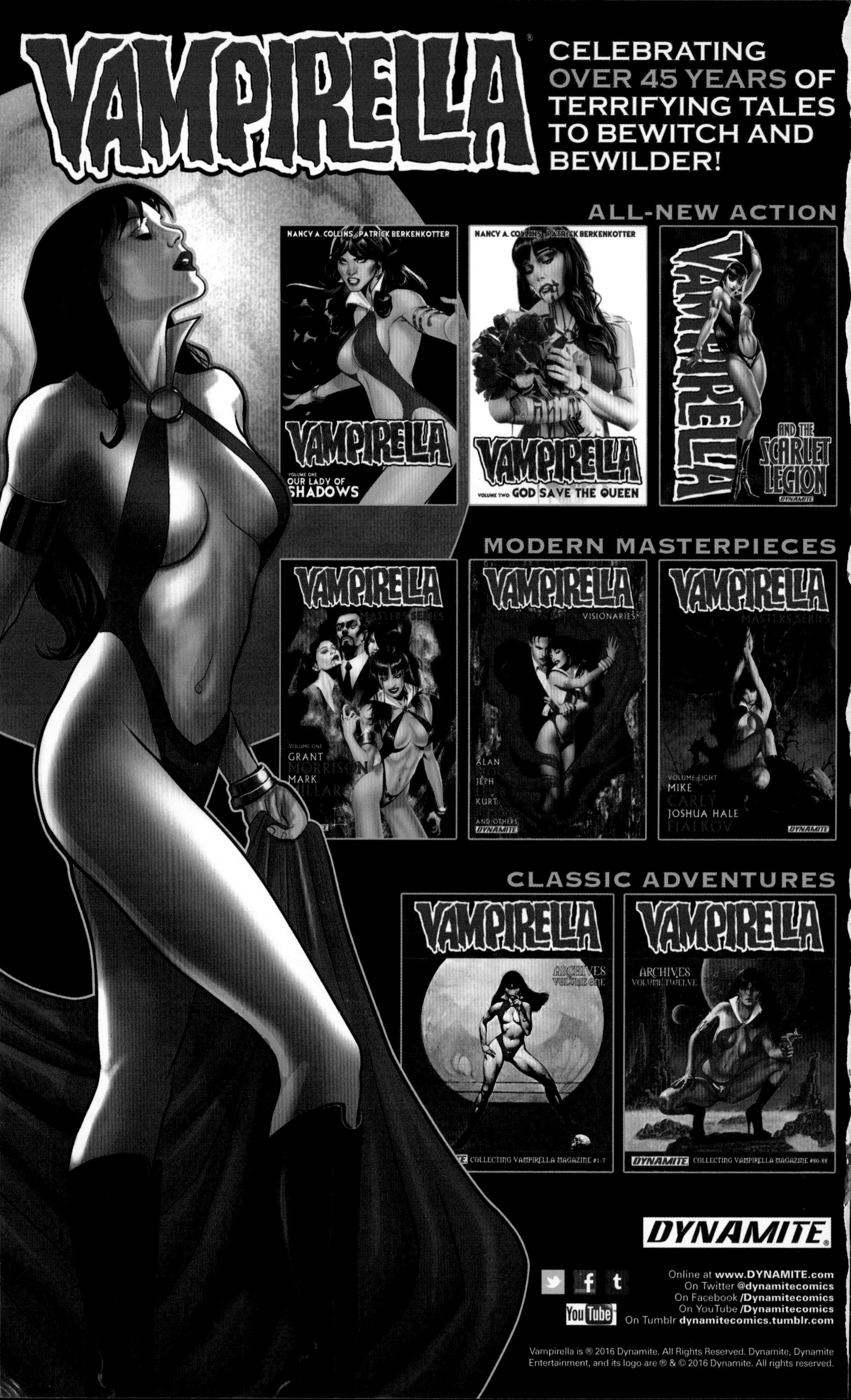
VAMPIRELLA®
CELEBRATING OVER 45 YEARS OF TERRIFYING TALES TO BEWITCH AND BEWILDER!
ALL-NEW ACTION
NANCY A. COLLINS · PATRICK BERKENKOTTER
VAMPIRELLA
VOLUME ONE OUR LADY OF SHADOWS
NANCY A. COLLINS · PATRICK BERKENKOTTER
VAMPIRELLA
VOLUME TWO GOD SAVE THE QUEEN
VAMPIRELLA AND THE SCARLET LEGION
DYNAMITE
MODERN MASTERPIECES
VAMPIRELLA
MASTERS SERIES
VOLUME ONE
GRANT MORRISON
MARK MILLAR
VAMPIRELLA
VISIONARIES
ALAN
JEPH
KURT
AND OTHERS
DYNAMITE
VAMPIRELLA
MASTERS SERIES
VOLUME EIGHT
MIKE CAREY
JOSHUA HALE FIALKOV
DYNAMITE
CLASSIC ADVENTURES
VAMPIRELLA
ARCHIVES VOLUME ONE
COLLECTING VAMPIRELLA MAGAZINE #1-7
VAMPIRELLA
ARCHIVES VOLUME TWELVE
DYNAMITE COLLECTING VAMPIRELLA MAGAZINE #80-88
DYNAMITE®
Online at www.DYNAMITE.com
On Twitter @dynamitecomics
On Facebook /Dynamitecomics
On YouTube /Dynamitecomics
On Tumblr dynamitecomics.tumblr.com
Vampirella is ® 2016 Dynamite. All Rights Reserved. Dynamite, Dynamite Entertainment, and its logo are ® & © 2016 Dynamite. All rights reserved.